Firewalls Don't Stop Dragons

A Step-by-Step Guide to Computer Security for Non-Techies

Third Edition

Carey Parker

Apress®

Firewalls Don't Stop Dragons: A Step-by-Step Guide to Computer Security for Non-Techies

Carey Parker
North Carolina, USA

ISBN-13 (pbk): 978-1-4842-3851-6
https://doi.org/10.1007/978-1-4842-3852-3

ISBN-13 (electronic): 978-1-4842-3852-3

Library of Congress Control Number: 2018953686

Managing Director, Apress Media LLC: Welmoed Spahr
Acquisitions Editor: Susan McDermott
Development Editor: Laura Berendson
Coordinating Editor: Rita Fernando

Cover designed by eStudioCalamar

Cover image designed by Freepik (www.freepik.com)

Distributed to the book trade worldwide by Springer Science+Business Media New York, 233 Spring Street, 6th Floor, New York, NY 10013. Phone 1-800-SPRINGER, fax (201) 348-4505, e-mail orders-ny@springer-sbm.com, or visit www.springeronline.com. Apress Media, LLC is a California LLC and the sole member (owner) is Springer Science + Business Media Finance Inc (SSBM Finance Inc). SSBM Finance Inc is a **Delaware** corporation.

For information on translations, please e-mail rights@apress.com, or visit www.apress.com/rights-permissions.

Apress titles may be purchased in bulk for academic, corporate, or promotional use. eBook versions and licenses are also available for most titles. For more information, reference our Print and eBook Bulk Sales web page at www.apress.com/bulk-sales.

Any source code or other supplementary material referenced by the author in this book is available to readers on GitHub via the book's product page, located at www.apress.com/9781484238516. For more detailed information, please visit www.apress.com/source-code.

Printed on acid-free paper

To my wife, my mother, my father, and my daughters.

Table of Contents

About the Author

Carey Parker, an only child who loved to tear apart his electronic toys and reassemble them in interesting ways, was born and raised in Indiana. He began programming computers in middle school when personal computers were just starting to become popular. For years, these twin interests percolated until he attended Purdue University and he learned you could get paid to do this stuff—it was called electrical engineering! After obtaining a bachelor's degree and a master's degree in electrical engineering, Carey launched his career in telecommunications software development at Bell Northern Research (aka the "Big Nerd Ranch"). Over the next 20 years, Carey wrote software for multiple companies, large and small, and lived in various cities across the southern United States. After the Edward Snowden revelations in 2013, he became deeply concerned about privacy, mass surveillance, and computer security. In 2014, he combined his passion for computers, cybersecurity, and fantasy novels with the long-time desire to write a book: *Firewalls Don't Stop Dragons*.

About the Technical Reviewer

 **Dean Keith** studied at Rutgers College in the early 1970s, when the faculty did not recognize computer science as a legitimate degree. Dean submitted a proposal for an individualized major with courses from the computer science major at Livingston College, a newly formed college in the Rutgers University system, and the existing economics major at Rutgers College. It was approved, making him one of the early graduates in the field at Rutgers. Later, as personal computers made their way into the business world, he remembers the day his company updated their one and only office PC to a 20MB hard drive, thinking they had it made. Writing databases in Lotus Notes and becoming a company expert for Excel were tasks he took on in addition to his normal responsibilities as a distribution center general manager. Now semiretired, he and his wife Kathy teach technology classes for senior citizens at Richland College. One of the popular classes Dean teaches is a computer security class using this book!

Preface

Let's take a little quiz. If I asked you right now to rate your personal computer security on a scale from one to ten—with ten being Fort Knox and one being a wet paper bag—what rating would you give yourself? Seriously, give that some thought right now.

Unless you're a techie person, I'm going to guess that you don't really know how to come up with that number, and that almost surely means your ranking is closer to the wet paper bag end of the scale. Do you really need to be as secure as Fort Knox? No, of course, not, and that's not what this book is about. However, there are many things you can do (or avoid doing) that will significantly increase your security and privacy, and this book is chock full of them. You don't have to do them all—even I don't do them all—but I firmly believe that everyone should at least consider the specific tips and techniques described in this book.

I'm guessing that a few questions are popping into your mind right now. Do I really need this book? Do I need to be a "computer person" to understand it? How much effort is this going to take? All good questions! Let's answer them right up front.

The answer to the first question is easy: yes! Okay, *why* do you need this book? Because so many important parts of our lives are moving to the Internet now—banking, shopping, paying bills, socializing, gaming, you name it. And it's not just our desktop computers that are connecting to the Internet, it's our laptops, smartphones, tablets, and even appliances. Unlike the days of dial-up modems, our devices are now connected almost 100 percent of the time. These facts have not gone unnoticed by the bad guys. As the famous saying goes, why do criminals rob banks? Because that's where the money is![1] You need this book because it will make you safer—significantly safer, if you follow most of the advice. In fact, not only will it make you safer, it will make those around you safer, even if they don't do any of the things I recommend in this book. (I'll explain that bit of magic later in the book.)

This book is for my mother, my friends, my neighbors, and all the other totally normal, everyday people like them: people who use computers and mobile devices but

---

[1]This line is often falsely attributed to bank robber Willie Sutton; see https://www.snopes.com/quotes/sutton.asp.

CHAPTER 1

Before We Begin

Before you can dive into the nitty-gritty details of how to seriously bump up your cybersecurity, you need to have a basic understanding of the landscape. In this chapter, I'll help you understand what your real risks are, how safe you can expect to be, and how to get the most out of this book.

"How Worried Should I Be?"

I'd say people fall into three camps when it comes to computer security. There's a large camp of people who are blissfully ignorant. They like their computers and gadgets but don't really worry about security. Let's call this Camp Pollyanna. "Why would anyone target me? Surely the computer and gadget companies have built in lots of safeguards, right?" The people in this camp have probably not had anything bad happen to them, and they feel safe enough. (They're almost surely not.)

There's another camp of people who are scared to death of computers and online life in general. They refuse to shop or bank online, but maybe they send some e-mails, surf the Web to look something up, and dabble in Facebook. This would be more like Camp Luddite.[1] In my experience, the folks in this camp tend to be older—they didn't grow up with computers and can live just fine without them, thank you very much. (You can live without "horseless carriages" too, but why would you?)

Then there's a small camp of folks who understand the likely risks, take proper precautions, and proceed confidently with a wary respect for the dangers. That's my camp. Sorta like Camp Goldilocks—not too scared, not too indifferent, just cautiously confident. (I considered going with "Camp Super-Amazing Awesome Cool" but figured that probably sounded a little biased.) The goal of this book is to bring everyone into my camp!

---

[1]A Luddite is someone who shuns new technology, usually due to fear and ignorance. The term comes from a group of English workers in the early 1800s who destroyed the new textile manufacturing equipment because they felt it was threatening their livelihoods.

© Carey Parker 2018
C. Parker, *Firewalls Don't Stop Dragons*, https://doi.org/10.1007/978-1-4842-3852-3_1

Computers and the Internet have already changed the world, and there's no looking back. Like any powerful tool, a computer can be used for good and for ill. We shouldn't shun the tool because we don't understand it, but we also need to learn to use it properly so that we don't endanger others or ourselves. Automobiles can be lethally dangerous, but the benefits of mobility are undeniably worth the risks. However, unlike with cars, where we are carefully trained before being allowed onto the highway with others, there is no "Internet surfing license." Also, the dangers of piloting a 3,500-pound metal box at 70 miles per hour are readily apparent to the driver: "If I crash, I'm going to seriously injure myself and probably others." But the dangers of surfing the net are not intuitively obvious, and people just don't have an instinctual feel for the dangers. Before computers were connected to the Internet, this lack of understanding didn't matter as much. If you had computer problems, they were probably caused by you and affected only you. Today, with everything connected 24/7, our computers are much more vulnerable, and a security lapse by one person can have perilous effects on many others.

So, what are the dangers, really? And just how bad is it out there? The next chapter will answer these questions in more detail, but let's break it down at a high level. Security experts call this process *threat analysis*.

Threat Analysis

At the end of the day, you have two things you really need to protect: your money and your privacy. While it's obvious why you would want to protect your money, for some reason people are extremely cavalier these days about their privacy. However, private information can also be used to get your hard-earned cash (more on that in a minute). Most bad guys are motivated by good old-fashioned money. While it's certainly possible that someone might want to personally do you harm, unless you're a politician or a celebrity, it's not the most common threat. There are lots of ways to get money from people, however, and hackers are extremely creative. Let's look at the most common direct threats to your money and privacy.

Credit Card Fraud. People worry a lot about their credit card information being stolen online, but in reality this is probably one of the least scary scenarios. Why? Well, as long as you report the fraudulent charges in a timely manner, you won't be liable for them. Sure, you might have to get a new credit card, which is annoying, but you haven't actually lost any money. It shouldn't even affect your credit score. The credit card companies have insurance, and they charge all sorts of fees to cover losses like these. They're also getting good at spotting suspicious activity—they will probably catch the bad charges before you do. So, while credit card fraud is a real problem for the credit card *companies*, it's really not a major problem for the *cardholders*.[2]

Spam and Scams. The Internet is a con artist's dream come true. You no longer have to find and meet your marks one at time; you can reach millions of gullible people for almost zero cost (and almost zero risk) via e-mail. It's estimated that about 60 percent of e-mails are junk or "spam." That's a staggering figure. Junk mail filters now catch most of these e-mails, and most of the rest are rightly ignored and deleted. But if I can send 100 million e-mails for almost no cost and only 0.1 percent of these e-mails are read, I've still reached 100,000 people! If I can convince just 1 percent of those people to bite on my scam, I've landed 1,000 "clients." And that's just today.

Using e-mail as a delivery mechanism, bad guys will try to trick you into sending them money, signing up for expensive services, buying phony products, or divulging online account credentials (a scam known as *phishing*).

The list of scams is long and limited only by the perpetrator's imagination. They will use "social engineering" techniques to capture your interest and play on your emotions: guilt, shame, fear, even generosity. It's a classic tale, just told via a new medium.

Phishing. Unfortunately, this has nothing to do with a rod and a reel and whistling the theme to *The Andy Griffith Show*. Phishing is a technique used by scammers to get sensitive information from people by pretending to be someone else, usually via e-mail or a web page (or both). Basically, they trick you into thinking you're dealing with your bank, a popular web site (PayPal, eBay, Amazon, etc.), or even the government. Sometimes they entice you with good stuff (winning a prize, free stuff, or a special opportunity), and sometimes they scare you with bad stuff (freezing your account, reporting you to some authority, or telling you that your account has been hacked). But in all cases, they try to compel you to give up information such as passwords or credit card numbers.

Unfortunately, it's extremely easy to create exact duplicates of web pages. There's just no real way to identify a fake by looking at it. Sometimes you can tell by looking at the web site's address, but scammers are good at finding plausible website names that look very much like the real one they're impersonating.

---

[2]Note that the same cannot be said for using debit cards online. I will cover that later in Chapter 9.

Viruses and Other Malware. E-mails are often used to lure unsuspecting people to fake and/or malicious web sites. These web sites use bugs in computer software to surreptitiously download software to your computer. Sometimes the e-mails have infected files or applications directly attached, as well. This *malware* may be used to steal information from you, cause senseless harm to your computer or data, or make your computer a slave in their army to wage war on some third party. That sounds like a science-fiction story, but it's very real. I'll talk more about this in the next chapter.

Identity Theft. When someone uses your private information to impersonate you for the purpose of gaining access to your money or your credit, this is called *identity theft* or *identity fraud.* This is probably the most serious threat for the average computer user. If someone can successfully pretend to be you to your bank or a credit card company, they can do anything you can do, including draining your bank accounts and opening credit cards and/or loans in your name. If someone can gain access to your bank accounts, they can simply withdraw all your money. If they can open and max out a new loan or credit card in your name, you will be stuck holding the bill. Now you have to convince the bank and the credit agencies that it wasn't really you and that you weren't somehow negligent in allowing it to happen. If you're lucky enough to get your money back and get the debt waived, you may still have a big black mark on your credit history. This is where privacy really comes into play—it's not just about someone reading your e-mails or knowing what you did last weekend; it's about someone using that information to convince someone else that they are you.

E-mail Hacking. While it's obvious why criminals would want to target your bank and investment accounts, it might surprise you how lucrative it can be to hack into someone's e-mail account. When you forget your password, how do you recover it? The most common method today, by far, is via e-mail. If a crook can gain access to your e-mail account, they can use the automated password reset service on your bank's web page to change your password—locking you out and giving them full access all in one fell swoop.

Furthermore, they can use your e-mail to get money from your friends and family. One of the more popular scams is to e-mail everyone in your contact list and tell them you're stranded somewhere—your wallet, passport, and cell phone have been stolen, and you need emergency money wired right away. If you got this e-mail from someone you didn't know, you would surely ignore it. But if you got it directly from your daughter, your best friend, or your brother—maybe even a reply to an earlier e-mail from them— you could very well be duped into believing it was real.

For these reasons (and others), it's important to lock down your e-mail accounts and take action immediately if you believe they've been compromised.

Tracking and Surveillance. I personally cannot fathom why people aren't more upset about the massive invasion of our privacy by corporations and governments. We freely give away all sorts of significantly important bits of information left and right in return for "free" services. And we collectively shrug when whistleblowers reveal astonishing levels of surveillance on the entire population by our governments. But I won't get on this soapbox just yet; I'll save that for a later chapter.

I will say, however, that our online activities are being tracked at unbelievable levels today. Personal information is gold to advertisers, and they are building massive profiles on each one of us and selling them to whoever is willing to pay (including the government). This includes your gender, income range, spending habits, political leanings, religious affiliation, sexual orientation, personal associations and connections, search history, web sites visited, and even medical and health information. I will cover this in detail in Chapter 7.

Indirect Threats

So far we've only discussed direct threats—bad guys targeting individuals (even if they sometimes do it on a massive scale, as with spam). While some crooks prefer to mug a series of people in dark alleys, more ambitious thieves might prefer to just rob one bank vault and be done with it. It's the classic risk vs. reward trade-off. While we've had centuries to figure out how to properly protect physical assets like jewels, gold, and cash, we're still trying to figure out how best to protect our digital assets.

That "we" doesn't just refer to you and me—it also refers to large corporations. It seems like nary a month goes by now without hearing about another massive security breach at a brand-name company...the stealing of credit card info from Delta Airlines and Target, the colossal breach at Equifax that divulged gobs of personal and financial data, and the realization that Facebook "overshared" the data of tens of millions of users with Cambridge Analytica. While those were high-profile breaches that made the headlines, there are many others that didn't make the nightly news, either because they were smaller and escaped notice by the mainstream press or because the companies just kept the breaches quiet.

As regular consumers, we can't do anything to improve the security of these corporate server farms. However, we can do a lot to mitigate the impacts of these now-inevitable breaches.

Privacy vs. Security

I'd like to take a moment to draw a distinct difference between security threats and privacy threats. Security threats have been around since humans have had possessions worth stealing. As long as you have something that someone else might want, you need to be thinking about how to prevent that thing from being taken for greed or destroyed for spite.

We've actually had privacy threats for a long time, too. Examples are nosy neighbors and peeping Toms, who snoop for their own personal reasons, as well as tabloid-style journalists who sell sordid stories and compromising photos of politicians and celebrities for profit.

Until very recently in human history, all of these threats required physical proximity. To steal something, you had to go get it. Spying on people meant following them around, without them noticing, for days and weeks at a time, snapping pictures with telephoto lenses, planting bugs, rummaging through their garbage, and so on.

That all changed shortly after the turn of the century with the advent of smartphones and broadband Internet (both home and cellular). Not only have we managed to digitize all our most personal data, but we have also put that information on computerized devices that are connected to a global communication network every hour of every day. What could possibly go wrong? I'll be discussing this at length in this book.

But here's the main difference between security and privacy: if someone steals your stuff, you can replace it; if someone steals *you*—your history, your preferences, your relationships, your communications, your biometrics—you can't get that back. That knowledge can't be unlearned. Privacy cannot be regained once it is lost.

Here's another key difference between security and privacy: most consumer-oriented companies are on your side when it comes to security—it hurts you both if something you entrusted to them is stolen or destroyed. The same cannot be said for privacy. For companies who make their money off of advertising (such as Google and Facebook), there is a direct conflict of interest between your privacy and their profits.

I make this distinction here because we will find several situations throughout the course of this book where this conflict of interest has a significant impact on my recommendations. My goal is to improve both your security *and* your privacy. If there is no clear way to do both in a particular situation, I'll give you the information you need to evaluate the trade-offs and make the decision that works best for you.

Summary

How scared should you be? How likely is it that you will be hacked or swindled or robbed? The bad news is that I can't really give you a solid answer to that—it's like asking me to predict whether you will get mugged on the street or have your home robbed. It's a risk we all face, and that risk depends not just on where we live but also on our behaviors. But even those risk factors can't predict whether a particular person will be the victim of a crime. The good news is that there are many relatively simple and affordable things you can do to significantly reduce your risks, and that's the point of this book.

As an added bonus, taking steps to protect yourself will also increase the security of those around you, even if they don't read this book. It's very much like getting your child vaccinated. (Let's leave aside the hot-button topic of inoculations causing autism and just focus squarely on the preventative aspects.) You're not just helping to protect your child, you're actually helping to protect everyone else, including those who have not been vaccinated. It's the same with computer security: if your computer or online accounts are compromised, they can be used to compromise others—particularly those with whom you are connected to directly. When you leave yourself vulnerable, you're not just risking your own safety—you're risking the safety of others, as well. Therefore, protecting yourself will actually help to protect your friends and family, too.

Finally, security and privacy are different things, and I would argue that in many ways, your privacy is more important because once it's gone, you can't really get it back. But this book seeks to address both issues, so either way, I've got you covered!

How to Use This Book

My primary goal is to make you safer. The most efficient way to do this is to just tell you what to do. While I strongly believe that you need to understand *why* you're doing these things, when all is said and done, that's secondary to actually doing them. It's like eating right and exercising. Sure, it's good to know why it will help you, but you can get all the benefits just by doing it, whether you understand it or not. If you're like me, though, I can't get properly motivated to do something unless I know why it's important and what the benefits will be. But I get it, not everyone is like me.

Each chapter has two parts: the part that tells you what to do and the part that explains why it's important. The "what" part is in the form of a checklist, which you will find at the end of each chapter. The "why" part precedes the checklist, and I strongly encourage you to read it. But if you are short on time or truly don't care about the "why" and you're willing to just trust me, then by all means just skip straight to the checklists. You can always come back later and read the other parts. You may also get what you need by reading the summary at the end of each chapter.

The order of the chapters is important, and you should tackle them in the order presented, even if you intend to skip the explanation parts and jump straight to the checklists. In the next chapter, I cover some essential information that you need to understand before you read anything else—mostly terminology but also some general philosophy on security and privacy. Even if you're planning to skip most of the explanatory parts of the other chapters, I highly recommend you read this chapter word for word.

I've tried to make this book as simple as possible to use, and that required that I make some key decisions to reduce the number of choices. I've made it clear in each place where I've made such choices, giving you pointers on how you can make different choices. But for the sake of simplicity and brevity, I had to just make the call in some cases.

Remember, you don't have to do all of the things in this book. In fact, everything in this book is optional. But you bought this book (or perhaps someone bought it for you) in the hopes of making you safer. The more things you do from this book, the safer you'll be. At the end of the day, it's up to you to decide which of these things make sense for you and how much effort you're willing to expend.

Reader Prerequisites

To keep this book a reasonable length, I've had to make some key assumptions about the capabilities of the reader. For example, I have to assume that you know how to restart a computer, use a web browser, and download and install software. *If you do not meet these requirements, please do not let this stop you from reading this book!* If you are truly a novice user, you probably need the advice in this book more than most. I urge you to either enlist the help of a friend or family member, consider taking a local computer class, or find a good entry-level computer book for your operating system to help you learn your way around your computer.

Operating Systems Covered

I tried to cover the most popular operating system (OS) versions as of the writing of this book, but I also had to draw the line somewhere. I'm sure I will need to revise this book as the years go by, but in this edition, the following OS versions are covered:

- Windows 7

- Windows 8.1

- Windows 10

- Mac OS X 10.11 (El Capitan)

- macOS 10.12 (Sierra)

- macOS 10.13 (High Sierra)

Note that Windows has multiple flavors of each numbered operating system such as... Home, Premium, Pro, Enterprise, Ultimate, and so on. This book will focus on the entry-level versions of Windows, which come with most PCs (usually called Home or with no designation at all). Windows 8 is similar to Windows 8.1, so if you have Windows 8, you should upgrade to 8.1—it's free. But even if you don't, the instructions for Window 8.1 should work in most cases. With the advent of Window 10, Microsoft has moved to a biannual update schedule with names like Creators Update. All of these fall under the Windows 10 umbrella.

I will generally refer to the Mac operating system as *Mac OS* to avoid having to type *Mac OS X/macOS* all over the place. Also, if you have a slightly earlier version of Mac OS, the instructions and screenshots haven't changed much—the info here will probably work just fine for you in most cases. The Mac OS look and feel tends to change less drastically from release to release, compared to Windows.

Don't worry if you're not sure what operating system you have—I will help you figure it out at the end of the next chapter.

Navigating the Checklists

The most important parts of this book are the checklists at the end of each chapter. I've tried to make them as easy to follow as possible. Each checklist item will have a number and a title, followed by instructions for how to complete the checklist item. In some cases, this will just be a short paragraph; in others, there will be a series of steps that you will need to complete in order. Wherever possible, I've included images for what you should see on your computer screen.

In some cases, the steps you need to take will depend on your particular situation such as what operating system or what web browser you have. In those cases, there are subsections under each tip for each possible situation—you just need to find the one that applies to you, and you can ignore the other sections.

Here are some examples.

Tip 1-1. Simple Tip

For simple tips, there may only be a short paragraph describing what you need to do (or in some cases, not do). In general, the tips in each chapter should be done in the order given. It's not always required, but I tried to put the tips in the order that makes the most sense. Of course, you can always skip any tip if you don't feel like it applies to you or makes sense for your situation—or frankly if you just don't feel like doing it. Remember, you don't have to do everything in this book!

Tip 1-2. Tip with Steps

A tip that has multiple steps will have number lists like the one shown here. You will need to follow these steps in order, completing one before going on to the next.

1. Do this first.

2. Do this second.

3. And so on.

Tip 1-3. Tip with Variations

A tip that has variations depending on your computer setup (like your operating system or web browser) will have subsections for each one. You just need to find the subsection that applies to your situation and ignore the other subsections. In the following examples, there are variations depending on your operating system type and version.

Tip 1-3a. Microsoft Windows 7

If I list a single, specific OS version, then these steps will apply to only that version. If you have a different version, skip ahead to the section that is for your version.

Tip 1-3b. Microsoft Windows 8.1/10

If I specify multiple versions, then the given steps will apply to all the listed versions. In this example, that's Windows 8.1 and Windows 10.

Tip 1-3c. Mac OS

If I don't specify the OS version at all, that means the instructions are similar for all versions of the OS. In some cases, where just one or two screens look slightly different, I might include multiple versions in the same set of instructions just to avoid repeating the rest of the steps, which are the same. In this example, *Mac OS* would refer to macOS 10.13, macOS 10.12, and Mac OS X 10.12.

Apple changed its OS naming convention from Mac OS X to macOS a few years back. If the banner says *Mac OS*, you can assume it applies to Mac OS X and macOS variants.

You'll see that the tips are also numbered with the chapter number, followed by the tip number within that chapter. If there are variations on a tip, then there will be a letter to distinguish them.

Note that I've also taken the liberty to crop some of the screenshots to focus on the important parts. In some cases, I actually cut out parts of the middle to eliminate a lot of wasted space. So if you see an image that looks a little odd, that may be why.

Let's look at an example, so you know what I mean. Figure 1-1 is the actual image I captured from my computer. You can see there's a lot of extra space in the middle there. To get all of that into the width of a page, it makes the image text smaller and harder to read.

Figure 1-1. *Actual screenshot (unaltered)*

To make better use of space and make the text easier to read in this book, I can edit this image to show the important parts and remove the wasted space. See the edited image in Figure 1-2.

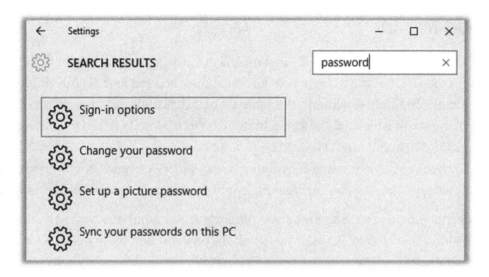

Figure 1-2. *Screenshot edited to eliminate extraneous white space for better readability*

Figure 1-2 still has all the important information, but it's more compact and therefore much easier to read. However, on your computer, you will see something more like the first image. So I just wanted to let you know that sometimes I make changes like this for the book, and hence some of the images here might look a little different compared to what you see on your computer.

Web Addresses and Staying Up-to-Date

All of the information in this book and the steps in the checklists were as accurate as possible when I wrote them. The wild and woolly world of the Internet is ever-changing. In just the time it's taken me to write this book, many things have changed. I actually had a hard time stopping writing because things kept happening that I wanted to write about!

Also, this book is full of web addresses. If you happen to have the eBook, you can just click these links. If you have the paper version, however, this is obviously not an option. And web links have a nasty habit of changing.

To stay as current as possible and to make it easier for you to find and click all the links, I've created a special page on my web site that gathers together all the links from this book (in order by chapter). See Tip 2-1 for details on this really handy web tool!

I also offer a few other ways to stay up-to-date. I have a newsletter and a blog, which often cover the same topics. I try to write something every couple weeks or so, either about something in the news or about an important topic. If you like having these things delivered to you on a regular basis, I strongly suggest signing up for the newsletter. If you would rather read the blog or perhaps catch up on past articles, you can get this on the main page of my web site. I also have a weekly podcast, if that's more your speed. In addition to timely news topics, I interview other experts in the field about current events, how the impact us, and what we can do about them.

On my blog, I offer straightforward analysis and advice on current topics. I also have a weekly newsletter that gives you tips on how to stay secure and guard your privacy—many of them will be from this book, but others will be targeted to new security concerns and the latest cool tools. Go to the following web site to stay up-to-date and safe!

`www.firewallsdontstopdragons.com`

For more up-to-the-minute security and privacy news, you can follow me on Twitter (my handle is `@FirewallDragons`). You don't even have to create a Twitter account to do this; you can subscribe to my Twitter feed via text messaging. The following link will give you instructions for this:

`https://help.twitter.com/en/using-twitter/sms-follow`

Always Go to the Source

For many of the tips in this book, you'll need to download something from the Internet. In most cases, I give you the link you need to do this. But in general, be sure to always go to the source whenever you download any piece of software. There are several popular software download sites that aggregate, rate, and review software, so feel free to consult them for information. But when it comes time to actually download the software, *don't use any download links on these sites*. Instead, go to the official web site for the software maker. These aggregator sites are a favorite target for bad guys and over-zealous marketers who will either taint the software with viruses or bundle additional software in the installer that you definitely do not want.

Feedback Welcome

If you find an error in this book or even if you just have ideas for ways I can improve the next edition, please send me an e-mail. I welcome any and all feedback, positive or negative. My goal is to make this book the best it can be, and I'm sure that I've missed some things or could have explained some things better.

```
https://feedback@firewallsdontstopdragons.com
```

I should head one thing off at the pass right now, though: grammar. I know I broke some rules in this book. I specifically tried to make this book very conversational and accessible. That means using "who" when it should be "whom," using "they" as a singular pronoun, and ending sentences with prepositions from time to time. If you are an English teacher, a formal writer, or just someone who is a stickler for grammar, I will just beg your forgiveness now and ask you to chalk it up to artistic license.

Spread the Word

If you find that you really enjoy this book, the blog, the newsletter, my Twitter feed, and so on—if you find this information valuable and believe (as I do) that the more people protect themselves the better we'll all be—then please help me spread the word! Take the time to share your book, forward them a newsletter, or just point them to my web site. From there they can also find links to several other helpful web sites, books, documentaries, and so on.

I also encourage you to socialize these issues with your friends and family. Talk about them over the dinner table. Post articles on your social media accounts. Engage people in constructive debate. Demand that your elected representatives (local, state, and federal) address these issues. The first steps to solving these problems are awareness, education, and transparency.

Not So Fast

Before we get to the good stuff, I'm compelled to offer a few caveats...

First, I promised that this book would make you safer—and if you do even some of the things I recommend, it will absolutely do that. But note that I did not say that it would make you *safe*. The topics of security and privacy are unbelievably vast, and the playing field is changing constantly. One book couldn't possibly cover every possible threat, and that wasn't my intent. There are so many small and simple things that everyone can do to mitigate most risks, and most people just don't know about them (or don't understand how important they are). Those are the things I want to cover in this book. Also, security and privacy are never, ever absolute. Look at the National Security Agency (NSA)—you'd think they'd be secure (it's right there in the name!), but they were still beaten by one guy (Edward Snowden). It's not about being 100 percent secure. That's impossible. It's about being secure *enough*. However, when it comes to computer security, most people have honestly done little or nothing to protect themselves. With this book, I will help you make sure you've been educated about all the simple, reasonable steps you can use to protect yourself. I'll even tell you some of the more arcane things you can do, if you really want to kick it up a notch.

Second, it's important to realize that you don't need to do all of the things in this book to be safer. Not all of these tips will make sense for everyone. That's why I went out of my way to explain the "why" first so that you can make an informed decision about which suggestions might do you the most good and which ones don't really apply to your situation. Don't feel like you need to race through this book and implement everything today. It's more important to take your time, understand what I'm telling you, and then start ticking things off the checklists.

Lastly, convenience is generally the enemy of security. That is, the more convenient something is, the less secure it probably is. Therefore, increasing your personal security is going to decrease your personal convenience and probably make your life more complicated than it is now—that's the hard truth of the matter. We're used to the inconveniences of real-world security; having to lock your house and lock your car all the time are inconvenient, but it's just the way things are and most of us don't give it a second thought. Having to show an ID to cash a check and enter a PIN to withdraw money from an ATM are things we're just used to doing. However, computer security is another story entirely. Most people are *not* used to doing the things that they really should be doing, and therefore some of the things that I'm recommending in this book are going to seem really inconvenient at first. Give them a try—you might be surprised how quickly you get used to doing them. It helps when you understand the benefits, so again, I encourage you to read the explanations before the checklists.

Now let's learn the basics of cybersecurity!

CHAPTER 2

Cybersecurity 101

Before we can begin to discuss security, we really have to define some key computer terms and concepts. You do *not* have to memorize this stuff, and it's okay if you don't follow everything here. There's a glossary at the end of this book that you can refer to for quick help, or you can return here if you want to refresh your memory. But for the rest of this book to make sense, I need to get you up to speed on the basics of how computers and the Internet work. I'm trying to cover all the bases here, so if you see a topic you already understand, feel free to skip it or just skim it. I've also taken the liberty of throwing in some fun little tidbits that will help to keep things interesting. There will be a wide range of people reading this book, and I just can't take the time to fully explain everything. But in this chapter, I give you a solid base to work from.

Here Be Dragons

Most people have no frame of reference for computer security—it's too abstract and too technical. I find that you can explain lots of aspects of computer security using the analogy of a castle. You have people and valuables you would like to protect from various types of attackers. To do this in the old days, people erected physical barriers like walls and moats. It turns out that these concepts work well to describe computer security, too. With that in mind, let's talk about the fundamentals of computer security using the classic medieval stronghold as an analogy.

I Dub Thee…

Congratulations! Your king, in his infinite wisdom and generosity, has granted you a lordship and has given you huge tracts of land! You have been charged with populating and protecting this new territory, all the better to generate more tax revenue for your liege. To this end, you have been provided a fixed budget of gold and raw materials. Now what? What do you do?

© Carey Parker 2018
C. Parker, *Firewalls Don't Stop Dragons*, https://doi.org/10.1007/978-1-4842-3852-3_2

Well, the first thing you need to do is to determine what and whom you need to protect. Obviously, you will need to protect your gold and other valuables. You will also need to protect the natural resources of your realm—farmlands, mines, quarries, forests, and sources of fresh water. You will want to control access to your realm, particularly the highways and waterways. The safety of the people within your realm is also paramount—not just because you're a good person but because these people are needed to farm the land, work the mines, create the goods, pay the taxes, and populate your army and personal guard.

The next thing you need to determine is what and whom you need to protect your people and resources from. Unfortunately, the threats to your people and assets are many and varied. Not only do you need to consider malicious marauders and adversarial armies, but you must beware of feral fauna, perilous pestilence, and even crafty con men. (Oh my!) It's also helpful to understand the resources of your opponent. Are they well-funded? What weapons do they possess? What attack techniques do they employ? Last but certainly not least, you need to understand the motivations of your attackers. Are they greedy or just hungry? Are they looking to make some sort of political or social statement? Do they have a reason to target you specifically?

You have a vast realm but only finite resources. You want to keep out the bad guys, but you must still allow for trade and travel. There are many possible attackers, but the risk of attack from each type of adversary is not the same. Likewise, while you have many different types of people and assets to protect, let's face it—you're of the strong opinion that some are more important than others (you and your gold, for instance). In short, you will need to make some trade-offs. Security is *always* about trade-offs. But now that we've done your threat analysis, you have a much better idea where to spend your limited resources.

As a consumer with a finite budget, you also need to evaluate your threats and decide where to spend your time and money. Luckily for you, I've done most of that work for you in this book!

It should be noted that if your attackers are much better funded than you are or have a lot more resources, then you're pretty much screwed. For example, if the Russian mob or the National Security Agency (NSA) wants to specifically target you, as an individual, you'd be hard-pressed to stop them. In our analogy, this would be like trying to defend your realm against a dragon. Prior to June 2013, I think many people would have put the likelihood of ubiquitous NSA surveillance on par with that of the existence of dragons—something crazy people wearing tinfoil hats might have raved about but almost surely wasn't true. But as the saying goes, just because you're not paranoid doesn't mean they're not out to get you.

If our fictional lord were to buy into the existence of dragons and decide that he must therefore defend against them, what could he really do? No wall could be built high enough to stop a flying beast. Regular weapons would be mostly useless against such a powerful creature. You could certainly *try* to construct some sort of domed fortress and an array of mighty, dragon-sized weaponry, but you would probably go bankrupt in the process. Even if this could be done, how exactly would you test these defenses? As if that weren't enough, it might well be that the act of attempting to create such a worthy stronghold would actually attract the attention of the dragon! Why else would someone build such a fortress unless they had something extremely valuable to protect (such as hordes of gold and jewels)? No, the only real hope of security in the face of such an adversary would be to hide in a deep, dark cave, strive to escape notice, and remain out of reach. But what sort of a life is that for your family and your subjects?

The point of this book (and the inspiration for the title) is that you shouldn't be trying to defend yourself against dragons. In our analogy, you're really not the lord—you're a commoner. You don't have a lot to protect compared to rich people or large corporations. And yet, what you have is yours, and you would like to take some reasonable, cost-effective measures to safeguard your family and possessions. Think about your current residence. You probably have tens of thousands of dollars' worth of stuff inside—clothes, electronics, jewelry, and furniture. But what stands between burglars and all that stuff? Probably a simple key lock that costs $25 at the hardware store. Could it be picked? Yes, without a doubt (you'd be surprised at how easily standard door locks can be picked—I learned how to do it in about 15 minutes). And yet, in most neighborhoods, this simple lock is enough.

By the same token, your goal isn't to protect your computer and its contents from the Russian mob or the NSA. The only way you could hope to prevent that would be to go "off the grid." Just in case you're curious, here's how that might work. First, buy a new laptop from a big-box store. Before you power it up, open the laptop chassis and completely remove any hardware necessary for wireless communication (for example, the Wi-Fi and Bluetooth chips). Set up your new computer in a windowless basement. Line the walls and ceiling of the basement with wire mesh to block radio signals. Never, *ever* connect the laptop to the Internet or to any sort of peripheral device (mouse, printer, or anything with a USB plug). Now...how useful would that be? A computer that can't connect to the Internet is almost useless today. But even if you could live with that, these drastic security measures still wouldn't stop someone from simply breaking into your house or serving you with a warrant. If you're a political dissident, corporate whistle-blower, or just uber-paranoid, then you need to read a different book. Oh, and you'd better buy the book using cash.

But the point here is that the Russian mob and the NSA are not likely to target you *specifically*. As we discussed earlier in the book, your most likely threats are e-mail scammers, hackers trying to access your financial accounts, and corporations or the government engaged in mass surveillance. For these threats, you can actually do quite a bit to protect yourself without spending a lot of time or money, and that is the focus of this book.

Prevention, Detection, and Recovery

Security generally has three phases: before, during, and after—also referred to as prevention, detection, and recovery. Prevention is about trying to keep something bad from happening, detection is about knowing definitively that something bad is happening or has happened, and recovery is about repairing or mitigating the damage after something bad happens. Obviously most people prefer to focus on prevention so that detection and recovery will be unnecessary. But no security plan is complete without all three.

Let's return to our newly minted lord and the defense of his realm. The most common defense mechanism in medieval times was the venerable castle. It's not practical to build a 75-foot-high wall around the entire realm, so a lord would build walls around the cities (particularly the one in which he and his family reside). Castles were usually built on high hills to better monitor the surrounding countryside for incoming threats and to put attacking armies at a disadvantage. In times of war, the peoples of the realm could come within the walls for protection. Castles were built mostly to defend against people on foot or on horseback. There were no airplanes, so you didn't really need to protect yourself from the air, but the walls had to be high enough to stop attackers with ladders, arrows, and catapults. In addition to walls, castles often had moats or trenches in front of the walls to make it difficult for opposing armies to attack or scale the walls. Because people still needed to come and go, the walls required at least a few openings—so you would fortify these openings with large wooden or iron gates, sometimes multiple gates per opening. Armed guards, charged with evaluating who would be allowed to pass through (in either direction), would protect these openings.

The walls and grounds were also patrolled by guards, trying to identify bad people who may have gotten through the outer defenses.

Castles had *defense in depth.* That is, they didn't have just one mechanism for keeping out attackers; they had many. Each mechanism was different, not just because different attackers had different capabilities but also to diversify the overall fortifications in case the attacker found some clever way to neutralize one of the defenses. Some defenses were passive, like the walls and the moat. Once in place, they required little to no maintenance. Other defenses were active, like the castle guard. The guards could think for themselves, take orders, and evaluate and respond to individual threats on the fly. Once given comprehensive orders and training, though, even the guards could function pretty well on their own.

It turns out that setting up defenses for your computer is similar in many ways to constructing a castle. First, your main gate is your Internet router. This is what separates you from the outside world, from both good people and bad. You need to have access to the outside world to get your food, water, and supplies, as well as to sell your goods, but you have to be careful not to let the really bad guys inside. Your router has a built-in mechanism for this called a *firewall.* Using the castle analogy, the firewall allows people from the inside to get out and come back, but it prevents all foreigners from entering unless you say it's okay. That is, the firewall allows your computer to initiate connections to the Internet (like google.com) and knows to allow the thing you contacted to reply (like giving you back your search results). But if something on the Internet tries to initiate contact with your computer, it refuses the connection (or simply ignores it), unless you've given it explicit instructions to allow the connection. By default, almost all external connections are refused by firewalls.

Antivirus (AV) software is sort of like your armed guards. They actively watch your system for suspicious behavior, and if they find it, they try to stop it. Often the AV software will then make you aware of the suspicious behavior and ask if you want to allow it. But if it's sure that it has found something bad, antivirus software will usually just go ahead and neutralize it for you.

But not all threats to your computer come from the Internet. Gaining physical, in-person access to your computer, while not as likely, is still a real threat. In this case, your "castle walls" are made of 2x4s and drywall, and your "moat" is really just a well-lit yard with some thorny shrubbery in front of the windows. As long as your computer is inside your home or some place you trust, you're counting on the locked doors, walls, and such to keep bad people away. However, if you have a laptop and you take it out of your home, then you probably have a lot less physical protection—maybe a locked car or just a laptop bag. At that point, *you* are the best protection—keeping the laptop with you, in a bag, probably over your shoulder. For laptops, you really need to set a password for your computer so that if someone does manage to steal or gain physical access to it, they can't actually access your data. You should also encrypt your hard drive, particularly on laptops. There are sneaky ways to get at the laptop data without having to log in, so encrypting the data on your drive will make that data useless if the attacker manages to circumvent the log in process.

This is defense in depth. You should have multiple layers of security for your computer and the data it contains. The more layers, the more secure you'll be. This book will help you add those layers.

We won't spend a lot of time in this book on detection. Actively determining that your computer is being attacked or has recently been attacked is tricky to do. Though you can buy some software that will monitor your personal computer for suspicious activity (usually by watching outgoing network traffic), most intrusion detections systems (IDSs) are typically marketed toward owners of large, public servers. Intrusion detection systems are similar to firewalls, but whereas firewalls are generally used to prevent intrusion in the first place, an IDS will monitor background activities and communications on the computer for signs that the attackers have already gotten in and are trying to do bad things.

In our analogy, castle guards are charged with monitoring the people moving around within the walls, looking for suspicious behavior and illicit communications with outside agents. When intruders are identified, alarms are sounded, and the rest of the guard is put on high alert until the threats have all been identified and neutralized. If regular guards are like antivirus software, then the elite castle guards are more like an intrusion detection system, but the two functions are similar, mainly different in scope and complexity.

While not particularly practical (yet) for home computers, the role of detection in security is quite important in other areas that we see every day. For example, the sealing wrappers and pop-up lids on food products are there to tell you whether the jar or bottle has already been opened. The paper or foil seals covering the openings of over-the-counter medicine were implemented as a direct result of the Tylenol murders in Chicago in the early 1980s. The seal is there not to *prevent* tampering but to make tampering *evident*. If you see the seal has been broken, you know someone has been messing with it, and therefore you shouldn't use it. In the old days, wax seals were used to secure important letters—not to prevent them from being opened but to make it obvious if someone had opened the letter prior to the intended recipient.

Despite your best efforts, you may not be able to prevent all attacks, so you also need a plan for handling the case where something bad does happen. In some cases, if you know your security has been compromised, you can take steps to mitigate the impact. You can run malware removal tools, change your passwords, close your accounts, or remotely wipe your data (in the case of a stolen computer or device). Sometimes your only option is to replace what was lost and move on with your life.

Computer Lingo

Computers are everywhere. I don't just mean desktop computers and laptops, either. Just about every piece of modern electronics has some sort of computer chip in it, and we're now entering the era where all of these computers are interconnected: appliances, thermostats, TVs, radios, even toasters (I'm not joking). Despite their ubiquity, computers are not well understood—and for good reason: they're phenomenal, intricate pieces of engineering!

My first computer was a Texas Instruments TI-99/4A (see Figure 2-1).

Figure 2-1. *Texas Instruments TI-99/4A personal computer (circa 1981)*

This computer had only 16KB of memory. My daughter's first iPod had more than 250,000 times as much memory! A guy named Gordon Moore (cofounder of Intel) wrote a paper in 1965 that predicted that computing power would double about every two years. This prediction turned out to be very accurate and was later dubbed Moore's law. The act of doubling is deceptively powerful. Let me give you a classic example. Let's say I gave you a penny on January 1, and I offered to double its value every day for the rest of the month. So on January 2 you'd have two cents. A week later you'd have a whopping $0.64. Two weeks later you'd be up to $81.92. Now we're getting somewhere, but it still doesn't seem like much. By the third week, however, the value of your stash would be more than $10,000, and by the end of the month, after 31 days of doubling, you would have a whopping *$11 million dollars!* It's hard to believe, I know, but that's the power of doubling. Using Moore's law, we can estimate that desktop computers today are more than 65,000 times as mighty as my little TI-99/4A.

I could write an entire book explaining how computers work (and maybe I will one day), but for the purposes of this book, I will cover only the essential terms and concepts, and I will discuss them at a very high level. Remember, you do not have to remember all of this; I'm just trying to get you familiar with some terms and concepts. Remember to check the glossary if you need a quick note to jog your memory.

Hardware and Software

You can't talk about computers without talking about *hardware* and *software*. Hardware refers to the physical computer and all its parts—basically the things you can see and touch. This includes not only the computer itself but the things attached to it, as well. We generally refer to these attached devices as *peripherals*, and they include the mouse, keyboard, monitor, printer, disk drives, and so on.

Software is the computer code that runs on the hardware—the complex set of instructions telling the hardware what to do in every possible situation the programmer could think of, including (and often especially) when bad things happen. The prime piece of software that runs the computer itself is the *operating system* (OS). Software *applications* are smaller, more-focused pieces of software that are meant to do specific things, like help you edit a document, listen to music, or surf the Web. The operating system handles things like starting and stopping applications, managing the computer files, connecting you to the network, and directing the peripheral devices like your mouse, keyboard, monitor, and printer. The OS is a special software application that must be there for the computer to run, and the applications are optional add-ons that perform specific tasks.

For most PCs, the operating system is Microsoft Windows; for Apple's Macintosh computers, the operating system is called macOS (previously "Mac OS X"). Examples of applications include Microsoft Word, Adobe Reader, Mozilla's Firefox, and Apple's iTunes.

You can sort of think of hardware and software in terms of a stage play. The hardware is the stage, set, curtains, lights, and sound system. The operating system is like a combination of a script, director, and stage crew—the OS controls the overall flow of the show, making sure the actors follow their lines and setting up the environment for the scene (props, costumes, lighting, sound effects). Finally, the actors are sort of like the applications, performing specific roles based on the script and using and sharing the props (data and peripherals) with other actors.

File Manager

When you're sitting at your computer and you want to look at the list of files stored on it, you do this with the *file manager*. In Windows, this is called Windows Explorer or File Explorer; on a Mac, it's called the Finder. When you double-click a folder on your desktop or open My Computer or Macintosh HD, you are launching the file manager. This may seem trivial, but some people aren't used to giving it a name.

Bits and Bytes

All the data on your computer—every document, every image, and every movie and song—is stored as bits and bytes. By the way, this includes all of your software applications and even the operating system itself. Bits and bytes are the building blocks of digital things. A *bit* is the smallest piece of information on a computer. A bit has two possible values—zero or one. A bit, therefore, is binary. That's just a fancy way of saying that it can have only two possible values (*bi* means "two"). We abbreviate bit with a lowercase *b*.

To build bigger things—like larger numbers, alphabet characters, and those fun little emoji icons—we need more than a single bit. The next largest chunk of digital data is the *byte*, which we abbreviate with a capital *B*. There are eight bits in a byte. So, since each of those eight bits has two possible values, if you do the math, there are 256 possible combinations of eight bits: 00000000, 00000001, 00000010, 00000011, and so on, till you get to 11111111.

We use various patterns of these bits to represent meaningful pieces of information—this is called *encoding*. There are a gazillion ways to encode things, mostly because you can do it any way you want as long as you spell it out clearly so that someone else knows how to *decode* it. One common example of this is ASCII encoding (pronounced "ass-key"). ASCII is used to encode characters—letters, numbers, and other symbols that you would find on a computer keyboard. For example, the letter *A* is encoded as 01000001 in ASCII. Because we want to tell the difference between uppercase and lowercase, we need an encoding for both. Lowercase *a* is encoded as 01100001. Basically, anything you can type using a computer keyboard has an ASCII representation. So, using ASCII mapping, "Hello" would look like this:

$$0100100001100101011011000110110001101111$$

The first eight bits, 01001000, represent the letter *H*, and so on. It looks ugly and complicated to you as a human, but this is the language that computers speak, day in and day out.

Now, let's talk about bigger data. One byte might be enough to encode a single key from the keyboard, but that's not terribly useful. To encode entire documents, images, movies, etc., we need lots of bytes. And just like we have shortcuts for large decimal numbers (thousand, million, billion, etc.), we have shortcuts to describe lots of bytes. These terms are based on standard metric prefixes: kilo- (thousand), mega- (million), giga- (billion), tera- (trillion), and so on. So, a kilobyte (KB) is a thousand bytes, a megabyte (MB) is a million bytes, and a terabyte (TB) is a trillion bytes.[1]

Storage

For your computer to store and process all these bits and bytes, it needs somewhere to keep them. There are all sorts of sophisticated levels of storage space on your computer, but the two most important ones are random access memory (RAM) and the hard drive. When you buy your computer, these are two of the most prominent specs you'll see on the box.

---

[1]Almost. Because computers are so tied to binary counting, they count things based on the powers of two. You frankly will probably never need to know this, but if some smart-ass tells you that 1KB is not really a thousand bytes, they're right...it's technically 1,024 bytes. Why? Because. Just trust me. For most purposes, you can just call it a thousand and be done with it. The same is true for the others (MB, GB, TB)—just go with thousand, million, billion, and trillion. It's close enough.

The best analogy I've heard for understanding how computer memory works is comparing your computer to a garage workshop. You garage holds all your tools and materials. You use the tools to work on the materials. You either make new things or modify old things. But you don't simultaneously use every tool and all your materials—you generally use one at a time, or a few at most. When it's time for you to work on a project, you fetch the specific tool and materials that you need for the moment and bring them to your workbench. When you're done, you put the tool and remaining materials back. If you try to work on too many things at once, you'll find that your workbench is full—you literally cannot use all your tools and materials at once; you have to choose. Maybe you can try to just move some to the floor nearby and swap them with something else when you need it again, but this is not very efficient.

Your computer works in a similar way. Your hard drive is like your garage—it holds all your data and all your apps, ready for you to use. When you launch a particular application or open a file, the data for the file and the application are copied from your hard drive into RAM where the computer can work with them directly and most efficiently. When you close the app, the data is copied back from RAM to the hard drive. That's why the hard drive is so much larger than your RAM. The hard drive has to hold everything, whether you're working on it right now or not; the RAM only needs to hold what you're actively working on. The more RAM you have, the more you can work on at one time—like having a bigger workbench. When you fill up your RAM, your computer actually moves things back to the hard drive to make room, trying to swap things back when you need it. That's why your computer becomes really sluggish if you try to open too many applications or big files at the same time.

If you have too much crap in your garage, you have two options: build a bigger garage or get some sort of external extra storage space, like a rented storage room or maybe a shed in the backyard. Similarly, if you want to work on more things at once, you need a bigger workbench. When this happens on your computer, you have similar choices. When you want to hold more data, you get a bigger internal hard drive or buy an extra external hard drive. When you want to work on more things at once, you need to buy more RAM.

Networks (Wired and Wireless)

When computers talk to one another, they do it over a *network*. Put another way, a network is a set of connected computers that are all communicating using a common computer communication language, or *protocol*. Most computer networks today use a communication language called the Internet Protocol (IP). Networks vary wildly in size but come in two primary forms: public and private. The public network we all know and love is the massive, globe-spanning network called the Internet (originally from the term *Internetwork*).

However, there are countless small, private (or semiprivate) networks that are attached to the Internet. These are usually referred to as *local area networks* (LANs). You might think of corporations being the primary owners of LANs, but if you have a router at home with more than one computer or device on it, then you have a LAN, too.

Networks can be wired or wireless or (often) both. Computers that are wired to the LAN use Ethernet cables (they look like phone cables with a wider plastic clip at each end). Computers that are wirelessly connected to the LAN use Wi-Fi.[2]

Figure 2-2 shows a picture of a standard Ethernet cable (wired connection) and the internationally recognized symbol for Wi-Fi (wireless connection).

Figure 2-2. *Ethernet cable (left) and Wi-Fi logos (right)*

You can't talk about cybersecurity without understanding some basic things about how computers communicate. I've devoted a whole section to this topic later in this chapter.

Bandwidth

When we move data around, we like to know how fast it can go. We measure this in "bits per second," usually megabits per second (Mbps) and sometimes gigabits per second (Gbps). This measurement is referred to as *bandwidth*. Most people run into this value

---

[2]The term Wi-Fi is just a marketing term someone made up. It was meant to sound like Hi-Fi but doesn't really stand for "wireless fidelity." It's just a lot catchier than 802.11, which is the technical name.

in two places: when they're buying Internet service from their Internet service provider (ISP) and when they're looking at networking products like Wi-Fi routers.

The best way to think about bandwidth is moving water through a pipe. You can move more water, faster, through a bigger pipe. The Internet is often referred to as a series of pipes (or tubes), and that's because of the water analogy. If you think about how water gets to your house from your town's main water source and back through the sewer system, that's similar to data moving on the Internet, at least in terms of speed (see the next section for the routing part). There are big pipes at the source that take lots of water to your neighborhood, then there are smaller (slower) pipes that come to your home, and finally there are much smaller pipes that take the water to your sink, shower, and so on.

It's much the same with your Internet service. The connections within your house are the slowest (the smallest pipes). The connection from your house to the neighborhood junction box is a good bit faster. The connection from the junction box to your cable provider is faster yet, and the connection between your service provider and the next service provider is the fastest—the biggest "pipe."

In the next chapter, I'll talk about how the Internet actually moves these bits and bytes around.

Bluetooth

Bluetooth is the funny name of a handy wireless connection technology. Its main purpose is to remove the need for pesky wires. Originally this was used mainly to connect peripheral devices to your computer over short distances like mice and keyboards, but it's gained a lot of popularity with sending and receiving audio; examples include hands-free car connections to your mobile phone, portable speakers, and, of course, wireless headphones. It is also used in some modern remote controls because it doesn't require line-of-sight like the more common infrared (IR) remotes. Figure 2-3 shows the official Bluetooth symbol so you'll recognize it when you see it.

Figure 2-3. *Bluetooth logo*

Clients and Servers

When two computers talk to each other, one of them is usually asking the other one to do something. The requester is called the *client*, and the responder is called the *server*. While it's possible for one computer to be a client in some cases and a server in other cases, in today's Internet age, almost all requests originate on your computer (client) and terminate at some big computer out on the public Internet (server). Example requests might include "show me the video with the cat playing piano" or "find all the web sites with pictures of Scarlett Johansson" or "post this totally cool photo of me for all my friends to see."

The Cloud

This has to be one of the most overused (and abused) terms in modern computer lingo. It's the latest industry buzzword, and it's being thrown around like crazy. So, what is it? When someone refers to *the cloud,* all they really mean is that it exists or is happening somewhere out in the Internet.

When engineers draw diagrams of computer networks, they often use a picture of a cloud to represent some vague grouping of things "out there"... we can't really see what's in there and don't really care. Things enter one part of this nebulous fog, and they emerge somewhere else. Sometimes they change in there, and sometimes they just come out the same. Sorta like the Internet, eh?

Today all of our computers and devices are connected via the Internet, and the connections have become so fast that we can actually send our data out there for processing instead of doing it all locally on your computer. When you send your data to the Internet for something out there to work on it, we call it *cloud computing.* An example of this would be Google Docs: instead of running Microsoft Word locally on your computer (modifying a file on your hard drive), you edit your document in a web browser, and all of this is happening on a faraway computer owned by Google. When you store copies of your data using a service like Dropbox or Google Drive, this is *cloud storage*—while the files exist on your local hard drive, they also exist on the Dropbox or Google server.

Net Neutrality

Unless you've been under a rock, you've heard the term *net neutrality.* You've also probably seen a lot of politicians and corporate spokespeople screaming about why it's going to destroy the Internet and e-commerce...or why it will save it. So, which is it?

Net neutrality, as a concept, means that no person or company on the Internet should be allowed to have preferential treatment. The Internet should be a level playing field. When you define it like that, it sounds pretty good, right? So, let's look at a real-world example and see how this definition holds.

Netflix is a popular movie-streaming service—so popular that by some estimates it accounts for over a third of all Internet traffic during peak hours! As you might expect, slinging all those bits around can seriously tax the servers on the Internet. If an ISP has to buy more equipment to handle all that demand, shouldn't Netflix have to pay them some more money to help cover the costs?

It's tempting to say yes, they should. But it's a slippery slope. The bottom line is that Internet service providers are selling a service, and if they can't deliver what they've promised, then they need to invest some money in their infrastructure. If that requires raising costs for the service, then that's what they need to do, perhaps creating tiers of service so that only the people using the most bandwidth pay the most money. But we can't be asking the companies providing popular services to foot the bill or it will turn into a money grab, and the only companies that will be allowed to play are the ones who can pay. The reason Netflix and other startups flourished in the first place was because they could compete on an even playing field. The little guys always want regulation to keep things fair because otherwise they could never compete with the deep-pocketed incumbent powerhouse corporations. But once you become a powerhouse corporation, you want to get rid of these regulations so you can tilt things in your favor and keep out the competition.

Net neutrality is not new. It's what we've had all along, at least to this point. We need to preserve it so that the next Google, Netflix, or Facebook can come into being. Unfortunately, as of the writing of this book, the U.S. government has rolled back regulations that would have ensured a fair playing field.

The Internet of Things

The term *Internet of Things* (IoT) refers to the current push to add Internet connectivity to everyday devices: toys, appliances, cars, water meters, even light bulbs, and thermostats. This allows you to control these devices from your smart phone or computer, even from outside the house. Of course, this means that others may be able to control them, as well, if they can find a bug in the software to exploit.

These devices are almost always tied to some sort of cloud service. These devices are constantly "phoning home" to the manufacturer or third parties to provide those cool Internet-connected features. The Amazon Echo and Google Home products are often brought up when discussing IoT—small Internet-connected devices that respond when you say the phrase "Alexa" (this is referred to as the *wake word*). You can ask for the weather forecast, get the latest news, order products from Amazon, and even control other IoT devices in your house. However, this also raises some obvious questions about privacy. I'll cover that later in the book.

Know Your Enemy

I'm willing to bet that you've heard most of those computer terms already, even if you didn't quite know exactly what they meant. But most people are a lot less familiar with the terminology of security. I will cover many of these terms in greater depth in future chapters, but I want to quickly define a handful of terms up front so I can at least make some passing references to them without losing you.

Malware

Malware is short for "malicious software," and it's a catchall term for software behaving badly. Much of this book is dedicated to helping you avoid malware. Protecting your computer and avoiding infections protects not just you but every other person you know (or at least all the people in your computer's address book).

As you might imagine, there are many different varieties of malware out there, and it's actually common for a single piece of malware to have multiple components/behaviors. The following are the most common types of malware out there today.

Virus/Worm: This is the term that most people have heard, and it's probably the first thing that popped into your mind when you read the definition of malware. A *virus* is a piece of malware is spread through infected files, usually requiring a user to open it to become infected. A *worm* is a special kind of virus that can replicate itself and travel autonomously to other computers over the network by exploiting bugs in the services that computers often make available remotely. Like a human virus, computer viruses tend to spread to the people you know and come in contact with. The virus can use your e-mail address book, browsing history, and other information on your computer to figure out who to infect next.

Trojan: A *trojan* is malware disguised or hidden inside "legitimate" software. The name comes, of course, from the classic tale of the Trojan horse that the Greeks used to sack the city of Troy. The Greeks hid a select group of troops inside a large, hollow wooden horse statue (Figure 2-4). They left the horse at the gates of the city as a trophy and then sailed away in apparent defeat. The people of Troy brought the horse into the city gates, and when night fell, the troops came out of the statue and opened the gates from the inside. The Greek army, which had returned under cover of night, was then able to enter the city and take it.

Figure 2-4. *Classic image of the famed Trojan horse*[3]

A trojan application or document works much the same way. You're presented with what appears to be a legitimate application or document, but the malware is hidden inside it. When you launch the app or open the document, the malware program runs and infects your computer.

---

[3]Image source: *Histoire des jouets* by Henry René d'Allemagne (1902)

Spyware: This is malware that is designed to spy on you—either to watch what you do or to look for sensitive information on your computer—and then relay what it learns to the bad guys. This might include things like account passwords, your contacts, or personal information that would allow the watcher to impersonate you (identity theft).

Scareware: Sometimes the bad guys take the direct approach to getting your money. This type of malware might surreptitiously do something bad to your computer and then offer to fix it (for a fee). Sometimes this type of malware disguises itself as a free antivirus scanner or something, and in reality this software is *causing* the problem and then offering to undo the damage. In other cases, the malware watches your online habits, waiting for you to do something potentially embarrassing, such as visiting porn sites or illegal download sites. At this point they pop up some sort of fake law enforcement warning, threatening to expose you unless you pay a fine.

Ransomware: With the rise of digital currencies like Bitcoin, we've seen an explosion in a specific type of malware called *ransomware*. Crooks infect your machine with software that effectively steals your data and holds it for ransom. The malware surreptitiously encrypts your hard drives, making the data completely unreadable—but also completely recoverable with a simple decryption key. It would be like crooks sneaking into your house, putting all your valuables in a vault (in your house), and then leaving you a note that says "If you want the combination, you must deposit $10,000 in my Swiss bank account." You technically still have all of your stuff... you just can't use it. Clever, eh? If you pay the fee, they give you the keys to decrypt and recover your data.

Note   I'll talk in Chapter 5 about how you can encrypt your hard drive to prevent someone from accessing your files if they were to steal your laptop or hard drive. However, encrypting your hard drive will not prevent ransomware... there's nothing preventing a file from being encrypted twice!

Potentially Unwanted Program (PUP): This is probably the most innocuous form of malware, though it can still be quite annoying and frustrating. This sort of malware commonly accompanies "free" software you download from the Web—you download the free app, but one or more PUPs come along for the ride—and the vendor makes money from the third-party vendors of the unwanted programs for installing their stuff on your computer. Most of these installers will warn you about the hitchhiker apps, if you dig in deep enough, but they don't make it easy to find. Assuming you find the installer configuration that shows you the extra software, you can usually deselect the additional, unwanted crap.

A more insidious type of PUP is called *adware*. Once installed, adware will pop up advertisements in some form or another. For every ad shown or clicked, a referral is paid, which is how they make their money. Sometimes adware will also collect information from your computer, as well, to be sold to marketers.

Bot: A bot (short for "robot") is a piece of software that automates something that a human would normally do. Bots are not always bad. For example, bots are used by search engines like Google and Bing to "crawl the Web" looking for new and interesting web sites to provide in their search results. Other bots might be used for slightly less benevolent things like beating real humans at online games, registering for online contests, or creating bogus e-mail accounts from which to send junk e-mail (or *spam*).

That's why many web sites force you to look at a seriously distorted picture of some letters and numbers and then ask you to enter what you see. (Those annoying tests are called CAPTCHAs.[4] See Figure 2-5.)

Figure 2-5. *Example of a web CAPTCHA form*

They're trying to prevent bots from automatically doing whatever it is that you're trying to do. They specifically create problems that they believe are easy for humans to solve but very hard for computer programs.

However, in the context of malware, bots can be used to do things on *your* behalf that you would *not* normally do—like send e-mails to everyone you know advertising pills for male genital enlargement. Some bad guys actually try to build up large networks of infected computers to form a *botnet*. A botnet is essentially an army of remote-controlled

---

[4]An acronym for Completely Automated Public Turing test to tell Computers and Humans Apart. A Turing test, named for Alan Turing, is a test that attempts to verify that you are communicating with a real human and not a computer.

computers, all pretending to be the owner of the computer but actually working for someone else. Worse yet, you may never even know that computer is doing this. One common use for botnets is to simultaneously slam some specific web site with requests in an attempt to bring their servers down (called a *distributed denial of service*, or DDoS, attack). They do this because either they don't like the owner of the web site or maybe they're trying to extort protection money from them.

Even worse, all of our wonderful new Internet of Things devices are also computers. Any computer connected to the Web is subject to hacker attacks—and because these devices are usually very cheaply made, their security is bad or nonexistent. IoT devices are favorites for creating botnets.

Cryptomining: With the meteoric rise of "cryptocurrencies" like Bitcoin, there's been a sort of digital gold rush to "mine" it. Bitcoins are mined by performing some very hard, very taxing computer operations—and as time goes on, these digital currencies are designed to be harder and harder to mine to control the supply. It didn't take long for the bad guys to turn their botnets into massive, networked mining rigs. Thankfully, the only real impact on you and your devices is a higher electric bill. Cranking up your computer's brain to work on these complex operations requires significant power.

Rootkit: This is a particularly nasty bit of malware that often attacks the operating system. It's specifically designed to hide from you and from malware detection software like antivirus programs. Sometimes the rootkit actually disables or breaks your security software, preventing it from working. To make matters worse, rootkits often find ways to hide copies of their code so that even if you do find the running copy and remove it, it just replaces itself and runs again. Rootkits are often used as a sort of beachhead on your computer, a safe landing point for other invaders. The techniques in this book will help to greatly reduce your risk for this (and all) malware.

Hardware Bugs

In recent years, a new class of threat has become popular: hardware hacking. Instead of finding bugs in the operating system, web browser, or other applications, hackers have managed to cleverly exploit vulnerabilities in the computer's processing chips, called the *central processing unit* (CPU).

Two bugs that garnered a lot of media attention (and rightly so) were dubbed Spectre and Meltdown. In an effort to eke every last ounce of processing power out of our computer chips, CPU manufacturers AMD and Intel devised techniques that allowed the CPU to precalculate various possible outcomes ahead of time and, when the particular choice of course was made, have the answer ready and waiting. This involved prefetching all the necessary data to make these decisions. It turns out that this mechanism wasn't properly locked down and a rogue application could actually peek at this data without proper permission, so this information leaked. And if that information contained private data, it could be harvested and used for nefarious purposes.

If that sounds complicated, that's because it is. These vulnerabilities and the hacks required to exploit them were devilishly crafty. But because AMD and Intel make the brains for just about every computer on the planet, it meant that just about everyone was vulnerable—Mac, PC, and even Linux (which is the dominant operating system for most big-time computer servers on the Internet). In this case, it was actually possible to patch the bugs with low-level software changes. But the day will surely come when a software fix won't cut it, and in that case, your only choice will be to throw your computer out and get a new one. Computer chips take many months to design, manufacture, and integrate into computer systems, so if this type of bug were to be found, it could be a long time before new computers would be available for purchase.

Exploit

Exploit is the general term for some sort of chink in your cybersecurity armor—a vulnerability that will allow bad things in. Exploits are usually software bugs in your operating system or an application like a web browser, PDF reader, or browser plugin. A bug is just a mistake in the code—some software engineer (like me) screwed up and missed something. It's actually easy to do, even for seasoned software writers, which is part of the reason we have so many problems with malware these days.

A *zero-day exploit* is one that was previously unknown to the general public, in particular the creator of the software containing the vulnerability. Essentially it means that the bad guys found it before the good guys did. It's important to note that many bugs go unnoticed for years before they're discovered. The vulnerability dubbed Shellshock, announced in September 2014, is one of the worst zero-day bugs ever found—and it was lurking in the software since 1989!

How the Internet Works

The Internet is a fascinating piece of technology (actually many different technologies, playing together more or less nicely). Entire books are devoted to explaining this stuff, but I want to focus here on how the data moves—because it's important to understand these concepts before talking about the things we do to protect the data as it moves.

When you surf the Web, send an e-mail, upload a video to YouTube, or stream a movie on Netflix, you are transferring data between your computer and some other entity on the Internet—often a big server owned by the likes of Amazon, Google, or Netflix, but sometimes another computer like yours (if you're doing a Skype session with a friend, for example). Data can travel in two directions, and we like to label these directions so we can talk about it. When data goes toward the Internet, we call that direction *up*; when data moves toward your computer, we call that direction *down*. So, when you are pushing a video file to YouTube, we call that *uploading*; when you are buying a song from iTunes to play on your computer, you are *downloading*. If you think of the Internet as "the cloud," then you can remember this by thinking that clouds are up.

But how does that really work? Glad you asked! It's actually really cool. As I said earlier, data is made up of bits and bytes. If you make a perfect copy of the bits, then you make a perfect copy of the data. To get data from one computer to another computer, you just have to find some way to reproduce the same bits, in the same order, on the other person's computer. Let's say you want to send someone a Microsoft Word file. You don't physically send your bits to someone else—you send *copies* of the bits. When you're done, the file exists on both your computer and on their computer, and the two files are 100 percent identical.

So, how do we do that exactly? Again, it would take an entire book to tell you the real deal here, so we're going to simplify things considerably. The Internet works a lot like the U.S. Postal Service's first-class mail system. The USPS is in charge of getting letters from point A to point B, and it does so using a vast array of methods and technologies—most of which you never see or know about. All you know is that if you put your letter in the mailbox, with the recipient's address on it and a stamp, they'll take care of the rest! If you want that other person to send something back, then you need to also include a valid return address. As far as you know, it's just magic—it somehow leaves your mailbox and ends up in the other person's mailbox, right?

Well, let's take a look at what really happens behind the scenes after you put that letter in the mailbox. Every so often, usually once a day, a mail carrier comes by to check your mailbox. If the mail carrier finds a letter in the mailbox, they take it and throw it in their pile of outgoing mail. At the end of the day, the mail carrier takes the pile of outgoing mail to a sorting facility that looks at all the "to" addresses and starts separating the mail into bins based on destination. Local mail may go right back out the next day with the same mail carrier, whereas mail to another state will likely be put on a truck or plane and sent to another post office for local delivery at the far end. They may split that pile up and send it different ways, even to the same destination. How they split this up might depend on how full the truck or plane is, on whether a particular truck or plane is out of commission, or even on the fluctuating costs of fuel. The route taken and the method of transport will also vary based on what type of service the user paid for (media mail, first-class mail, or special overnight delivery). There may be multiple stops along the way and multiple methods of transport. Again, as the sender, you don't know or care how it gets there—only that it does get there, and in a reasonable amount of time.

Internet routing works very much the same way. Every computer on the Internet has a unique address. It's called an *Internet Protocol address*, or IP address for short. An IP address is set of four numbers separated by periods like 74.125.228.46 or 72.21.211.176.

FUN FACT

Each one of those four numbers in an IP address ranges from 0 to 256. So if you add up all the possibilities, that's more than 4 billion possible unique addresses…and, believe it or not, we're already running out! There's an expanded addressing scheme that is slowly being rolled out that will save the day called *IPv6* (which stands for Internet Protocol version 6, which will replace the current *IPv4*). IPv6 has a truly stupefying number of unique addresses.

$$340,282,366,920,938,463,463,374,607,431,768,211,456$$

Yeah, that's one number. I've heard it said that every single atom on the planet Earth could have its own IPv6 address… and there would still be enough left over for 100 more Earths!

To make those numbers easier for humans to remember, we give them aliases like "google.com" or "amazon.com"—we call those aliases *domain names* or *hostnames*. When your web browser or e-mail application is told to use one of these aliases, your computer invokes a service called the Domain Name Service (DNS) to convert the alias to an IP address.

So, when you tell your computer to send some data across the Internet, it packages that data up, slaps on the destination IP address, and puts the data in a sort of digital mailbox, waiting to be picked up. Your return IP address is automatically added so that the computer at the other end can send you a reply. Once the data is picked up for delivery, it's dispatched through a series of special computers called *routers* that figure out how to get your info from here to there. The exact route it takes may be different each time, based on how busy the routers are, the costs charged by the various carriers, and any special handling that your computer may have requested. More on that in a minute.

Now, as fancy as the Internet is, it doesn't have the notion of shipping large things in a single package—like shipping a big box full of stuff at the post office. Basically, everything is letter-sized. Why is that? Well, when you're dealing with bits and bytes, you can deconstruct anything into small pieces and reconstruct them perfectly at the other end! (It's sorta like that scene in *Willy Wonka* where Mike Teavee is transported across the room.) Since the individual pieces may take different routes, they may actually arrive out of order at the far end. So, how do we fix that problem? As you chop up the big thing into little pieces, you give them a number, counting from zero to whatever. At the other end, they can use the numbers to put everything in the proper order when reassembling the data.

To think about this, let's go back to our analogy of the post office. Let's say you want to ship a copy of the Oxford Dictionary to someone across the country, but you can ship them only one page at a time. How would you do that? Well, first you'd have to copy all the pages and stuff each one into its own envelope. Every one of those envelopes would need to have the recipient's address on it. Instead of putting a stamp on each one, you just pay the USPS some sort of bulk mail rate and they take care of that for you. The pages are already numbered, so if they arrive out of order, your friend will be able to put them back in the proper order.

However, now you realize that your mailbox isn't actually big enough to hold all of these letters at once. Now what? Well, you just have to do this in batches, maybe 100 letters at a time. Once the mail carrier empties your mailbox, you can put in 100 more. The person at the other end opens all the envelopes and reassembles them in order (using the page numbers). When the last letter arrives, they will have the complete book!

Now, the U.S. mail service (like the Internet) isn't perfect…sometimes letters get lost. So, how do you handle that? Well, you ask the person at the other end to send a letter back every so often telling you what they've received so far. If they find that some pages are missing, they can ask you to resend them.

That—in a nutshell—is exactly how data is sent across the Internet—but instead of taking weeks, it takes fractions of a second! Your computer breaks the file or e-mail or whatever into small chunks called *packets*. Each packet is labeled with a "from" address and a "to" IP address. Those packets are then numbered so that the computer on the receiving end will a) know in what order to reassemble them and b) know if any packets are missing and need to be re-sent. See, it's not that hard!

Why do you need to know all of that? I'll explain in later chapters. We'll revisit this analogy when we talk about privacy, authentication, and encryption.

Tools of the Trade

Now that we've reviewed the basics of computers and we've learned the fundamental operation of the Internet, it's time to turn to the really cool stuff! Okay, I will stipulate here and now that normal people may not share my deep-seated fascination for the mechanics of cybersecurity. But I'm going to do my best to win you over. One of the important takeaways from this book is that you can trust the math. The media and pop culture like to make it look easy to hack into secure systems, cracking passwords and breaking encryption with ease. In reality, modern computer security algorithms are extremely robust and nearly impossible to crack, if implemented properly (which turns out to be a crucial "if"). Despite the billions of dollars spent on supercomputers at places like the NSA and GCHQ,[5] the tools that cryptographers have created hold up surprisingly (and thankfully) well. In this chapter, we're going to discuss the processes and tools that allow us to shop and bank online, as well as communicate privately and keep our computer data from being read by others.

Encryption and Cryptanalysis

What problems are we trying to solve here? Why do we need cryptographic tools in the first place? Let's consider the classic case of a personal diary. I would like to be able to write some thoughts down and save them in such a way that only I will ever be able to read them. You could just hide this journal somewhere and hope no one finds it. This is a form of *security through obscurity*, something that is secure only because its existence isn't known. In the realm of cryptography, this is never sufficient, at least not as the primary means of security. No, what you really want is some sort of mechanism by which we can render the words completely incomprehensible by a third party, even if they steal the journal—and yet somehow be fully readable by you.

---

[5]Britain's version of the NSA, which is called Government Communications Headquarters

---

SECURITY THROUGH OBSCURITY FAIL

Security through obscurity is used way more often in the real world than it should be. For anything important, it should simply never be used. Here's a real-life example of how the implementation of security is just as important as the underlying technical aspects. A tech startup company debuted a new Wi-Fi-controlled "smart" light bulb. This would be part of the Internet of Things: connecting everything to the Internet so that users can control them remotely using their smartphone or computer. The idea was that once you set up your first bulb (where you must give it your Wi-Fi credentials so it can connect to your home network), any added bulbs would talk to the "master" light bulb and automatically connect to your Wi-Fi network. How convenient! These amazing little devices had a private "mesh" network that allowed them to talk to one another. Since wireless communications are broadcast over the airwaves, hackers can easily eavesdrop on the signal. Well, the engineers at this company understood this, so they used "military-grade" encryption to prevent eavesdroppers from tapping into these communications. Unfortunately, the encryption key they used—the lynchpin for any successful encryption—was a fixed, hard-coded value! That is, *there was only one key for all of their products*. But they hid this key away inside the memory on their light bulbs... who would ever figure out how to extract it? Hackers, of course. They were able to take one of these light bulbs, hook up some wires to the computer chip inside, and pull out the key. All a hacker needs to do is come close enough to your house to "hear" the light bulbs talking to each other, and they can decrypt the transmissions and see your household Wi-Fi login ID and password. The company counted on no one bothering to poke around in their devices to find the encryption key—security by obscurity. Once this key is made public (i.e., no longer obscure), the jig is up for all customers who bought these bulbs. The company updated its software with a fix, but it still requires the customers to get around to updating their light bulbs to remove the vulnerability... which is not very likely.

As you may have guessed, what we need here is *encryption*. We need to somehow transform the words we wrote into some other representation that appears to be pure gibberish to someone else. In cryptography, the original text is referred to as the *plain text*, and the garbled output is called the *cipher text*. We call it that because to convert the plain text to cipher text, we run the plain text through a *cipher*. A cipher is a secret code or algorithm that maps letters in the plain text to letters, numbers, or symbols in the cipher text. These types of cyphers are referred to as *substitution cyphers* because you substitute each letter of the regular alphabet with one character from a cypher "alphabet."

This is the classic "secret decoder ring" from bygone years. If you're not familiar with the secret decoder ring concept, it's basically two wheels, side by side, connected together on a common hub. Each wheel has a sequence inscribed on its edge so that if you rotate the wheels, you can align the letters or numbers in multiple ways. When the letter sequence is the same on both wheels, we call this a *rotational cipher*. Let's say that each wheel just has the alphabet in the proper order so that if you align the letter *A* on one wheel with the letter *A* on the other wheel, then they are in perfect alignment all the way around... *B* on the first wheel maps to *B* on the second wheel, all the way to *Z* mapping to *Z*. That's a crappy cipher, so let's give the wheel a spin... let's say now that *A* maps to *N*. That would mean that *B* would map to *O*, *C* would map to *P*, and so on. Because the wheels are round, when you get to *Z*, the next letter is *A*, and it continues. This is actually a special rotational cipher referred to as *ROT13*, which is short for "rotate 13 places"—because the letter *N* is 13 places away from the letter *A* in the alphabet. Since the English alphabet contains 26 characters, if you run ROT13 encoding on something *twice*, you end up back where you started (because 13 + 13 = 26).

Figure 2-6 shows an example of this. You can see the entire alphabet mapping and also see how the word *Hello* would be encoded using this scheme.

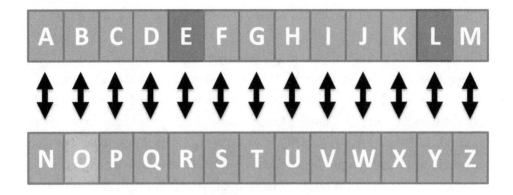

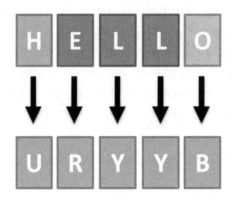

Figure 2-6. Alphabet character mappings for the ROT13 rotational cipher

My favorite pop culture example of the secret decoder ring comes from the classic movie *A Christmas Story*. The primary character, Ralphie Parker, has just received his Little Orphan Annie secret decoder pin in the mail, and now he's part of the Little Orphan Annie "Secret Circle." At the end of each radio broadcast of the classic adventure series, announcer Pierre Andre would read off a secret, ciphered message that only kids with the decoder could interpret. In this case, the cipher mapped letters to numbers, so one wheel had the alphabet while the other wheel had numbers. (See Figure 2-7.[6])

---

[6]This is my personal decoder pin, obtained from the A Christmas Story House and Museum in Cleveland, Ohio. If you're a fan of the movie, it's a must-see (https://www.achristmasstoryhouse.com/)!

Figure 2-7. *Little Orphan Annie decoder pin from A Christmas Story*

To decode the message, you needed to know how to align the two wheels—and Pierre informed his listeners to set the dials to B-2. In other words, the letter *B* mapped to the number 2. This is the simplest conversion possible because *B* is the second letter of the alphabet. Therefore, *A* is 1 and *Z* is 26. Ralphie's first message as part of the Secret Circle was as follows[7]:

2-5-19-21-18-5-20-15-4-18-9-14-11-25-15-21-18-15-22-1-12-20-9-14-5

Using his decoder pin, Ralphie painstakingly decoded the message. We know that 2 maps to *B*, so the first letter is *B*. The fifth letter of the alphabet is *E*, so that's the second letter of the message. The 19th letter is *S*, and so on, until we ultimately get this:

B-E-S-U-R-E-T-O-D-R-I-N-K-Y-O-U-R-O-V-A-L-T-I-N-E

At this point, Ralphie slowly reads the message, figuring out where the word boundaries are… "Be sure… to drink… your… Ovaltine. Ovaltine? A crummy commercial?"

Now let's flip this whole process on its head. Let's play the bad guy now. You have intercepted this secret message, and you want to know what it says. How would you go about trying to break the cipher? The process of trying to break a cipher is called *cryptanalysis.* Modern cryptography is performed by computers and is essentially beyond the capability of a mere mortal to break unassisted, but in the olden days, ciphers were performed by hand and broken by hand.

---

[7]As you can see in the figure, the actual decoder pin wasn't a true rotational cipher. But I've simplified it here for the purposes of our example.

Figure 2-8. *German WWII Enigma machine (photo by Karsten Sperling)*

Modern Cryptography

Modern ciphers revolve around the notion of a secret key. You take your plain text, plus some sort of text key (much like a password), and run it through an encryption algorithm. The result looks like complete gibberish. Unlike our simple substitution cipher previously, the output may not have a direct character-for-character mapping—it might well not even be representable as English characters at all. But, if you take the same secret key and apply the algorithm in reverse (the decryption algorithm), you get the original plain text back. This sort of cipher is called a *symmetric cipher* because the same key is used to both encrypt and decrypt (see Figure 2-9).

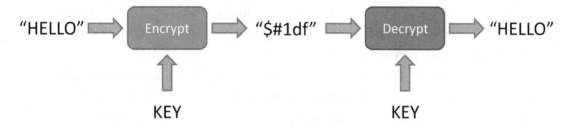

Figure 2-9. *Symmetric encryption flow diagram*

It's crucial to note here that the encryption and decryption algorithms themselves are public and well known. That is, the process for mangling and unmangling (demangling?) the text is *not secret*. In the past, people have argued that we would be more secure if the algorithms themselves were secret. That sort of sounds intuitively correct—like a magician not telling how his tricks are done. But that's exactly the point— it's not really magic if there's a trick to it. If I could break your encryption just by knowing how you did it, then the entire process is dependent on that secret never being leaked or discovered—not just for one person but for everyone who ever used that algorithm—and therefore, every message or file ever encoded with that algorithm. In today's world, that's just not good enough. Any encryption scheme worth using must be secure even if the detailed mechanics of the scheme are well known. This also allows the algorithm to be exhaustively tested and scrutinized by crypto experts.

If you're just using a cipher to encrypt personal data, like your diary, the symmetric cipher works quite well. You choose a password, commit it to memory, and use it as the secret key to encrypt the text of your diary. No one knows the key but you, and as long as you picked a strong password, that diary is completely unreadable by anyone. But again, you have to notice the caveat I slipped in there...you must choose a strong password for this to work. We'll discuss this in depth in a later chapter, but for now just realize that computers are so powerful that they can guess millions or even billions of passwords per second in an attempt to crack your diary open—so choosing your granddaughter's name or favorite football team is not going to cut it.

You can think of symmetric encryption as a trunk with a strong lock—you have the key, and only you can open the lock. It doesn't matter if people have the trunk in their possession—unless they have the key, they can't access the diary kept inside. It shouldn't even matter if they know how the locking mechanism was made. For this analogy to compare well to modern cryptography, we must assert that the trunk would be completely impenetrable, and the lock would be effectively impossible to pick.

The crucial element then is the key for the lock. As long as you have the key in your possession and there are no other copies of the key, then only you can open the lock, and therefore only you can access the contents.

Having the ability to lock up your diary is a good thing, but there are other situations in the real world that require security. In cryptographic parlance, we've covered the case of *data at rest*, but what about *data in motion*? That is, what about communications? In this new scenario, we've crucially increased the number of people who need to be able to access the information from one to more than one. We've also added the requirement that we need to be able to send this data across some distance, in the hands of third parties that we can't necessarily trust. To use a symmetric cipher for this purpose, you must now share your secret key with the intended recipient. But how will you do that securely? You can't just send it to them—someone might intercept it along the way. You might tell them over the phone, but what if your phone or their phone is being tapped? You would have to meet them in person and whisper it in their ear. And yet, that's not always practical or even possible.

Thankfully, some really sharp researchers devised a radical new approach to encryption in the mid-1970s that revolutionized secure communications and encryption in general. They essentially invented a lock with two keys: a public key that is used to close the lock and a private key that opens the lock. This is referred to as *asymmetric encryption* because different keys are used to encrypt and decrypt. In this scheme, copies of the public key are given away freely and indiscriminately, while only the owner holds the private key. Anyone wanting to send a message will use the recipient's public key to lock the message, and the recipient will use their private key to unlock it. What a brilliant and elegant solution! With this technique, it is now possible for two people to communicate securely without ever having to physically exchange a single, shared key.

You can think of it like this. Let's say Alice wants to send some confidential documents to a colleague across the country, Bob.[9] While Alice could get on a plane and hand them off in person to Bob, that's way too expensive and inconvenient—she wants to just ship them via U.S. mail. Alice has a nice little box that she can secure with a lock, but she can't just send Bob a copy of the key in the mail—after all, anyone along the way could make a copy. Being a smart woman, she knows that she doesn't have to rely on a symmetric locking mechanism—she can use an asymmetric method. To accomplish this, Alice tells Bob to send her an open padlock. She then takes Bob's padlock and

---

[9]Alice and Bob are well-known in the cryptographic world. These are the names used when describing communication scenarios in lieu of saying "Party A" and "Party B."

fastens it on the box. She didn't need Bob's key to close it; anyone can close the lock simply by clicking it shut. However, only Bob can open the padlock because only he has the key. If Alice was really smart, she could even include one of her own padlocks with the box when she ships it so that Bob could return the documents to her using the same technique.

So, how does all of this apply to you and your computer? As we discussed in an earlier part of this chapter, whenever we send an e-mail, watch a video on YouTube, shop at Amazon.com, pay bills using our online bank account, or just surf the Web, we're sending data to and receiving data from the Internet. That data is chopped up into bite-size pieces called *packets*, and those packets make their way from your computer to some other computer (or vice versa). Along the way, those packets go through potentially dozens of other computers, routers, switches, and servers. The key thing to remember here is that those digital missives are a lot more like postcards than letters. That is, any person (or computer) along the way who takes the time to look at them can see whatever they contain.

For some of what we do on the Internet, that may be acceptable, but obviously there are situations—like banking and shopping—that will require a secure connection. The communication protocol used by the Internet is HyperText Transfer Protocol (HTTP). You've seen this many times when looking at web addresses like `http://yahoo.com/`. If you are observant, you may have noticed that sometimes it's not `http` but `https`. That extra *S* stands for "secure." When your web browser is communicating via HTTPS, you should see some sort of indicator like a padlock icon that indicates that your communications with that web site are secure. That means that no matter how all your packets are bouncing around the Internet, only the computer at the far end can actually decipher them.

Authentication and Message Integrity

Hurray! We have asymmetric encryption! Problem solved, right? Not quite. It's not sufficient just to prevent someone from seeing the contents of your communication. Let's go back to our document shipping analogy with Alice and Bob to see why. How did Alice know that she was actually shipping the documents to Bob? If I were a crafty spy, say Mallory, I could try to insert myself between Alice and Bob—pretending to each of them to be the other party. This is called a *man-in-the-middle attack*. The crucial step here is to intercept communications between Alice and Bob. Let's say that Mallory infiltrates the U.S. mail service so that she has access to all the correspondence between Alice and Bob. When Bob sends one of his open padlocks to Alice, Mallory intercepts the package and replaces Bob's open lock with her own open lock. She doesn't have Bob's key, but she also doesn't need it. When Alice sends the classified documents to Bob, she has unwittingly locked the box with Mallory's padlock, not Bob's. Mallory intercepts the package and opens the box using her key. If she wants to be really sneaky, she can simply copy the contents and relock the box with Bob's lock (which she saved). Bob receives the package, unlocks the box using his key, and wrongly assumes that the contents have not been viewed by anyone else.

As a man (or in this case, woman) in the middle, Mallory can create all sorts of mischief. For example, not only could she copy the contents of the messages and packages, she could *change* them. Let's say Bob asks Alice to send him $10,000 in cash. Since Mallory has intercepted this communication, she could alter the message to say $20,000 instead. When Alice sends the $20,000, Mallory can remove half the money and send the remaining $10,000 to Bob, who will receive exactly what he asked for and no one would be the wiser. Better yet, Mallory could replace the cash with counterfeit bills and pocket everything!

So, how do we solve this problem? We now need to come up with some way for Alice to convince Bob, beyond a shadow of a doubt, that not only was she the only person who could have sent this package but also that the contents of the package have in no way been altered. To solve this problem, we need to not only use our public and private keys, but we need to introduce a new tool called a *cryptographic hashing function*. (I know... it sounds super technical... just hang with me on this.)

First of all, for simplicity, let's just talk about sending a document from Alice to Bob. Alice has a set of pages that she needs to send to Bob securely, with complete confidence that no one has altered or intercepted them along the way. What sort of tool would we need here?

Let's say there exists a document X-ray machine that can effectively merge multiple pages into one. It stacks up all the pages and shoots a magic ray through them all, capturing what is essentially a shadow of all the text on the pages, merged into a single composite "X-ray" image. We'll call this machine a *Dox-Ray machine*!

To see how this marvelous Dox-Ray machine works, let's use a simple example. Figure 2-10 shows five sentences of about the same length.

> Once upon a midnight dreary, while I pondered, weak and weary,
>
> Over many a quaint and curious volume of forgotten lore--
>
> While I nodded, nearly napping, suddenly there came a tapping,
>
> As of some one gently rapping, rapping at my chamber door.
>
> "'Tis some visiter," I muttered, "tapping at my chamber door--
>
> Only this and nothing more."

Figure 2-10. *Five phrases*

Now let's stack these five phrases on top of each other (Figure 2-11).

Figure 2-11. *Five phrases stacked on top of one another*

This is the Dox-Ray image of all five phrases, the merging of all the lines, one on top of the other.

This Dox-Ray image has some very interesting properties. First, it's completely unique and predictable, based on the input. The one and only way to get this *exact* X-ray is to use these exact same words, in the exact same order. If you changed, added, or deleted even a single character, the X-ray image would also change.

Second, there is no way for you to get the original five phrases back from this Dox-Ray image. This is a "lossy" conversion: information is lost in creating it. It's therefore a one-way conversion. Given the input (the five phrases), you can always reproduce the output (the X-ray image); but given the output, you cannot get back the original input.

Finally, this process produces something small and a fixed size. If you imagine that we run this X-ray process on a set of pages of a book, the output will be the size of a single page, regardless of how many pages are in the original book. You're basically squashing the entire tome into a single sheet of paper.

So, our Dox-Ray machine can take a set of document pages and produce a unique image of all those pages—a single page that represents dozens or even hundreds of input pages.

Now let's give this Dox-Ray machine to Alice and Bob! With this nifty device, Alice could take an X-ray of her document and include that image with the package. When Bob receives the package, he could use his own Dox-Ray machine to create an image of the document he received. He can then compare his image with the one sent by Alice. If they're identical, then Bob can be assured that the document hasn't been altered in any way. If Mallory attempted to alter the document in any way—removed a page, used Wite-Out correction fluid, replaced a page with different text, or tried to add a new page—the Dox-Ray machine would produce a different image. So, even if Mallory could intercept and inspect the package, she can't alter the document in any way without being detected.

This is essentially how a cryptographic hashing function works. You put in a bunch of text and out comes a short value. If you alter just one letter of that input text, the value changes completely. It's also effectively impossible to find another set of words that will end up with the same hashing result.

Let's test that theory, just to prove the point. Using a popular crypto hash function called SHA-256, here is the hash output using this entire 300+ page book as input:

4a939d318741a70f67af9e3fbb28d5f2ebeccc799c0ee6bf0de59628bbcc7178

Now here's the hash of this book after altering just a *single character*:

1fd4094a7780cdc18c54c339bc4011669656455e7a64a32b4769aafa6516e6b7

Do you see any similarities in those two numbers? Nope. They're completely and utterly different. So, this is even better than our Dox-Ray machine—one tiny change in the input creates a massive change to the output.

If I've managed to make you properly paranoid, you will realize that there's still a problem here. Why wouldn't Mallory, who obviously has access to the contents of every package, just swap out the X-ray image that Alice included with the package? She could alter the contents, re-create the X-ray with the new document, and include *that* image in the package. This is where the public key crypto comes back into play, and this is where the padlock analogy breaks down.

Now we need to imagine a different sort of lock, one that doesn't exist in the real world—let's call it a *SuperLock*. This lock has two key slots: one to lock it and one to unlock it. The keys to work this special lock always come in pairs. One is a public key, which is copied and given out to anyone who wants to have one; the other is a private key, which is never copied and held only by the owner. Either key can be used to close the lock, but once locked, only the other matching key can open it. The same key cannot do both things—one key locks it, and the other must unlock it. Any two keys will work, which is the beauty of the SuperLock, but the keys have to be a matched pair. With me so far?

SuperLocks are available in fine stores everywhere, but to have a pair of matched keys made you must go to a very special locksmith—a SuperLocksmith, naturally. This locksmith will create a pair of matched keys, one public and one private. The locksmith will also keep a copy of your public key and make a duplicate for anyone who asks, free of charge. Finally, this locksmith will also vouch for the fact that he made the lock for you, specifically, and can prove that he gave the single, private key directly to you. Basically, the SuperLocksmith is verifying and vouching for your identity.

Okay... assuming you followed all of that and bought into the concept, we can now say two powerful things. First, if I lock a SuperLock with someone's public key, then that someone is the only person on the entire planet who can open that lock (because they are the only person who has the private key). That is to say that I know for a fact that if I were to lock this special lock with one of Alice's public keys (which I could pick up for free from the locksmith), then I can be sure that Alice, and only Alice, could unlock it. Second, if I were to receive something with a lock on it and Alice's public key could open that lock, then it must have been Alice who locked it—and therefore I can guarantee that whatever is in the locked box did in fact come from Alice.[10]

Now we have all the tools we need to resolve our dilemma. We're in the home stretch here! Hang with me just a bit longer...

Let's start from the top again and see how this works with our new tools. Alice wants to send Bob some confidential papers. She wants to make sure that no one else will be able to read these documents, even if they were to intercept them in transit. She also wants to make sure that Bob will know beyond a shadow of a doubt that Alice was the one who sent them. Finally, just to be safe, Alice wants to also give Bob the means to verify that the documents have not been altered in any way.

So, Alice and Bob both buy a Dox-Ray machine and a SuperLock. Alice and Bob take home their private keys and order a copy of the other person's public key online or pick it up from a local locksmith. Alice puts the confidential papers in the box. Then she takes out her Dox-Ray machine and scans the documents. She puts the Dox-Ray image into another smaller box. She then locks this smaller box with one of her own SuperLocks using her private key. Since the box was locked with Alice's private key, anyone can open it using one of Alice's freely available public keys. The point in this case is not to protect the contents (the X-ray image)—the point is to declare that Alice was the one

---

[10]This provides something called *nonrepudiation*. That's a fancy legal term that basically means Alice can't plausibly deny that something digitally "signed" with her private key came from someone else.

who X-rayed the documents and therefore the one that sent the package. Now Alice puts the little box inside the big box, along with the documents, and locks the big box with another SuperLock using Bob's public key. At this point, the only person who can unlock that big box is Bob. Alice confidently hands her package to her new mail carrier, Mallory.

When Bob receives the box, he unlocks it with his private key. He then removes the smaller box that contains the X-ray image. Using Alice's public key, he opens the smaller box and removes Alice's X-ray image. Because the SuperLock opened using Alice's public key, he knows that Alice was the one who locked the SuperLock on the smaller box. He then whips out his Dox-Ray machine and takes his own image of the documents he received. The image exactly matches the one Alice sent! Now he knows that even if the box was somehow compromised, the contents have not been altered.

And there you have it! At a base level, these are the same mechanisms used to secure just about all communication on the Internet today. There are many different algorithms and complex combinations of these mechanisms, but the fundamental principles are the same. The public and private key pairs are negotiated behind the scenes by your computer (the client) and the far-end computer (the server). While you could actually create a public/private key pair and register them with a formal key authority (the locksmith in our analogy), most average people have no need for this. You prove your identity when you first set up your online account, and from then on you use a combination of user ID or e-mail address and password.

Triple-A

We're almost done with the basics of security, but we need to take a minute to explain AAA, or Triple-A. No, not the American Auto Association. Not Anti-Aircraft Artillery, either. In the world of cybersecurity, AAA stands for "authentication, authorization, and accounting." We've already discussed authentication, so let's quickly talk about authorization and accounting.

Once you have a mechanism to definitively identify someone (authentication), you may also want to restrict what that person is allowed to do. For example, if you've ever worked for a large company, you may have been issued an ID badge that can be swiped to give you access to different areas within the company's buildings. The ID badge provides authentication under the assumption that only the person to whom the badge was issued would be in possession of the badge. At this point, you can allow or deny that person access to certain areas by either allowing or disallowing their badge to unlock certain doors. This allows you to compartmentalize access to sensitive regions within a building. Knowing that only a handful of people can get through a given door means that you have a limited set of suspects if something is stolen from that area, for example.

You can also use these badge swipes to keep a record of who has accessed the restricted region and when they were present. This is the third *A* of Triple-A: accounting. If a new piece of lab equipment is reported missing from a restricted lab, the security team can see who was in that room around the time it went missing.

Newer Isn't Always Better

In the realms of security, there is a constant struggle between using the latest and greatest technology while at the same time not trusting anything until it has been proven using the test of time. Let's say you were in a castle with an angry horde outside your gates and I came to you with a new-fangled magical force field that I guarantee will be stronger than any stone wall you could build. Would you tear down your walls and install the force field based on my word? Probably not. What if I showed you reams of laboratory data where I tested my force field against a stone wall with simulated attacks? If you were properly worried about your safety, this would still not be sufficient. Yet, if this product were truly better than what you have now, you'd be wrong to ignore it. So, what would you do?

Well, you'd probably deploy the new force field *in addition to* your existing walls and see how it held up during some actual assaults by actual adversaries. And you would probably do this for some time before you decided it was safe to rely solely on this new technology. Stone walls are something you know and trust. You know how they're built; you know how to build them well because you've gone through many iterations of building them. You know their weaknesses, and you've figured out how to shore them up. But this new force field thing... it's never been used. You really have no idea how it will perform in the real world. What if the designer missed something crucial? What if it works great in the lab where you can control everything but works poorly in the real world where there are many variables outside your control: having unfailing and unlimited access to magical energy, for example.

The same is true for security. New encryption schemes, new authentication systems, and new security processes are generally shunned until they've been around for at least a few years. This gives independent security teams a chance to kick the tires, take it for a spin, and see how it performs in the real world. It's all well and good to come up with a new encryption algorithm that's mathematically sound on paper, but it's quite another to actually implement this algorithm in software and hardware.

While there is certainly a lot more to know about cybersecurity tools and processes, this chapter has introduced you to the primary conceptual building blocks that underlie information security.

Privacy and Tracking

We can't discuss computer security without discussing privacy. As we've discussed in earlier parts of this chapter, bad guys having access to your private data can greatly increase their ability to crack your passwords or convince someone that they're you (identity theft). For these reasons alone, you need to be very careful about how much information you give away about yourself online to Google, Facebook, Instagram, Twitter, LinkedIn, and so on.

But there's much more to privacy than what you knowingly and willingly give away. In fact, the truly scary part is what you're giving away every day without really knowing it. Your credit cards and debit cards are convenient for making purchases, both online and at brick-and-mortar stores. It won't surprise you that MasterCard, Visa, and American Express know all about where you shop, what you buy, and how much you spend. It also shouldn't surprise you that major retailers also keep similar records.

After the Cambridge Analytica scandal, no one should be surprised at the amount of information social medial companies like Facebook and LinkedIn have on you. You should probably also realize that Google has more than any of them. Google is not a search engine, an e-mail provider, or a document collaboration service... Google is an advertising company, period, end of story. More than 90 percent of its revenue is from selling ads, and it can charge a premium for its ads because they're highly targeted. And they're highly targeted because they know unbelievable amounts of things about all of us.

What you, as a consumer, need to realize is this:

If the product is free, then you are probably the product.

That is, all of these "free" online services have to make money somewhere. If they're giving you some service for free, then they have to make money somewhere else.

What you may not realize is that many of these companies sell your data to other companies, as well. These are companies we call *data brokers*. I've seen estimates that there are 2,500 to 4,000 data brokers in the United States alone. These companies are essentially unregulated (as of the writing of this book...changes may be coming soon). You don't own your data, and in most cases, you can't even look at your data. Have you considered why grocery stores have "loyalty cards"? Whenever you present your card, you are allowing them to associate all your purchases with you.[11] While they will almost certainly use this information to better target you with store promotions, they are probably also selling this information to third parties.

Want to know what info they have on you? Acxiom, one of the largest data brokers, has created a web site that lets people view the profile they have on you. If you want to see what your profile looks like, go to aboutthedata.com. You'll have to create an account by giving them your e-mail address. (Don't worry about giving away that information... trust me, they already have it.) If you go to this web site, you will see that they have collected a treasure trove of information about you: income range, house and car value, marital status, number of children, education level, political party affiliation, types of products purchased, debt levels, household interests, and so on. While you may be surprised at the information you find there, what you need to realize is that this is just the tip of the iceberg. This site only shows you the "core" information they collect. It doesn't show things like sexual orientation, propensity for gambling, and known health issues. It also doesn't show you the correlations and associations they've made about you...whether you have a sick mother, a rich uncle, or a shopaholic spouse.

One of the most lucrative consumers is a newly pregnant one. New parents spend tons of money, and locking in brand loyalty at this stage is paramount to product sellers. In February 2012, Forbes ran a story about how Target correctly predicted that a woman in a household was pregnant based on the types of products she was buying: unscented lotion and soap, large quantities of cotton balls, washcloths, and particular vitamin supplements. Based on a high "pregnancy prediction score," according to the story, Target took it upon themselves to send some unsolicited baby product coupons to the woman in the mail. Unfortunately, this "woman" was a teenage high school girl living with her parents, and she had not yet told her father the news. Some of the specifics of this story have been called into question, but this is precisely the sort of situation that can arise from broad data collection and correlation. This is the world in which we are currently living, and it's just getting worse.

---

[11]Here's a fun workaround to giving your personal info. If your store allows you to find your loyalty card using your phone number, try your local area code plus 867-5309. If you were a 1980s teenager, you'll recognize this as the telephone number for "Jenny" from the one-hit-wonder song by Tommy Tutone.

Though the stated purpose of gathering this information and creating these detailed personal profiles is to provide supposedly anonymous demographic information to advertisers, you have to realize that you have no real control over the buying and selling of this data. You can attempt to "opt out," but you're relying on these unregulated companies to voluntarily comply with your wishes—not just now but forever. As if this weren't bad enough, you must also realize that because someone is maintaining this information and saving all of this data, that means the government and law enforcement agencies will also have access to this information—and they probably don't even need a warrant to get it. In fact, you can access some of this information yourself. Your IP address, because of the way these ranges of numbers are administered, can tell a lot about you—who your ISP is and where you are physically located (at least city and state[12]).

And just to completely demoralize you, I must state one more fact: even if you do pay for a service, that doesn't guarantee that the company providing the service still won't turn around and try to make extra money off your personal information. It was revealed a couple years ago that both AT&T and Verizon were adding tracking information on all of their users' Internet usage. Basically, any time you browse the Web from your smart phone, AT&T and Verizon were tagging all of your requests with a marker (sometimes referred to as a *supercookie*), which can be seen by any web site you visit. This marker changed periodically, allowing AT&T and Verizon to basically sell subscriptions to your online activity. But even if web sites don't pay for this information, they can still use that ID to track you. If they can find some other way to independently figure out who you are, then it has the same effect. The only good news here is that the tracking happens only when using the cellular network for Internet access, and it works only on unencrypted web surfing. When you go to web sites that support HTTPS, the communication is protected, and no tracking IDs can be added.

After a consumer backlash, AT&T and Verizon eventually gave their users a way to opt out of this tracking. In fact, Verizon was fined $1.3 million by the FCC over this (which is nothing to Verizon). But this just goes to show that even paying a lot of money for a service doesn't guarantee that they won't sell your information to make more. Sadly, as of March 2017, the rules that were put in place to stop these practices were gutted. ISPs are now totally free to collect as much info on you as they can to use and/or sell as they please.

---

[12]You can try this yourself. Go to ip2location.com.

Here's another story that will make you cringe. A story in Salon by Michael Price[13] tells about a marvelous new "smart TV" that he purchased to replace a failing, old "dumb" TV. This TV came with all sorts of wonderful, built-in features like web browsing, e-mail, social media, streaming TV services, apps, and games. Then he made the mistake of reading the fine print.

> *... I'm now afraid to use it. You would be too—if you read through the 46-page privacy policy. The amount of data this thing collects is staggering. It logs where, when, how and for how long you use the TV. It sets tracking cookies and beacons designed to detect "when you have viewed particular content or a particular e-mail message." It records "the apps you use, the web sites you visit, and how you interact with content." It ignores "do-not-track" requests as a considered matter of policy.*

It gets worse. This TV has a built-in microphone and camera that are used to provide face and voice recognition. The privacy policy actually states the following: "Please be aware that if your spoken words include personal or other sensitive information, that information will be among the data captured and transmitted to a third party."

Of course, we now live in the age of virtual assistants like Apple's Siri and Amazon's Alexa. We purposely buy products that listen to us all the time so that we can ask them for the news or the weather, buy stuff, and even turn things off and on.

This is the world we live in now, filled with smart devices that track our every move, physically and virtually, and report that information to some nebulous "third party." As the Internet of Things becomes a reality and many more dumb devices become smart devices, the potential for tracking and breach of privacy will grow by leaps and bounds.

The real issue today with monetizing your data is that most people are simply not aware of what is actually happening and they have little to no control over the data once it's collected. We need more transparency, and we need the option to "opt out"[14] of data collection, even if taking that option costs money. People should have the choice, and it should be an informed choice. As consumers and as citizens, we need to compel our government representatives to stand up for our interests. These companies must

---

[13]https://www.salon.com/2014/10/30/im_terrified_of_my_new_tv_why_im_scared_to_turn_ this_thing_on_and_youd_be_too

[14]The term *opt out* refers to a situation where a company signs you up for something but gives you the option to back out if you make some effort. For example, they might automatically include you in some data-gathering program but allow you to "opt out" if you change some preference on your account or send them a signed form. An *opt in* program is the opposite: you have to explicitly ask to be in.

provide free and easy access to the profiles they keep on us (much like credit companies must provide free copies of our credit reports) and allow you to edit this information or completely remove it, if you ask. I would go further and say that you must "opt in" for any data collection, but it's frankly too easy to get this approval. How often have you actual read the end user license agreement (or EULA) that comes with all the software you install or the online services you use?[15] Buried in there somewhere is language that allows the software maker to pretty much do as they please. The only way we're going to change this is to elect representatives that will enact regulations to keep these companies in line.

While the European Union has taken some big steps in the right direction with the General Data Protection Regulation (GDPR)—addressing most if not all the aspects I listed earlier—the United States is actually *deregulating* the data collection industry. It remains to be seen whether the Equifax, Facebook, and Cambridge Analytica scandals will finally reverse this trend and foster some commonsense regulations in the United States.

Who Can You Trust?

So, who *can* you trust these days? That's a critical, fundamental question, and as a society, we need to be asking it a lot more than we are. Unfortunately, there's no easy answer. If you think about this too hard, it quickly becomes deeply philosophical. But my job here is to try to simplify things for you, so let's look at this from a practical standpoint.

First, we need to decide what we mean by *trust*. Violating trust is not just about intentionally trying to do you harm. Online service providers and marketing firms are certainly not trying to harm their customers by gathering and selling mass quantities of "anonymized" personal data. In fact, they would (and do) argue that they're helping you by trying to tailor the ads you see on the Web to your specific interests. By better targeting the advertisements presented to you, they increase the likelihood that you will actually want to know about the products and services for sale, while avoiding showing you ads for things you don't want to see. Because targeted ads are more valuable to marketers, they can also make more money per ad, meaning they should be able to (theoretically) reduce the overall number of ads to make the same money. They view

---

[15]There's a great documentary on the topic of these EULAs and the data being collected on all of us called *Terms and Conditions May Apply*.

this as a win-win situation (or at least this is what they claim). You may very well decide that you're willing to sacrifice some privacy to get free web content and services. But it's important that you realize how you're paying for these services and to realize that your data is probably getting sold to other third parties, as well, who may have entirely different purposes.

At the end of the day, you need to try to determine the motivations of the person, corporation, or entity behind the advice or service being offered. In many cases you just need to ask, how do they make their money? Are you paying a fair price for what you're getting? If you're paying nothing or if the price is too good to be true, then you should think carefully about trusting the source. Many online services that are "free" make their money by selling advertising and by getting kickbacks when you click links that take you to other sites. They also make money off selling your information to interested third parties—which you probably agreed to when you signed up for the service, in cryptic language buried deep in the license agreement. Sadly, as we discussed in the previous chapter, we also know that paying a fair value for a service does not mean you can trust the provider, but the odds are at least better.

Besides "following the money," you also need to think about other motivations and ask deeper questions. Is it in this service provider's own best interest to be open, honest, and transparent with you? Or do they stand to gain more if they confuse, mislead, or scare you? Let's think about that one for a minute. Before the advent of the Internet and before CNN came into being, most people got their news from newspapers and the nightly TV news. In the "old days" (like 30 to 40 years ago), TV news was not about making money—it was about providing a public service. (This wasn't out of the goodness of their hearts; it was actually mandated by the Federal Communications Commission under various "public interest" requirements for broadcast licensees.[16]) However, in the intervening years, as Nielsen ratings and advertising dollars have become the driving force in television, our "news" programs have become "infotainment." The focus is not educational or informational; it's about getting (and keeping) eyeballs. Boring facts don't rivet people in their seats. "Will watching the nightly news actually kill you? The answer will shock you! Tune in at 11!" The more sensational, the better.

---

[16]http://benton.org/initiatives/obligations/charting_the_digital_broadcasting_
future/sec2, reference 32. Amendments to Delegations of Authority, 59 FCC 2d 491, 493 (1976)

Summary

- Cybersecurity is analogous to physical security. To be truly secure, you need understand your adversary's capabilities and motives. You need to know where your weaknesses are. And you want to have several layers of defense, not just one.

- Security is never absolute, and there are always compromises. You'd go broke trying to be completely secure, so you have to make intelligent trade-offs.

- We reviewed all the basic computer and cybersecurity terms. If you forget something, remember to turn to the glossary for quick help.

- Encryption is a marvelous tool that allows us to keep our data safe and secure—both on our hard drives and as it traverses the public Internet.

- The real threat today is to our privacy. In the United States, corporations and third-party data brokers are harvesting vast amounts of personal data with little or no regulation. This data is ripe for abuse and begging to be stolen by hackers or misappropriated by overzealous agencies.

Checklist

It's time to start doing stuff!

Tip 2-1. Know Thyself

We need to take a moment to jot down some key information that you will need to have handy. This information will be needed for you to choose which sets of directions to follow in the checklists. You'll want to make note of the following information:

- What sort of computer do you have—is it a desktop computer or a laptop? A desktop computer is always plugged into the wall for power; a laptop has a built-in battery so that the computer is portable and does not need to be plugged in all the time.

- What operating system (OS) is running on your computer? This book covers modern versions of the two most popular OSs: Microsoft Windows and Apple macOS (formerly called OS X). One quick way to check the type and version of your OS is to simply go to this web site:

  `http://whatsmyos.com/`

- At the top of the page, it will tell you its best guess at your OS type and version. The page will also explain how to "manually" determine your operating system. This is crucial information, so you might take the time to verify it manually. Examples of Windows versions are 7, 8, 8.1, and 10. Mac OS versions have numeric versions as well as code names. Examples of macOS are Sierra (10.12) and High Sierra (10.13). For older Macs, you might find Mac OS X version 10.11 (El Capitan) or 10.10 (Yosemite). If you do not have any of these versions, then your OS is pretty old, and you will have some trouble with the OS-specific recommendations in this book. However, other recommendations will still be useful.

Tip 2-2. Know What They Know

I've tried to explain to you how much data is being collected on you, but I doubt the magnitude of this has really sunk in. Did you know many popular services give you the option to download all the information they've collected on you? Now, realize that in many cases, they only give you the raw data, not all the things they've *derived* from this data. They also don't share the information they may have from other sources. Nevertheless, seeing this data for yourself is quite eye-opening, and I strongly encourage you to download as much of this data as you can and take a long hard look at it.

Note that in just about every case, they will arrange to send you a big "zip" file to download. A zip file is a compressed archive of a bunch of files and folders. Once you download this file, you can double-click the `.zip` file, and it should expand to a folder that is full of other files and folders.

Google:

1. Go to `https://takeout.google.com/settings/takeout`.

2. You'll see dozens of Google services there. I would leave all the boxes checked, except perhaps Gmail; you already have all your e-mails, and there's no need to download them all again.

3. Scroll to the bottom and click Next.

4. The default settings here should be fine, so just click Create Archive.

Facebook:

1. Go to Settings on the Facebook web site.

2. Click "Download a copy of your Facebook data" at the bottom of the General Settings page.

3. Click Start My Archive.

Twitter:

1. Go to your Account Settings on the Twitter web page.

2. Click the Request Your Archive button.

LinkedIn:

1. Go to your Account settings for Privacy.

2. Click How LinkedIn Users Your Data at the left.

3. Click Download Your Data.

4. Click The Works.

5. Click Request Your Archive.

Apple:[17]

1. Log in to Apple's Privacy web site: `https://privacy.apple.com/`.

2. Under "Obtain a copy of your data," click Getting Started.

3. Select the data you want to download. You may want to skip things you already have like e-mails.

4. Select the chunk size for the data, that is, what the maximum size of each file download should be.

5. You'll get an e-mail when your files are ready for download.

---

[17]Note that this feature will initially be available only in the European Union but should roll out to other countries soon.

CHAPTER 3

The Three Ups: Back Up, Clean Up, and Update

With the key background knowledge from the previous chapter, we're ready to really dig in and start taking some truly important steps to being more secure. If you were to do nothing else but follow the tips at the end of this chapter, you would be miles ahead of most people.

Backups

What if you had a time traveling device...Doctor Who's TARDIS, Hermione's Time Turner necklace, Doc Brown's DeLorean, or the classic HG Wells contraption? Then you really wouldn't have to worry about security, right? If something bad happened, you just go back in time, before it happened, and then avoid it the second time around. Short of maybe death, there would be really nothing from which you couldn't recover. You would have the wondrous power of the Do-Over!

This is the same principle behind backing up your data. If you keep regular backups of your data, then you can really never lose anything. While backing up your data can't prevent someone from copying and abusing your data (for example, identity theft), it can at least prevent you from losing your data to a virus or a crashed hard drive or even a natural disaster. Backing up your data is one of the best techniques for mitigating the damage from an attack or random stroke of bad luck. Luckily, in today's world, it's pretty easy to do, though it does cost money. Think of it as insurance, and it's money well spent.

You have two main options: a local external backup hard drive or an online backup service. Let's look at the local external backup hard drive option first.

As we discussed in the previous chapter, all your data—your files, documents, digital photos, downloaded music, and home movies—lives on your computer's hard drive. Unlike all the crap in your garage, you can create perfect and free copies of all of this data anytime

© Carey Parker 2018
C. Parker, *Firewalls Don't Stop Dragons*, https://doi.org/10.1007/978-1-4842-3852-3_3

you want. Keeping a backup copy of this data is as easy as buying an external hard drive, plugging it into your computer, and then telling your computer to use this drive for backup.

Both Windows and Macintosh computers come with software built-in for this purpose. This software is even smart enough to keep multiple backups. It's not just a single copy of your data—it's a rolling copy of your data as it changes. The first backup will obviously need to make a copy of every single file, but subsequent backups only need to make copies of the files that have changed. This technique will allow you to get older versions of files, in case you realize that you somehow messed up a file or just want to undo a bunch of changes you made. Having a full backup of your entire hard drive, with multiple versions, is really just like having a time machine (and in fact, Apple cleverly dubbed its backup software Time Machine). You can return your computer to just about any point in time—on a per-file basis, if necessary. You can even completely restore your entire system to a new computer if your current computer bites the dust.

Sounds pretty foolproof, right? The external hard drive option is a good solution for most people. However, there are at least two problems with this option. First, it doesn't protect you from natural disasters. If your house burns down or floods with water, the hard drive sitting right next to your computer is going to suffer the same fate as the hard drive that's inside your computer. Second, viruses and malware can mess up an attached external backup drive just as easily as they can mess up the drive inside your computer. However, external drives are still excellent protection against hard drive crashes, accidental file deletion, or any problem that affects only the main computer. They also tend to be the cheapest solution over time because they require only a one-time cost (buying the external hard drive).

Now let's look at the second option: online backup (also called *cloud backup*). This includes services such as Carbonite, iDrive, Backblaze, and many others. This sort of service is slightly easier than the external hard drive option in that you don't have to buy an external drive. You sign up for the service, you download their application, and you tell it to start backing up your stuff. The cost varies from service to service and even varies over time for a given service because of competition and falling costs of storage. (At the other end of your Internet connection, they have a hard drive with your name on it—so essentially you just paid them to buy the external drive and keep it off-site for you.) Unlike the fixed cost of buying your own external hard drive, these services make money by charging you an ongoing fee to keep your data for you. So over time, this option is going to cost more than the previous option.

Online backups solve the natural disaster problem because the storage is outside your home. It also usually solves the malware problem because there is no direct access to the external backup drive from your computer. But the online backup solution has other drawbacks. First, there's just the problem of logistics. Let's do the math. (Don't worry, *I'll* do the math; you just follow along.) Let's say you have a one terabyte hard drive, which is fairly common. Let's also assume you have a modest Internet connection that allows you to upload two megabits per second. That means when everything is working perfectly, under ideal conditions, you can upload two megabits of data to your online backup service every second. How long would it take you to copy your entire hard drive to the online backup provider? First, note that your drive is one tera*byte*, but your upload speed is measured in mega*bits*. If you recall from the previous chapter, there are eight bits in a byte—so one terabyte is eight terabits. If you divide eight terabits (8 trillion bits) by two megabits (2 million bits) per second, you will see that it will take *four million seconds...* which is more than 46 days! Recall that this assumes ideal conditions, which will never happen for 46 straight days. If you have better broadband service, you can cut that time down quite a bit, but just realize that it may take quite a while for that first backup to complete. And what happens when you need that data back? Luckily, most people's Internet connections are much faster for downloads than for uploads, but it could still take many days to get all that data back.

So, why would anyone bother with an online backup solution? First, you're probably not going to upload your entire hard drive to the cloud. For example, you don't really need to back up your operating system, which takes a lot of space. You probably don't need to even back up most of your software applications, since you can probably just reinstall them from disk or re-download them from the Internet. You might not even need to back up your music, if you have it all on CD somewhere or you bought it online. This could greatly reduce the amount of data you really need to back up. Most people really only *need* to back up the files that they simply cannot replace—documents (which are usually very small), personal photos, and maybe home movies. Second, you only need to upload everything one time. It will take a long time, but once it's done, you only need to upload the changed files and new files. So while it may take a few weeks for that initial backup, it will be much faster after that. Finally, your hard drive is probably not 100 percent full. Our calculations were based on worst case.

The second problem with online backup is the creepy factor. That is, you're giving all your data to a bunch of complete strangers...those embarrassing spring break pics, the "love letters" from that psycho you dated from Match.com, your tax returns, and potentially even things like your browsing history and e-mails. If you back up your cell phone data to your computer, you could be exposing your text messages, contacts, and location history, too. But wait, surely all your data is encrypted, right? Probably. Sorta.

It may be locked up, but who holds the key? Any service worth considering will encrypt your data during transit (from your computer's drive to their off-site drive), which will prevent someone like your Internet service provider from seeing any of the data as it flies by. And my guess is that most services will tell you that they're encrypting your data on their hard drives, too. If they do this properly (and that's a big "if"), this would protect your data from anyone hacking into their system or from a nosy employee. However, if served a warrant[1] from the police or FBI or a National Security Letter from the U.S. government, they would be required by law to decrypt your data and hand it over (and probably also be strictly prohibited from telling you that they did it). And if they're able to decrypt it for legal reasons, then they can decrypt it for any reason.

So... which option is best? Honestly, if you can afford it, I recommend you do both. They each solve the same problem but in slightly different ways, with various pros and cons. If you do both, you get the best of both and address the shortcomings of each.

However, if cost is a problem, I recommend using an external hard drive. It's quicker, it's cheaper over the long run, and it keeps your data in your own control. If you want to go the extra mile to protect against natural disasters or anything that could destroy both your computer and your external hard drive at the same time, then use *two* external hard drives: swap them once a month and keep one drive off-site somewhere.

If the computer you're backing up is a laptop, having an external hard drive that is always connected can be a pain. If you don't mind paying an ongoing fee and want to know that your data will always be safely held off-site, then using an online backup solution is a viable option. The first backup will take some time, but after that, it should perform similarly to a local hard drive. As competition heats up and storage prices fall, these services will become cheaper and add more features. If you want to ensure your privacy, you can find services that will allow you to encrypt your data before you upload it, too—meaning that all they will see is an indecipherable blob of bits. However, that means if you lose the key, your data is effectively gone; even though the online service technically still has your information, neither you nor they can read it. However, I will show you in a later chapter how to solve this problem.

I would like to make one further recommendation. Computers need electricity to run, and if that electricity gets yanked with no notice, it can really cause serious problems for your computer, including corrupting your data. It doesn't have to be a complete power outage, either—just a flicker or "brown out" can cause your computer to

---

[1]Thanks to the CLOUD Act, passed in early 2018, they may not even need a warrant.

shut down abruptly. For this reason, if you have a desktop computer, I strongly suggest buying an *uninterruptable power supply* (UPS). This is basically a big battery that can be used to power your computer if the power to your house goes out. You plug this battery into the wall and then plug your computer into the battery box. When the power goes out, the box will supply power to your computer for a short amount of time—the bigger the battery you buy, the longer it will let your computer run. But all you really need is enough power to give your computer the time to properly shut down. Most of these UPS boxes have a data connection to your computer, as well, and can tell the computer when it should shut down. This means it will work without you being there to monitor it.

Spring Cleaning

It's time for a spring cleaning of your computer! It's time to purge the things you don't need or don't use. If the software in question was a free download or something you've installed from a disk, then you can just reinstall it if you find later that you need it. Also, you have a complete backup of your system (right?), so in the absolute worst case, you can always dial the clock back and get right back to where you were.

Awww, but I don't wanna clean my computer! Do I hafta?

As we discussed in the previous chapter, one of the most important things you can do to protect yourself is to reduce the number of places where you are exposed (in the security biz, this is referred to as your *attack surface*). Every single piece of extra software you have installed—every application, toolbar, utility, plugin, and extension—is just one more place that an attacker can probe for vulnerabilities. All software has bugs. Adding more software adds more bugs, and bad people can exploit those bugs. Therefore, you should take every opportunity to close the gaps, reduce the number of vulnerabilities, and lower the risk of bad guys getting in.

There are actually other good reasons to clean up your system. First, those extra apps take up space on your hard drive. Second, many applications and utilities have components that run in the background, whether you're actively using them or not. That chews up memory resources, for sure, and potentially processing power and Internet speed. Finally, many of these utilities and extensions are started automatically every time you boot your computer, which can significantly increase the time it takes to start up. Have you felt like your system has been running more slowly than it used to? Do you find it slower to surf the Web? Does your computer take forever to restart? Getting rid of the junk might very well speed things up.

Update Everything

Once you've backed up all your stuff and you've gotten rid of all the excess stuff, then the last thing you need to do before we proceed is to update the stuff that's left after the dust settles.

It's *extremely* important to keep your software applications and utilities up-to-date, particularly your operating system and Internet applications. New bugs, holes, and other vulnerabilities are found in software *all the time, every day... 24/7/365.* The bad guys are plentiful and highly motivated, and they don't honor business hours or national holidays. Mature and responsible software companies are diligently patching these holes and making updates available as soon as they can. While it's true that any time you change software—even if you're trying to fix a bug—you may well end up creating some new bug, it's still best to keep up-to-date.

Both Microsoft and Apple have made keeping your operating system up-to-date easier over the years, even automating the process. If you turn on the right options (and I'll show you how), your computer will keep itself up-to-date. Apple has even managed to provide a mechanism to keep non-Apple applications up-to-date automatically, as well. Individual software companies have implemented proprietary methods for keeping their software updated—usually popping up a dialog that tells you there's a newer version of your software and giving you the option of installing it. While sometimes annoying, this is a good thing.

I strongly recommend you enable these automatic update mechanisms. Yes, it's possible that an updated version of your operating system or cherished software application will remove some feature you love or totally change the look and feel, but from a security standpoint, it's essential that you stay up-to-date.

If you're a Mac OS user, I highly recommend updating your operating system to the latest and greatest. Apple stopped charging for these upgrades, so there aren't many reasons *not* to upgrade. The main reason you might not want to upgrade is if you're running a really old but crucial piece of software that is not compatible with the newer OS version (and doesn't have a free update that makes it compatible). Nevertheless, there are many important security features in the newer OS versions, and if possible, I would upgrade. And that may mean buying a new version of those critical applications or finding a different application that can take its place.

Microsoft charges a pretty penny for major OS updates. Upgrading to Windows 10 will cost you about $120 as of this writing. But unless you have a real reason to stick with whatever version you have now, I strongly recommend that you go ahead and update to Windows 10; it has some really nice security features, and Microsoft appears to be giving away even the major updates for the OS. Windows 7 and 8.1 will stop being supported very soon.

The recommendation to upgrade to the latest OS is purely for security reasons. The most recent OS will almost always have the best security technology. While Apple and Microsoft will also try to patch older versions with security updates, there are quite often key new security techniques built into the OS that are not included in those updates to older versions.

Sadly, there is a privacy trade-off with these upgrades. Part of the reason Apple and Microsoft are giving away the operating system updates is because they're making money in other ways, including gathering valuable information about you. Nevertheless, this is pretty much unavoidable because there's nothing stopping them from adding these same "features" to older version of the OS, too, via the regular software update mechanism. So, on balance, it's best to stay current on the OS version.

Upgrading your operating system is outside the scope of this book. So if you decide to do this and you have any reservations about doing it yourself, you might want to find a tech-savvy friend or relative to help you. Before you upgrade, be sure to set up your backup! See the first section of this chapter's checklist for instructions.

If you don't want to turn on automatic updates, then you will need to periodically run through all your software and update it manually. I recommend at least once a month for most applications and weekly for your operating system and crucial applications like your web browser, e-mail program, and any "office suite" software (word processing, spreadsheet, or presentation software).

Summary

- One of the best ways to ensure yourself against catastrophic loss is to make full backups of all your files, or at least the truly irreplaceable ones. You can do this using an external hard drive or using a cloud backup service.

- Once you've backed everything up, you should take some time to clean up your hard drive—remove unused applications and utilities. Every piece of software has bugs and holes, so if you're not using something, it's safest to just get rid of it. You can always reinstall it later if you find that you do want it.

- You need to keep your operating system and key applications up-to-date. Software bugs and security holes are discovered all the time, and keeping up-to-date should help to mitigate your risk.

Checklist

For this checklist and every checklist in this book, I will assume that you have not read the preceding parts of the chapter that explain why you should do the things listed in the checklist. Nevertheless, I highly recommend you do read the explanation part of the chapter, if you can find the time. For you to know which of these tips will make the most sense for you, you'll need to understand why they're important.

Operating System Configuration

For many of the operations in this book, you will need to be able to open the system settings to configure something. To do this, follow these instructions.

Microsoft Windows 7

In Windows 7, the general system settings are in the Control Panel. To access the Control Panel, click the Windows Start menu at the lower left and then click Control Panel, as shown in Figure 3-1.

Figure 3-1. *Accessing the Windows 7 Control Panel*

Microsoft Windows 8.1

Windows 8.1 has two locations for system settings: the Control Panel and a new Settings window. The easiest way to open the Control Panel is to right-click the Windows menu icon at the lower left and select Control Panel (Figure 3-2).

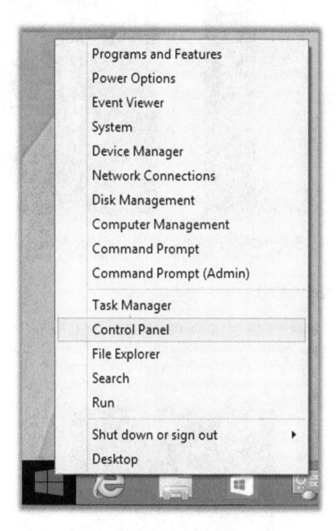

Figure 3-2. *Accessing the Windows 8.1 Control Panel from the Windows menu*

You can get to both the Control Panel and the Settings window by moving your mouse to the lower-right corner of the screen to pop open the right-side menu. From here, you can click the gear icon (below left) to bring up Settings or click the Control Panel menu option (below right) to bring up the Control Panel (Figure 3-3).

Figure 3-3. *Accessing Windows 8.1 Settings (left) and Control Panel (right)*

Microsoft Windows 10

In Windows 10, there are two places to change settings: Control Panel and Settings. To get to Settings, click the Windows icon in the lower left and select Settings (pictured in Figure 3-4).

Figure 3-4. *Accessing Windows 10 Settings*

Once the Settings window is open, you can search to find the Control Panel (Figure 3-5).

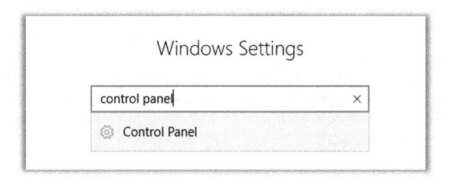

Figure 3-5. Accessing the Windows 10 Control Panel

Mac OS

Mac configuration is done via System Preferences, which is accessed via the Apple menu in the upper left (Figure 3-6).

Figure 3-6. Accessing Mac OS System Preferences

Tip 3-1. Back Up to an External Drive

Backing up your computer is one of the best ways to protect your important computer files and data from getting lost or messed up (either maliciously or accidentally). If you have a solid backup of all your important files, you can always replace them if something should go horribly wrong.

You have two main options for backup: an external hard drive or an online (*cloud*) backup service. If you can afford it, I would do both. If you feel you have to choose just one option, I would read the section of the chapter on backups to help you choose which one would be best for you.

Buy an External Hard Drive

External USB hard drives have gotten very affordable, and the prices are constantly falling (in terms of cost per byte). These boxes come in various shapes and sizes but are generally rectangular and are between the size of a paperback book and an oversize deck of cards. These devices are frequently on sale at places like Best Buy, Office Depot, and Fry's. You can also buy them online at many places, such as Amazon.com or newegg. com. I would look for a sale on a name-brand drive such as Western Digital, Toshiba, LaCie, or Seagate. If you need help, I would go to a local store and ask someone in the computer department to make some suggestions. You have three main choices to make: type of drive, USB version, and size of drive.

- *USB-powered ("portable") versus AC-powered*: Hard drives require power to run. This power can be provided by the computer itself (USB-powered portable drives) or via a standard AC wall adapter. I recommend a USB-powered drive because they reduce a lot of clutter and tend to be a lot smaller in overall size. However, if you go with a USB-powered drive, the drive must be plugged into a *powered* USB port. That would be a port on the computer itself or a port on a powered USB hub (i.e., one that is itself plugged into the wall via AC adapter).

- *USB version*: Be sure to get a USB 3 drive (not USB 2), even if you have an older computer. Most recent PCs and Macs support USB 3. USB 3 drives will still work on older USB 2 ports, and it will "future proof" your next computer upgrade. USB 3 is a *lot* faster than USB 2. If you have a choice, USB 3.1 is faster than USB 3.0.

- *Drive size*: I would plan to buy a drive that is at least twice the size of your computer's internal hard drive. If you have very few files, you can probably get away with a drive that's the same size as your computer's drive, but you might want to also plan for the future.

Connect the Drive to Your Computer

Once you have the new shrink-wrapped hard drive box in your hands, open it up and take out the contents. The drive will almost surely come with some instructions for attaching the drive to your computer—a "quick-start guide" or similar. Follow these instructions for connecting the drive to your computer, but it's pretty straightforward: the USB cable can connect only one way. That is, the ends of the cable are different—one will connect to your computer (or USB hub), and the other will connect to the hard drive.[2] If the drive requires wall AC power, then it will have a separate power cable: one end will fit into the hard drive, and the other will be a typical AC wall plug. Note that you will need to leave this drive connected at all times so that the backup software can do its thing when it needs to.

Note 1   On a Mac, when you first plug in a new hard drive, it may automatically ask you if you want to use it for Time Machine. *Don't click anything yet*—wait until the "Configure Your Backup" section. You can close this window for now.

Note 2   Many external drives come with bundled software, often including backup software. In this book, I will walk you through using the free and effective backup software that already comes with Microsoft Windows and Mac OS. If you decide to use the included backup software, then you can ignore the rest of the steps for this tip and just use the instructions that come with your hard drive. However, I strongly

---

[2]If you happen to get one of the newer USB-C drives because you have a new computer that supports this newer standard, the USB-C cables have a much smaller tip that can be inserted on either end and in either direction; it doesn't matter.

suggest you *not* use the proprietary backup software. It usually has all sorts of extra stuff you don't need and just confuses matters. Some drives also come with some cloud backup service, as well—often free or discounted to begin with, and of course the cost goes up later. Again, I would *not* use anything that comes with it. It's probably more expensive, and I doubt it's functionally better than the ones I will refer you to in this book.

Configure Your Backup

This will differ depending on your operating system and OS version. Choose the following section for the OS type you have. Be sure that your new external hard drive is connected properly before continuing.

Tip 3-1a. Microsoft Windows 7

Note   It's possible that Windows will ask you for your system installation disk for this process. This disk should have come with your computer when you bought it. If you do not have this, you can still do backups, but you won't be able to create a system restore disk (i.e., back up your entire computer including operating system). That's not ideal, but it's okay—the most important things to back up are your irreplaceable files.

1. When you first plug in your new hard drive, you will probably see some messages about the drive being set up and drivers being installed. Just let this process complete until it says your device is "ready for use" (you'll see a little pop-up window at the lower right of your screen).

2. You should then see a pop-up dialog like the one in Figure 3-7. If so, click "Use this drive for backup" and skip to the next step.

Figure 3-7. *Window 7 dialog for setting up new backup drive*

3. If you do not see this AutoPlay dialog within a minute or so of
    connecting your hard drive, you will need to manually launch
    Backup and Restore. To do this, go to the Start menu and search
    for *backup*. Select Backup and Restore (see Figure 3-8).

Figure 3-8. *Windows 7 Search for backup*

4. In the next window, click "Set up backup" at the right side
    (Figure 3-9).

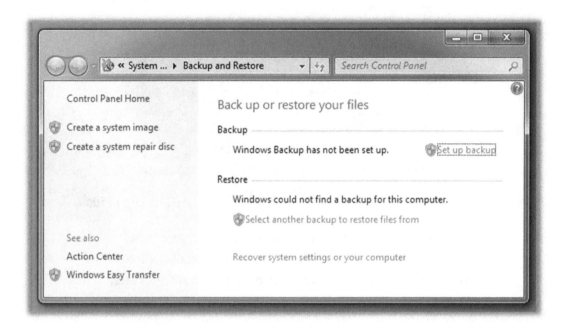

Figure 3-9. *Windows 7 Backup and Restore dialog*

5. At this point, regardless of how you launched the setup, you
    should see a window asking you to wait while Windows Backup
    starts (Figure 3-10).

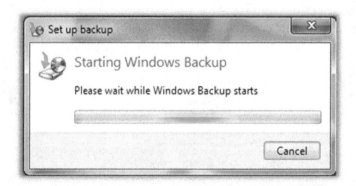

Figure 3-10. *Windows 7 Backup starting dialog*

6. If you are asked which drive to use for backup, select the new hard drive you just connected and then click Next.

7. Windows will then ask you which files to back up. Select "Let Windows choose" (the default option). Click Next (Figure 3-11).

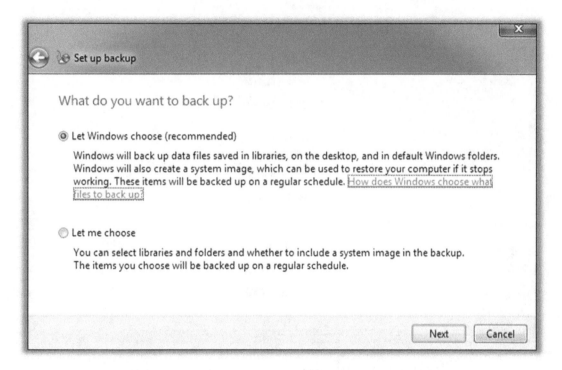

Figure 3-11. Windows 7 backup selection dialog

8. You will then be asked to review your settings. The default settings here should be fine, but you can tweak the schedule if you'd like. When done, click "Save settings and run backup."

9. At this point, Windows will create your first backup. You should see a progress window like the one shown in Figure 3-12.

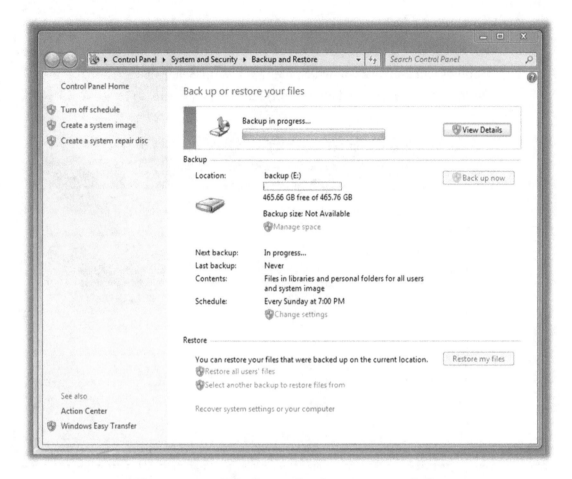

Figure 3-12. *Windows 7 backup progress dialog*

10. When the backup completes, you can close this window. Backups will now occur automatically in the background, as long as you have the external hard drive plugged in.

Tip 3-1b. Microsoft Windows 8.1

1. Open your Control Panel. See the earlier "General" section for help with this.

2. Search for *history* to find File History. Click "Save backup copies of your files" (Figure 3-13).

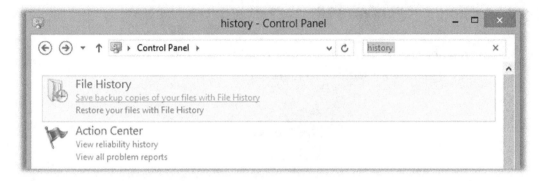

Figure 3-13. *Windows 8.1 Search for history*

3. In the File History dialog, you should see your new hard drive,
    perhaps with a generic name. If not, click the "Select drive" link
    at the left to find and select your new hard drive. Then click the
    "Turn on" button to enable file backups. Windows will begin
    backing up your files. You can close this window before the
    backup finishes—it will complete in the background (Figure 3-14).

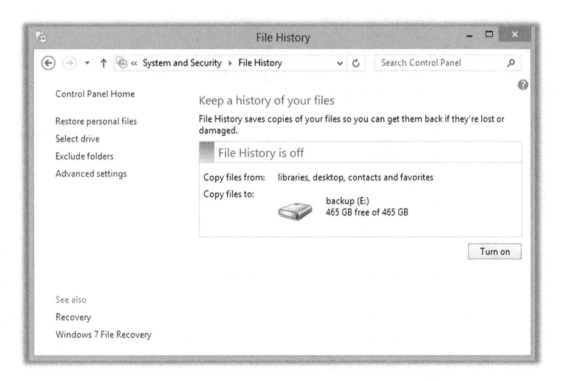

Figure 3-14. *Windows 8.1 File History dialog*

Tip 3-1c. Microsoft Windows 10

1. Open Settings. Search for *backup* to find File History Settings.
   Click "File History settings" (Figure 3-15).

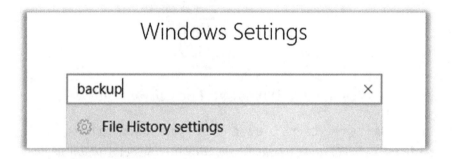

Figure 3-15. Windows 10 Search for backup

2. This should bring up the Backup settings. Click "Add a drive." You
   will see your hard drive there—select it (Figure 3-16).

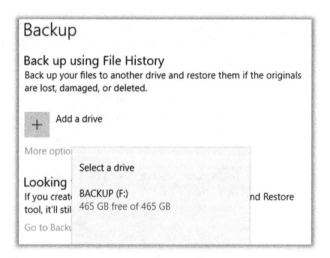

Figure 3-16. Windows 10 backup drive selection dialog

3. When done, your screen will look like the one in Figure 3-17.
   You can click "More options" to customize the backups, though
   by default it will just back up everything, every hour, forever
   (Figure 3-17).

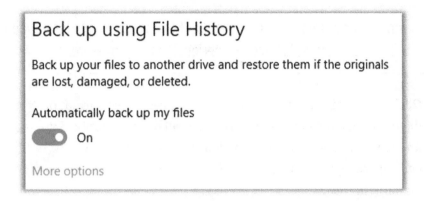

Figure 3-17. *Windows 10 backup confirmation dialog*

Tip 3-1d. Mac OS

1. Setting up backups on a Mac is easy. When you first plug in a new hard drive, you will be presented with a dialog asking you if you'd like to use this drive for Time Machine, Apple's backup utility. Figures 3-18 and 3-19 are for OS X 10.13, but they look pretty much the same in 10.12 and 10.11.

Figure 3-18. *Mac OS Time Machine backup confirmation dialog*

Note   For now, do *not* select Encrypt Backup Disk. We'll do this later when I explain how to create and safely store a seriously strong password.

2. Click Use as Backup Disk button. You may see the confirmation dialog shown in Figure 3-19. This drive will be solely for backup, and anything else on the drive will be permanently erased. So, click the scary Erase button. If this is a new drive, there's obviously no harm in this.

Figure 3-19. Mac OS Time Machine disk erase confirmation dialog

3. Mac OS will then prepare your drive for backup and start your first backup. You will see a progress window like the one in Figure 3-20. Be sure that the Back Up Automatically box is selected! You can also select the "Show Time Machine in menu bar" option so you can quickly see when it's backing up and check on your backup status periodically (Figure 3-20).

Figure 3-20. *Mac OS Time Machine progress dialog*

4. You can close this window at any time; you don't have to wait for the backup to finish. That's it, you're done!

Tip 3-2. Back Up to the Cloud

Recommending a specific cloud backup service is tough. The features and prices for online backups are changing all the time. This is good because the features are increasing, and the prices are decreasing, but trying to do a cost-benefit analysis when the costs and the benefits are in a constant state of flux is like trying to hit a moving target. I've done a good bit of research, and I believe that the best option currently available for the average user is *Backblaze*. It's dead simple to use, and the company has an excellent reputation. If for some reason Backblaze doesn't work for you, I suggest either iDrive or Carbonite as alternatives. However, I'm going to go with Backblaze for this tip. The screenshots look the same for both Mac OS and Windows.

1. Download the free trial of the personal backup software from Backblaze. Create your account and then download the installer.

   `https://www.backblaze.com/`

2. Run the installer. It will go through a phase of "analyzing your drive" that may take a while. It's figuring out what you have to back up; just wait for it to complete.

3. When done installing, it will automatically begin backing up all of your files. It's that simple! If you open up the Backblaze app, you will see something like Figure 3-21.

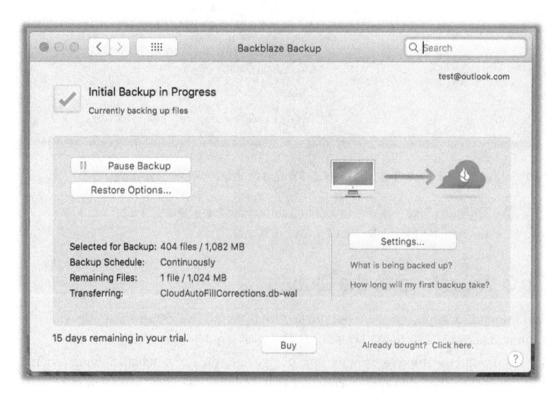

Figure 3-21. *Backblaze Initial Backup in Progress dialog*

4. If you decide to stick with the service, you will eventually give them your credit card or other payment information. Shortly after clicking "create account," you will receive an e-mail with instructions.

5. In most cases, you can simply accept the default settings, which will back up all the data for the current computer user (documents, photos, music, etc.). However, one option you might want to seriously consider is setting a private encryption key (on the Security tab in Settings). Even though your files will be encrypted in the cloud, Backblaze will have the key. If you'd like to make sure that even they cannot access your files, read Chapter 4 and then use your password manager to generate a killer password and store it safely—then enter it via the Settings page shown in Figure 3-22.

Figure 3-22. *Backblaze Preferences dialog*

Tip 3-3. Buy a UPS

If you have a desktop computer, you should seriously consider buying an uninterruptible power supply (UPS). (Laptops have built-in batteries and do not need this.) Most UPSs are just big lead-acid batteries (like the one in your car) that sit between your computer and the AC wall outlet. (They are starting to make Lithium-Ion UPSs, too, which are smaller but more expensive.) When there's a power spike, glitch, brown-out, or complete outage, the device provides juice to your computer from the battery. Most UPSs have a separate data cable that allows it to talk to your computer so that if the power is out *and* the battery is running low, the UPS can tell your computer to shut down gracefully before power runs out. A UPS can be expensive, but suddenly cutting the power to a computer while it's running can cause real harm, including corrupting data on the hard drive. Look for name brands like APC or CyberPower. Generally speaking, the more you spend, the bigger the battery—and the longer your computer can run without wall power. However, for most of the protection benefits, you just need one that will smooth out the power glitches and give your computer a chance to shut down gracefully. If possible, buy a UPS that has automatic voltage regulation (AVR).

Tip 3-4. Clean Up Your Apps

The goal of this step is to remove software you're not using. This includes utilities, games, and anything else you might have added over the years. I wouldn't remove any applications that came with your operating system—I would focus on the ones that you (or someone) installed. If you are unsure of what a particular application is or what it does, use your web browser to search for more information. If you're not sure about any specific piece of software, just leave it be.

Note 1   Be sure to complete the previous step (backing up) before moving on to this one! And by "complete" I mean that a full backup has occurred. If you accidentally "clean up" something that you later realize you actually need, you can recover it from your backup. If necessary, skip ahead and come back to this step later.

Note 2   Before uninstalling anything, exit all other applications. Some applications have strange interdependencies, and it's best to quit everything while you're uninstalling stuff. (If you're reading the electronic/digital version of this book on your computer, you might want to print out these few pages so you can quit your book reading app, as well.) If you really want to be sure, you might restart your computer here and then quit any applications that automatically start.

Tip 3-4a. Microsoft Windows 7

1. Open your Control Panel. See the earlier "General" section for help with this.

2. Select "Add or remove programs." Search for *programs* to find it (Figure 3-23).

Figure 3-23. *Windows 7 Search for programs*

3. Uninstall programs. Scroll through the list of applications and double-click any applications that you would like to remove. Depending on the thing you're removing, you might see a different type of confirmation screen. Figure 3-24 shows the most general type—in this case, just click Yes to remove the unwanted app. Some applications will launch a special, custom application. In this case, just follow the instructions to remove/delete the application.

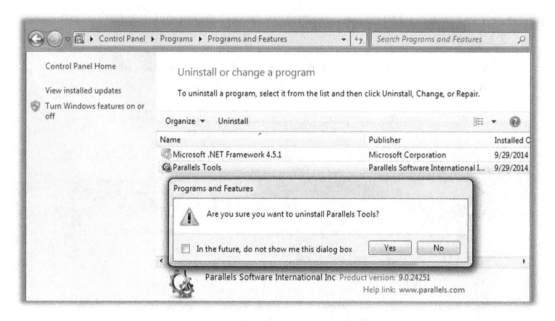

Figure 3-24. *Windows 7 uninstall confirmation dialog*

4. Repeat this process for every app you want to delete.

Tip 3-4b. Microsoft Windows 8.1

1. Open your Control Panel. See the earlier "General" section for help with this.

2. Select "Uninstall a program." Search for *programs* to help find it (Figure 3-25).

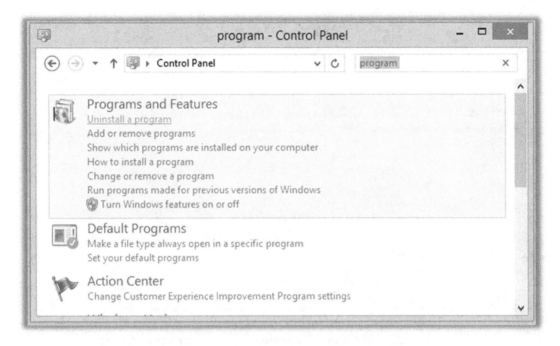

Figure 3-25. *Windows 8.1 Search for program*

3.   Uninstall programs. Scroll through the list of applications and
     double-click any applications you want to remove. Depending
     on the thing you're removing, you might see a different type of
     confirmation screen. Figure 3-26 shows the most general type—
     in this case, just click Yes to remove the unwanted app. Some
     applications will launch a special, custom application. In this case,
     just follow the instructions to remove/delete the application.

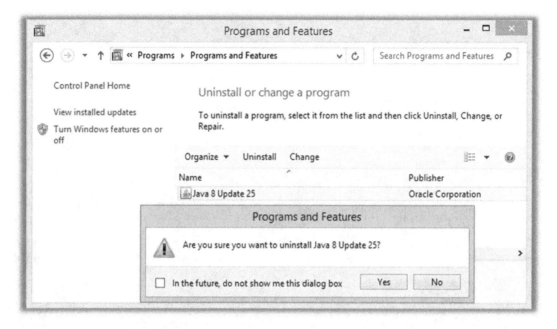

Figure 3-26. *Windows 8.1 uninstall confirmation dialog*

4. Repeat this process for every app you want to delete.

Tip 3-4c. Microsoft Windows 10

1. Open Settings. See the earlier "General" section for help with this.

2. Select "Add or remove programs." Search for *remove* to help find it (Figure 3-27).

Figure 3-27. *Windows 10 Search for remove*

3. Uninstall programs. Scroll through the list of applications and uninstall any applications that you would like to remove. To remove a particular application, select it by clicking on it with the mouse. This will give you the "Uninstall" option. Some applications will launch a special, custom uninstaller application. In this case, just follow the instructions to remove/delete the application (Figure 3-28).

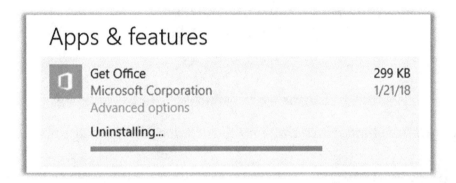

Figure 3-28. *Windows 10 uninstall progress dialog*

Tip 3-4d. Mac OS

While in most cases you can simply drag unused applications to the trash in Mac OS X, sometimes applications leave little extra bits lying around. The free application AppCleaner helps to find those extra tidbits and remove them. It's probably not necessary, but if you'd like to be squeaky clean, this app will help.

1. Download and install AppCleaner. You can find this application here:

    `https://freemacsoft.net/appcleaner/`

2. Drag and drop apps to delete them. Open the newly installed AppCleaner application. Then open your Mac's Application folder and simply drag and drop every app you want to delete onto this window (Figure 3-29). It will not only delete the app itself but find all the little extra files that the app may have scattered around. When you drop the app, it will show you all the files that it found and will delete.

Figure 3-29. AppCleaner drag-and-drop dialog for removing applications

Update Everything

You should try to keep your operating system and key software applications as up-to-date as possible. Operating system updates in particular are important because they usually contain important bug fixes, particularly security fixes. The most popular applications and utilities are often the target of hackers, and therefore you should be sure to keep these applications up-to-date.

Note   Many hackers will attempt to trick you into installing "updates" that are really just malware. If you get a pop-up message telling you to "click here" to update anything, just close the window without clicking anything. If you think it might have been legitimate, you can go to the proper web site to download the update and install it manually.

This section covers the more common applications and utilities. Some other applications (like web browsers and their plugins) will be covered in later chapters. If you get through this book and find that there is still an application you have that you believe needs updating, use your web browser to find the maker's web site and download the software updater application directly from the source. If the application has a "Check for updates" menu option, that's another good way to go.

Tip 3-5. Turn On Auto-Update for Your OS

Both Microsoft and Apple have mechanisms for automatically updating their operating systems. In more recent versions of their operating systems, both Apple and Microsoft also have methods for updating applications purchased through their official "app" stores. I strongly recommend you turn on all OS updates, at least critical and security updates. Application updates can be handy, too, though the most important apps are not currently within the purview of the App Store. We'll cover those next.

Tip 3-5a. Microsoft Windows 7

1. Open the Control Panel. See the "General" section for help with this.

2. Open the Auto Update Configuration. Search within the Control Panel window for *update*. Select "Turn automatic updating on or off" (Figure 3-30).

Figure 3-30. *Windows 7 Search for update*

3. Enable automatic updating. Select the "recommended" option of automatically installing updates (Figure 3-31).

Figure 3-31. *Windows 7 automatic update dialog*

Tip 3-5b. Microsoft Windows 8.1

1. Open the Control Panel. See the "General" section for help with this.

2. Open the Auto Update Configuration. Search within the Control Panel window for *update*. Select "Turn automatic updating on or off" (Figure 3-32).

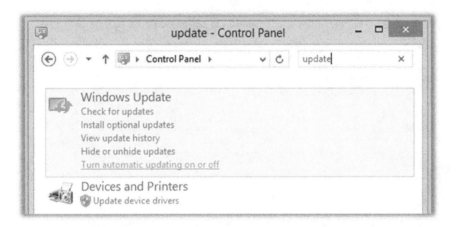

Figure 3-32. *Windows 8.1 Search for update*

3. Enable automatic updating. If necessary, select the option "Change settings" at the left (Figure 3-33). Select the "recommended" option of automatically installing updates. You can elect to check the other boxes at the bottom, as well (I would).

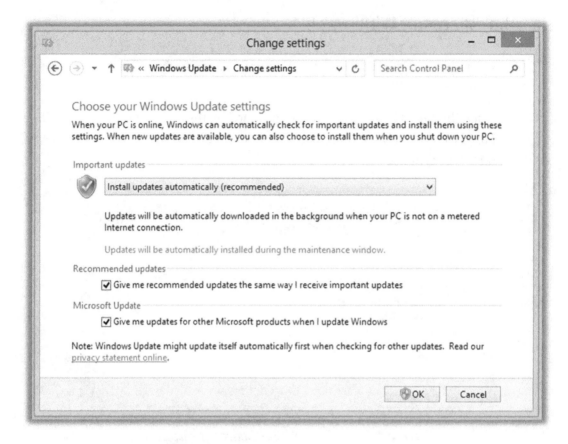

Figure 3-33. *Windows 8.1 automatic update dialog*

Tip 3-5c. Microsoft Windows 10

Windows 10 Home is now automatically set to download and install Windows updates for you. I'm not usually in favor of your operating system taking choices away from you, but in this case, it's the right move.

You can verify this setting by searching for *windows update* in Settings and opening the Windows Update Settings panel. It should look something like Figure 3-34.

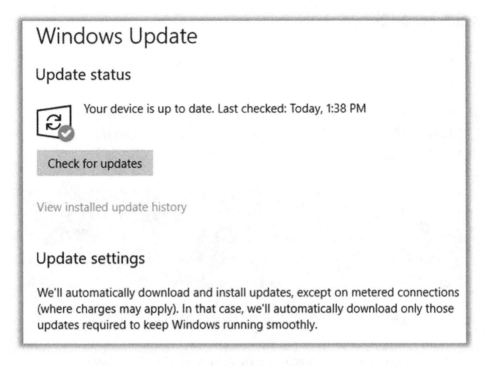

Figure 3-34. *Windows 10 Windows Update dialog*

Similarly, the Microsoft Store also has a setting for automatic updates that should be enabled by default. You can verify this by searching for *Microsoft store* in Settings and opening the Microsoft Store Settings panel (the little ... menu at the upper right). See Figure 3-35.

Figure 3-35. *Microsoft Store Settings App updates dialog*

Tip 3-5d. Mac OS

1. Open System Preferences. See the "General" section for help
    with this.

2. Open the proper updater preference. Open App Store toward the
    bottom of the screen (Figure 3-36). You can use the search bar to
    find it quickly.

Figure 3-36. *Mac OS App Store in System Preferences*

3. Enable automatic updates. From this window, check the boxes to
    automatically check for updates, automatically download them,
    and automatically install security updates (Figure 3-37). If you
    would like to also update your apps and your OS, that's fine, too.

Figure 3-37. *Mac OS App Store automatic updates preferences dialog*

Tip 3-6. Update Adobe Flash (If You *Really* Need It)

Adobe Flash Player is a web browser plugin that enables all sorts of snazzy animations and interactive content. Unfortunately, it's also one of the absolute worst offenders when it comes to security problems. I mean, it's horrible. Fortunately, web developers are moving away from requiring Flash on their web sites and Adobe has announced that Flash will be going away. But some web sites still haven't gotten with the program. In later chapters, I'll show you how to uninstall Flash and still have a backup plan for the few sites that require it. But if you know for a fact that you truly need Flash, then you need to keep it up-to-date.

Note   If you ever get a pop-up message that says you need to update your Flash plugin (or really any plugin), *do not click the provided link or button!* Go directly to the source to get the latest software. These pop-ups are often fake and trick you into installing malware!

---

1. Download the Adobe Flash installer. The safest way to update Flash is by going directly to the source. Use this web address:

    `https://get.adobe.com/flashplayer/`

2. If this link doesn't work, search the Web for *adobe flash download* to find the site. *Make sure you pick the actual adobe.com site.* Sometimes other sites will show up at the top of the search results, and you no *not* want these. When you go to the official Adobe Flash Player web site, you should see something like the screen in Figure 3-38. (If there is any "optional offer," be sure to *uncheck* it.) Click the Install Now button at the lower right. This will download the installer, which you should save.

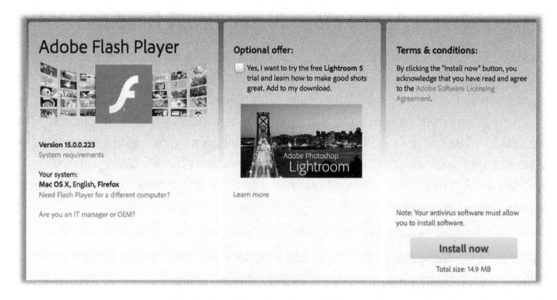

Figure 3-38. *Adobe Flash install/download web dialog*

3.   Run the installer.

   •   On Windows (see Figure 3-39 for Mac), you should get a warning
       asking whether you want to run or save the installer. In this case,
       you can select Run. (Generally this practice is bad, but in this case
       we know exactly what we're running because we requested it.)

Figure 3-39. *Windows installer confirmation dialog*

- On Mac, the installer will download as a file that is named something like "AdobeFlashPlayer install," and it will end with .dmg. Open this disk image file to show the installer, which should look something like Figure 3-40 (they change it all the time). Then double-click the Install Adobe Flash Player area. If necessary, click through any warning dialogs and enter your login credentials to authorize the installation.

Figure 3-40. *Mac disk image installer window*

4. Turn on auto-updates. When presented with the choice, select the option "Allow Adobe to install updates." Click Next, and the installer will run (Figure 3-41).

Figure 3-41. *Adobe Flash Player preferences*

Tip 3-7. Update Java (If You *Really* Need It)

Most people, quite frankly, do not need Java (the app...people will kill for the drink). If you don't already have Java installed, then *do not install it*.

However, if you do have it installed, you need to keep it up-to-date. To check whether you have Java installed and whether you are up-to-date, you need to find the Java Control Panel.

1. Open Java Control Panel. If you cannot find it using the steps here, then you can assume that you don't have Java installed and you can skip this section.

    *   For Mac OS, open System Preferences. See the first checklist item in this chapter for help with this. Find the Java Control Panel. This will be on the bottom row. You can also search for it in the System Preferences window.

    *   For Windows, open the Control Panel. See the first checklist item in this chapter for help with this. Find the Java Control Panel. You can use the search feature to find it.

2. Update Java. Click the Update tab within the Java Control Panel. It should look something like the Figure 3-42. First, make sure that the Check for Updates Automatically button is checked. If you see a button labeled Update Now, go ahead and click it. Follow the instructions to update Java on your system.

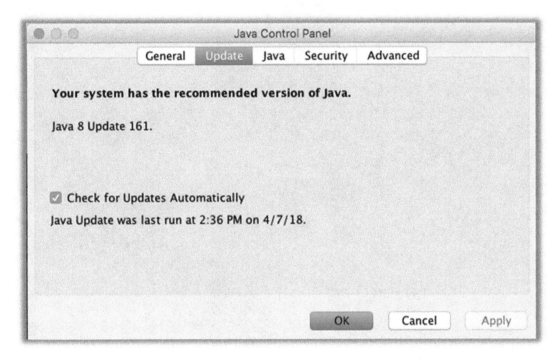

Figure 3-42. *Java Control Panel update preferences*

CHAPTER 4

Passwords

We can't go much further in this book without discussing passwords. I *hate* passwords. I hate them with a passion. And I know I'm not alone. But despite a lot of new-fangled technology, I'm here to tell you that they're still our more secure option for authentication, particularly if you use them correctly. By the time you finish this chapter, you'll know everything you need to know.

How Did We Get Here?

Passwords have become the bane of our modern computer existence. Just about every web site we visit requires that we create an account to use any of its features. That means creating and remembering yet another password. To make it interesting, every web site has a slightly different set of rules for its passwords. Your password has to be long, but not too long. You have to use mixed case and throw in a least one number. Some require you to use a "special character," but only certain ones. Some sites don't let you use special characters at all. Some of them are even more restrictive. You can't use any dictionary words. It can't have repeated letters. It can't contain your name or user ID or anything that looks like a date. In short, they all require that your password be very hard to guess and yet somehow also be something you can easily remember. And just to add insult to injury, some systems require that you change your password on a regular basis.

It would be bad enough if we had to do this only once, but in our modern online world, most of us have dozens if not hundreds of different web sites that require us to log in. And so we all do the same thing: we come up with one or two favorite passwords that meet all the stupid rules, and we use them for *everything*. How else can we possibly remember them all? And yet, that's precisely what you should not do. I'll explain why in a bit.

© Carey Parker 2018
C. Parker, *Firewalls Don't Stop Dragons*, https://doi.org/10.1007/978-1-4842-3852-3_4

So, how did we get into this horrid state of affairs? Why do we need all of these passwords? In some cases, it's obvious—you don't want just anyone to have access to things like your online bank accounts. Somehow you need to convince your bank's web site that you are who you say you are and prevent someone else from impersonating you. This process is called *authentication*. We use these credentials (username and password) to prove our identity. It's not foolproof, of course—someone could steal or guess your password and then gain access to your account. It's like the key to your house. Ideally, only you have the key that opens your front door, but if you lose your key or lend it to someone who secretly makes their own copy, then someone else can open the lock. It's better than nothing, but it's not perfect.

However, there are many web sites that have nothing of yours that needs protecting, and yet they still require you to sign up for a "free" account, meaning you have to create a set of login credentials. Why is that? Because they want to track you and they want to be able to send you e-mails with advertisements. They may tell you it's for your own benefit— allowing you to customize your settings, share things with your friends, save info for later, get customer support, etc. But in the end, it's probably about tracking what you do and building up a profile on you that they may use for themselves or sell to others or both.

There has to be a better way, though, right? Isn't there something else besides passwords? Let's look at this a bit because it's good to understand how we got where we are.

Proving your identity usually involves one or more of the following three types of proof:

- Something you know (like a password or PIN)

- Something you have (like a key, a badge, or your smartphone)

- Something you are (like your fingerprint, your face, or your eye's iris pattern)

Most people immediately think that the best method is "something you are." You can't forget it! You can't lose it! However, *biometrics* have some serious drawbacks as a primary means of identification. What if you have a disfiguring accident? Or what if someone manages to make a viable copy that fools the system? For example, you may be able to fool a simple facial recognition system with a picture of the authorized user's face. Or why not simply remove someone's finger to fool a fingerprint scanner? You can't control something that you are. If that method of authentication is somehow compromised, you're screwed for life. But it's more than that—you also can't hide or change who you are. There are many situations where you want to prove to the web site that you are the same person who was here last time, but you don't actually want them to know who you are specifically. That is, you want anonymity. Nevertheless, biometrics are used in many hypersecure environments, and the technology is becoming cheap enough to be used on laptops and smartphones. Biometric identification can be useful as a second authentication factor, but it's not good as a primary or sole factor. In truth, biometrics are really more like user IDs than passwords.

What about "something you have"? The problem with this solution is that, until recently, it was not common for computers to have any sort of mechanism for detecting and identifying something you have in your possession. Computers were pretty much guaranteed to have only one form of user input: a keyboard. Whatever technique they came up with had to be something that every computer could do, which is why they settled on a string of characters (i.e., a password or a personal identification number, or PIN). However, most devices today now have wireless technologies like Bluetooth and Wi-Fi built in, which will allow us to start using things like our smartphones to authenticate ourselves. In fact, there's a promising new technology called Secure Quick Reliable Login, or SQRL[1] (pronounced "squirrel"), that will allow you to simply scan a code on your phone, tablet, or computer to log in to web sites. It automatically generates a secure code for each web site and remembers them all for you! Best of all, there are no secrets that need to be saved on the servers, so there's nothing to steal! There will undoubtedly be other such technologies coming out of the woodwork in the years to come because passwords are so bad... but for now, passwords are what we're stuck with.

Understanding Password Strength

So, if we're stuck with passwords as our primary form of authentication, then we need to understand what constitutes a "good" password. To truly understand this, first we need to understand how the bad guys try to guess our passwords and hack into our accounts. There are two key scenarios to consider: I will call them *online attacks* and *offline attacks*. I think when most people consider the threats to their accounts, they think of online attacks: a live human being sitting at a computer somewhere trying to log into your bank account. They try to guess your password over and over till they either get in or give up. That's actually not very common, but let's discuss it because it does happen. In this case, a human has somehow picked you out of the billions of people out

---

[1]https://www.grc.com/sqrl/sqrl.htm

there and decided they want to hack your accounts. So, they figure out where you do your banking (somehow), guess your user ID (maybe it's just your e-mail address), and then slowly and methodically try to guess your password. If they know you (or maybe if they've found your Facebook page), they can make some educated guesses: your pet's name, your kid's name or grandkid's name, your address, your anniversary, your alma mater, your favorite sports team, etc. While this is a real risk, it's actually a small one, and I think most of us realize this. What are the chances that someone is going to target little old me? Unless you're rich or famous or you ticked off a wacko, there's really not much of a reason for someone to attack you, personally. This sort of attack is also just not that efficient—it's hard to pull off.

The more common threat for John Q. Public is the offline attack. Surely by now you've seen the news stories about companies having their servers hacked and then asking all their customers to reset their passwords. In these situations, hackers break into the computer systems of a large company, and they steal their customers' information. This often includes names, addresses, phone numbers, credit card numbers, and passwords. The passwords are almost always scrambled, but unfortunately it's not always done properly. So at this point, the bad guys have this juicy vault full of information in their possession, and they have all the time in the world to try to crack it open. That is, they have copied thousands or millions of encrypted passwords to their local computer and can now try to crack them all.

Let's compare this to the previous case. In the online attack, a human (or perhaps a computer) is trying to log into a single person's online account by guessing individual passwords. The web site is slow, so you can't roll through a long list of different passwords quickly. And if the web site is secure, they will cut you off after you fail too many times anyway. But in an offline attack, the bad guys have a massive collection of scrambled passwords in their hot little hands, and they can just crank up a computer to guess billions of passwords per second until they start finding matches.

Now do you see the difference? Hang on, it gets worse because people are notoriously bad at choosing good passwords. Table 4-1 contains a list of the top 25 most-used passwords, based on sets of passwords that were recovered from stolen databases in 2017.[2] The number-one hacked password was 123456. The second most popular was *password*. Scanning the list, you will see just how bad people are at choosing good passwords.

---

[2]According to Splash Data: `https://www.splashdata.com`

Table 4-1. *Most Used Passwords from 2017's Hacked Passwords*

Rank	Password
1	123456
2	password
3	12345678
4	qwerty
5	12345
6	123456789
7	letmein
8	1234567
9	football
10	iloveyou
11	admin
12	welcome
13	monkey
14	login
15	abc123
16	starwars
17	123123
18	dragon
19	password
20	master
21	hello
22	freedom
23	whatever
24	qazwsx
25	trustno1

So, the bad guys aren't starting from scratch. They know human nature, and they know that most people will choose something they can remember, probably something pronounceable. That *significantly* reduces the number of guesses they have to make. The scrambling process for the passwords they've stolen is not directly reversible, but the scrambling process (known as *hashing*) is well-known and repeatable—so all they need to do is take a guess, scramble it, and see whether it matches one of the other scrambled passwords.

That is, if I take *password* and hash it, I get something like this:

$$\textbf{5f4dcc3b5aa765d61d8327deb882cf99}$$

So if I find 5f4dcc3b5aa765d61d8327deb882cf99 somewhere in my stolen list of scrambled passwords, then I know the password for that account is *password*. (There are techniques that make it harder to do this, but sadly they're not used as much as they should be.)

The first passwords the bad guys try are the popular ones, based on much larger lists like the one in Table 4-1. In fact, this list is so useful that hackers usually have all the scrambled versions of these passwords precalculated to save time. If these don't work, they move on to dictionary words, common names, phrases from pop culture, sports-related terms, and so on. They try them all forwards and backwards. They replace some letters with numbers or symbols (zero for O, @ for *a*, etc.). Believe it or not, this process is usually enough to guess most of the stolen, scrambled passwords.

But surely this must take a lot of time, you say. It doesn't. Computers can crank out these guesses and compare them to every stolen password millions or even billions of times per second. Using common guessing techniques like this, hackers can usually recover most of the stolen passwords in a matter of *hours*. This is why companies that have been hacked will often immediately lock all their user accounts and force everyone to reset their password.

That would seem to be very effective, right? If we just invalidate all the stolen passwords, then this must stop the hackers dead in their tracks. What's the point of guessing these passwords if they're almost immediately reset? The problem is that people tend to reuse their passwords. If you used "CowboyUp!" as your password for one web site, the bad guys know that it's very likely that you used that same password for some of your other online accounts. While hacked-site.com has invalidated that password on their system, what about other-site.com where you used that same password?

This is why it's crucially important that you use a strong, *unique* password for each and every online account you have, at least the ones that are important. Important ones would be your financial accounts, any web site that has your credit card info, your social media accounts, and your e-mail accounts. You might not think your Facebook and Gmail accounts are that important, but they can be used to impersonate you, luring people you know into clicking links or giving up information that will get them in trouble. Also, when you forget your password, almost all web sites use your e-mail account to send you a link to reset your password. If a bad guy can get to your e-mail account, they can log into your banking site and request a password reset—and then intercept the e-mail and set the password to whatever they want. Worse yet, they can change your e-mail password and lock you out, preventing you from fixing the problem. It's very hard to convince your e-mail provider that you are the true owner of your account when you can't even log in. (And good luck getting them on the phone.)

Now we come to the crux of the chapter: what makes a strong password? When choosing a new password, many web sites will tell you to include numbers, uppercase and lowercase characters, and "special characters," like punctuation marks. They will often have a little password strength indicator that will indicate, as you type, how strong your password is. These "strength meters" are handy, but they're sometimes too simplistic and may give you a false sense of security. So I want to educate you on what truly makes a strong password. We're going to get into a little math here, but don't be afraid...I've got you covered.

Let's start with a simple case: a personal identification number (PIN). These are most often used with ATM and debit cards, but we also use them on our phones and tablets. They're usually four digits long—some sequence of numbers from 0000 to 9999. Each character in this PIN has ten possible values: 0 through 9. If you take all possible combinations of four digits, that's 10,000 total possible values. To get that value (10,000), you take the number of possible choices for each digit (in this case ten) and multiply by itself for each digit in the PIN (four). That's 10 times 10 times 10 times 10, or 10,000. This is the same as 10 to the 4th power. (I know, your eyes are starting to glaze over and you're having horrible flashbacks to middle school math...just bear with me a bit longer; I promise you won't actually have to think this stuff through.)

Ten thousand possibilities may seem like a lot, but a computer can crank through those values in a fraction of a second. However, PINs are almost always used in cases that require human input, and that's why they're good enough. That is, trying to guess a PIN would be an example of an "online" attack—the hacker would have to be there, in person, entering all of these guesses by hand. The attacker would need to steal or somehow copy your card, as well. Finally, most systems will lock the user out (and probably keep the card) if there are too many wrong guesses. For these reasons, PINs are usually good enough for these situations.

Now let's consider the case of passwords. Remember that the worst-case scenario for guessing passwords is an offline attack where the bad guys can just sic a computer on the problem and walk away. Assuming we avoid the common passwords as we discussed earlier and choose a truly random password, then the attackers have no choice but to just try to guess all the possible passwords...that is, start with *a*, then *b* ... eventually *aa* and *ab* and *bb*, and so on, and on, and on. This is known as a *brute-force attack* and is limited only by the speed of the computer and the complexity of the password. This is enormously more difficult to do, as long as the password is sufficiently long and random. In fact, for all practical purposes, if you choose a strong password, then it's effectively unbreakable.

To understand this, we have to use the same mathematical approach we used earlier on PINs to judge the strength of a password. First, we're adding more possible values for each character—not just numbers but letters and other keyboard characters. There are 10 numbers and 26 letters in the English alphabet. Each letter can be uppercase or lowercase. If you're keeping count, we're now at 62 possible values (10 letters + 26 lowercase letters + 26 uppercase letters). Let's stop right there and check our math. If we have an 8-character password that is only made up of letters and numbers, that means we have 62^8 (62 to the 8th power) possible values.

If you whip out your scientific calculator, you'll see this:

$$62^8 = 221{,}919{,}451{,}578{,}090$$

That's more than 200 trillion! Wow, surely that's good enough, right?

Not really. A fast computer performing an offline attack could conceivably guess 100 billion passwords per second, meaning that it could try all 221 trillion values in just under 37 minutes. That's not really good enough, especially when you have to assume that the supercomputers at the NSA are probably at least 1000 times faster (100 trillion guesses per second). Such a computer could chew through all those possible values in just *2.21 seconds*. In the age of government surveillance, we need to consider the worst case—and we need better passwords.

This is why adding more types of characters to the mix is so important. If you add punctuation characters (period, comma, semicolon, etc.) you can add about another 33 possible values, bringing the total number of possible characters to 95. If you raise

95 to the 8th power (95^8), you can lengthen the guessing time for our regular hacker's computer from 37 minutes to almost 19 hours. For the supercomputer, we go from a paltry 2.21 seconds to a little over a minute. Hmm…still not good enough for me. The answer is to make the password longer—with all due respect to our intrepid Mr. Bradford from 1970s TV, eight is simply not enough! Look at Table 4-2 to see how much difference a few extra characters makes, and you'll see why longer passwords, even just a little longer, are so important.[3]

You can see from Table 4-2 that at ten characters, we've pretty much gone beyond what regular hackers might be able to guess. But we need to use at least 12 characters to really feel good about protecting ourselves from the big boys! Remember that computers are doubling in computing power about every 18 months and realize that you might want to protect certain things at least until you're dead.

Table 4-2. *Estimated Brute-Force Time to Crack Passwords by Length*

Password Length	Computer Time	Supercomputer Time
8	18.62 hours	1.12 minutes
9	2.43 months	1.77 hours
10	19.24 years	1.00 weeks
11	18.28 centuries	1.83 years
12	1,074 centuries	1.74 centuries

So, how can we possibly come up with dozens if not hundreds of unique, strong passwords and expect to remember them? The simple answer is: you can't. That's where password managers come in.

Managing Your Passwords

The bottom line is that you should not know any of your web site passwords. Any password you can remember will have some sort of inherent pattern, and the bad guys have gotten really, really good at predicting those patterns. The human brain is just

---

[3]Special thanks to Steve Gibson's excellent web site for these figures: https://www.grc.com/haystack.htm

not up to this task. The only possible way to create an unguessable, unique password for every online account you have—and be able to instantly recall them all—is to use a *password manager*.

What is a password manager? A password manager is a software application or web browser plugin that helps you to generate truly random passwords and then remembers them all for you. A good password manager will automatically fill in these passwords for you on web sites that require a login and even synchronize your "password vault" across multiple computers and devices so you can access them anywhere.

Now, if I've done my job here, there should be all sorts of sirens going off in your head. If you're properly paranoid, you must be screaming right now: "Why on Earth would I trust all of my passwords to some unknown third party? What if *they* get hacked? All my eggs are in one digital basket!" And guess what...you're absolutely correct. However, I'm here to tell you that it's still the best option available to you. The pros far outweigh the cons; the benefits trump the risks. Think of putting all your valuables in a big safe. Yes, all the goodies are in one box... but that one box is really, really strong. People who make these vaults are experts in making them secure; it's what they do, and they wouldn't be in business very long if they didn't do it well.

Password managers are built for the express purpose for being secure. Password managers will encrypt all of your precious data on your local machine, using a master key or password that you provide. The password manager people will have no way to access your passwords, and neither would a hacker that got hold of your password database. That's the whole point, really. You open your vault with one master password that only you know, and then you put all your other passwords and sensitive information inside this vault and lock it. The locked (encrypted) vault can be safely sent between your devices and even stored on the password manager's company servers. Yes, it's scary— and you should be nervous about trusting any third party with all your passwords. But in reality, they don't have your passwords; they have a blob of scrambled data that is completely inscrutable to them or to any hacker that manages to steal it.

As a side note, many cloud storage companies will tell you that they lock up your data with "military-grade" encryption. That may well be true, but the real question is: who holds the keys? Here's a little test for whether you can trust a third party with your sensitive encrypted data. Call up their technical support staff and ask them what they can do to recover your data if you forget your password. The answer better be "we're sorry, we can't help you." If they have any way to get to your encrypted data back for you, then they can get at your data any time they want because you don't have the *real* master key—they do.

Dropbox is a good example of this. If you haven't heard of Dropbox, it's a cloud storage provider that allows you to synchronize files and folders across multiple computers through the Internet. If you place a file in your Dropbox folder at home, it will magically appear in your Dropbox folder on your work computer—and vice versa. It's sort of like having a magic folder that can be seen by any computer where you've installed Dropbox. It's an extremely useful tool if you want to share files between multiple computers and devices. I have no doubt that they use heavy-duty encryption on the copies of your files that they store on their servers, but they also have full access to those files. That is, they can decrypt them whenever they want. They need to be able to decrypt them in order to provide many of the services they offer, such as letting you log into a web page where you can see the file names and search the content of the files. If the feds come knocking with a search warrant, Dropbox can give them full access—even though they are locked with "military-grade encryption." This is true of most services that I've seen, including Apple's iCloud. (We'll talk about ways to work around this later.)

A password manager can also hold other sorts of sensitive information for you: credit card and bank account info, PINs, medical and healthcare data, Wi-Fi passwords, driver's license and other key ID numbers, passport info, lock combinations, Social Security numbers, and any other secrets you may want to write down in a safe place. Where do you store this info now? Slips of paper in your wallet? Notes in your address book? Sticky notes on your computer monitor? This information is much safer in a secure digital vault, and as an added bonus, your passwords will be accessible anywhere you have a computer or a smart phone (even without an Internet connection).

Some password managers will allow you to securely share specific bits of information with friends and family, as well. It's even possible to allow someone else to log in to one of your online accounts without actually letting them see your password! When hooked up to your web browser, you can use password managers to automatically fill in credit card and address forms, saving you the hassle. Once you've installed a password manager, you'll be amazed at all the things it can do for you, and you'll wish you had done it sooner.

You might know that most web browsers will also offer to store your passwords for you and automatically fill them in. Some will even sync them across computers for you. But I strongly recommend you do not use these built-in services—use a separate password manager and turn this feature off in your web browser. We'll talk about that more later.

Spoiler alert: when we get to safe web surfing later in the book, we'll learn about how the bad guys often try to trick you with fake web sites. Another major plus for using a password manager is that they aren't fooled by look-alike web addresses!

Choosing a Master Password

While a password manager can be used to remember all your web site passwords, you will still need to memorize at least one password: the master password for your password vault. So now we're back to the drawing board, right? You still have to find some way to come up with a really tricky password that you can easily remember but the bad guys can't guess. However, you only need to remember one such password, not hundreds.

There are various techniques for generating a really good password that you can still remember easily. I'm going to discuss some options here to get you started, but you should then come up with your own algorithm. It can be a combination of these ideas, or something you come up with on your own that's similar. The key is to find a string of letters, numbers, and special characters that do not have any obvious patterns, like words in the English dictionary, dates, ZIP codes, phone numbers, and so on.

A popular method for coming up with the base for your password is to think of a phrase from a movie, poem, song lyric, or book—a phrase that you can easily memorize, perhaps one you already know by heart. It shouldn't be a phrase that people would associate with you, though, because you don't want anyone to be able to guess it. Then take the first letter of every word in that phrase to create your password. Include things like punctuation that exists in the phrase—capitalization, commas, question marks, and exclamation points. Change some letters to numbers or symbols, too—like 3 instead of *E*, $ instead of *S*, and so on.

It's probably easiest to explain this with an example. Let's choose the first line to "Stairway to Heaven" by Led Zeppelin:

There's a lady who's sure all that glitters is gold.

That phrase has ten words in it. If we take the first letter of each word, plus punctuation, we get:

Talwsatgig.

That brings us to 11 characters. Now, let's change some letters to symbols.

T@lw$@tg1g.

I changed *a* to @, changed *s* to $ and changed *i* to 1 (one). Now, you don't have to do all of these changes, you might just do some of them. The key is that you must remember which changes you made.

That's a pretty good password. But we can do better, without adding hardly any complexity. I could include the possessive parts, for example:

`T's@lw's$@tg1g.`

But we can do something else that's even easier...just add some characters at the end, even if it's all the same character. Semicolons are fun, and they're easy to type. Let's add three semicolons!

`T@lw$@tg1g.;;;`

That's a 14-character password that includes uppercase and lowercase letters, numbers, and symbols. That's plenty strong enough for our purposes. The semicolon trick may seem trivial—it may even seem wrong. It's a repeated character! Isn't that a no-no for passwords? Yeah, sure. Sorta. But you just made your password three characters longer with almost zero effort. This is the concept of *password haystacks*, which I referenced in the previous section. If a bad guy is trying to guess your password and can't figure it out using the standard English dictionary type attacks, then they will have no choice but to brute force it (that is, try every possible combination of letters, numbers, and symbols). And at that point, every character you add multiplies the guessing effort by almost 100. Adding three semicolons to your already-hard-to-guess password just made it almost a *million times* harder to guess!

Now you need to come up with your own technique. Maybe you put your three extra characters at the beginning. Maybe you put a period between every letter. Maybe you repeat every punctuation character twice. But just make sure that whatever you come up with is something you'll remember, something that "makes sense" to you.

Doing the Two-Step

Earlier in this chapter, we talked about the various *factors* we use to prove our identities: something we know, something we have, or something we are. When you require more than one of these, we call it *multifactor authentication*. In the case where two factors are required, we call it *two-factor authentication*. Many web sites and services are starting to offer a two-factor authentication option, which is a fantastic way to increase security with only a little extra effort. The primary factor is your password (something you know). The second factor is either something you have (like your smartphone) or something you are (like your fingerprint).

Let's look at a couple of examples to see how it works. Google offers various ways to add a second authentication factor to your Gmail account. This second factor can be required all the time or, more commonly, only for "untrusted" computers and devices. That is, the first time you try to log in from a new device, Google will require that you use a second factor to prove you are really you. At that point, you can decide to tell Google that this device is trusted and whenever you log in from this device in the future, you can skip the second factor. But if you were logging in from a public computer, say at a library or a cybercafe, you would not "bless" this device, leaving it as untrusted.

One method Google offers for second-factor authentication is to send you a text message. After registering your cell phone with Google, it can send you a text message with a special one-time PIN that you will have to enter in addition to giving Google your regular login credentials.

Another method Google offers, which is very cool, is a smartphone app called Google Authenticator. This app, once properly registered and synchronized with Google, will generate a six-digit PIN that you will need to enter along with your regular credentials. The cool thing is that this PIN changes every 30 seconds. Google is generating the same series of PINs on its end so that they always match. You can use this tool for other services besides Google, too—Dropbox and LastPass both offer Google Authenticator two-factor authentication. Each service has its own PIN, and all your PINs are accessible in a single window of the Google Authenticator smartphone application.

The key thing to realize about two-factor authentication is that now the bad guys have to beat you *two* ways in order to crack your accounts. Even if they somehow manage to guess or hack your password, now they also need to have your cell phone. That makes their job a hell of a lot harder. Also, if you have an account that is protected with two-factor authentication and that company's servers are hacked, you don't have to rush to change your password.

Note that there have been several successful attacks against the texting services. It's not easy, but it's possible. A technique involves a person convincing your cellular provider that they are you and claiming they've lost their phone. They convince your provider to give them a new phone... and now your phone no longer works, and the new phone is getting all your calls and text messages. Another technique is to hack the cellular communication network itself, which isn't as hard as it should be. So... if you have the choice, you should always go for the time-based PIN (e.g., using Google Authenticator app) over text/SMS.

Periodically Changing Passwords

If you've ever worked at a large company with an information technology (IT) department, then you've probably had to have a password to log in to your work computer. Furthermore, you've probably also been required to change that password every three to six months.[4] You can't reuse old passwords, and sometimes they even check to see that your new password is sufficiently different from your previous one.

You're probably wondering a) why they do this and b) whether you should do the same thing yourself for your personal passwords. For companies, the real issue is not preventing employees from getting access to sensitive information; it's to prevent nonemployees from getting in, not just hackers but previous employees. Companies also will compartmentalize information so that some people can access things and others can't. If your personal login credentials were somehow stolen or cracked, then someone could get to whatever company resources that you can access. Someone with these credentials in hand would try to snoop around without being caught—that is, they probably wouldn't do anything that would draw attention. If they allow themselves to be discovered, then your IT department will lock your account, and they will lose their access. Your password will be reset, and you will be allowed back in, but they won't know that new password. To combat this, companies try to limit these windows of opportunity. Forcing you to change your password every so often will also mean that someone else who managed to figure out your password will have only a short time to use it.

For your personal accounts, the problem is usually different. Someone who wants access to your accounts will probably want to use them (as opposed to just spying on you without leaving a trace). They may buy things in your name or try to transfer your money to their accounts, for example. If they were breaking into your e-mail account, they may be satisfied to just read your e-mails, in which case changing your password every so often would help. But generally speaking, you will probably know if someone hacks your account because they will probably do something with it.

So, should you periodically change your passwords? And if so, how often? This is completely up to you. Generally, I don't think it does much good to change passwords periodically for no reason. If you're worried that someone might be lurking on your account, just reading information but not actually changing anything, then you might

---

[4]Most people attribute this to a 2004 policy written for the National Institute of Standards and Technology by a guy named Bill Burr. He got it from a whitepaper from the 1980s! He's since apologized for this.

want to change that password. If you have ever given out your password to someone else for any reason, you should change your password when they're done using it. When one of your online service providers is hacked and the password database is compromised, they should send you an e-mail telling you to change your password, and of course you should do that right away. They may even reset it for you or lock you out until you re-authenticate. But beyond that, you can probably just leave your passwords alone, as long as they're strong (and particularly if you have two-factor authentication turned on).

Summary

- Passwords and PINs are used to authenticate us to someone else: an online account, our computer, our mobile device, an ATM, etc. Passwords are "something we know" and currently are the best primary form of authentication. Other factors like "something you have" and "something you are" are good as secondary forms of authentication.

- Password strength depends on a few things. First, you should never use regular words, phrases, or common numbers. Second, you need a wide variety of characters: uppercase and lowercase letters, numbers, and special characters. Third, you need at least 12 characters to prevent a brute-force attack.

- You should have a unique password for every web site. If you reuse a handful of passwords and one of those passwords is compromised (possibly without you knowing it), then bad guys will try using that same password for your other accounts.

- You should not know any of your online passwords—you should instead generate and save passwords using a password manager. It's impossible for humans to remember more than a few truly strong passwords, and we all have dozens if not hundreds of online accounts.

- You will still need to remember at least one strong password: the master password for your password vault. We discussed some techniques for generating a strong password that you can still remember.

- When possible, protect your critical accounts using two-factor authentication. These include e-mail and financial accounts, social media web sites, and any sites that have your credit card information on file.

- While it's fine to change your key passwords periodically, it's not that crucial, especially if you have two-factor authentication enabled.

- You should use two-factor authentication wherever you can, at least for your most important accounts. It greatly increases your protection over just a password. Prefer using a time-based rolling PIN for this (like Google Authenticator) versus text, SMS, or e-mail.

Checklist

This checklist covers one of the most important, most powerful defensive steps in the entire book. Please do not skip this one!

There are a handful of good password managers out there, each with their own pros and cons. You are of course free to choose whatever password manager you want, but for this book I am recommending LastPass. LastPass has been vetted by people I trust: independent third parties who know a lot about security were given access to the source code and spent serious time scrutinizing the tool for security holes. LastPass has some really nice features that we will be using that may not be available with other products. LastPass is supported by all major web browsers on all major operating systems and also has strong support on both iOS (iPhone and iPads) and Android devices. For web browsing on a computer or mobile device, the service is completely free. This includes securely synchronizing your password vault to multiple computers and your mobile devices. This service is sufficient for just about everyone. It offers some premium features for a few dollars a month that are worth considering, but the basic service is totally free.

So, feel free to use the password manager of your choice, but all the examples and suggestions in this book will use LastPass. Some other options to consider, if you'd like to do some research and make your own choice here, are 1Password, Dashlane, Roboform, and KeePass. KeePass in particular is a good option if you can't stand the thought of saving your passwords to the cloud, but if you have multiple computers, you'll have to figure out a way to take your password vault with you (like on a USB thumb drive) or use some other cloud service to sync your vault.

Note that we have a little bit of a chicken-and-egg situation here. The LastPass installer will install a plugin for every web browser you currently have installed, but in a later chapter, you may be installing a new web browser. At that point, you'll have to rerun this installer. Unfortunately, we need LastPass before then to help us generate and save some kick-butt passwords. But I'm just giving you a heads-up that you may have to do this more than once.

Tip 4-1. Choose a Strong Master Password

Use the techniques we discussed in this chapter to come up with your master password. You will use this password to log in to your password manager. (If you skipped the chapter, then you should at least go back and read the section on choosing a good master password.) Do not use this password for anything else! If necessary, you can write this password down on paper and store it in a safe place where you can find it but where others won't see it. You don't need to label this piece of paper, just write the password on it—you'll know what it's for. Don't keep it right next to your computer, but know where you can find it if you get stuck.

Tip 4-2. Install LastPass on Your Computer

1. Go to the LastPass web site: `https://lastpass.com/`.

2. Take a look around the web site and learn what LastPass can do and how it works. Trust me, this is important—you'll want to know this information, and I'm not going to try to repeat it here.

3. The exact process for installing and signing up for LastPass changes too often for me to explain it here in detail. But basically you need to do two things: install the browser plugin and sign up for a free account. Use the kick-butt master password you just created! It will give you the option of storing a password hint...I would avoid this. You're honestly better off writing down your password and storing it somewhere safe.

4. Once you have the LastPass plugin installed and you've signed up for your account, you're ready to start adding passwords! You can access your password vault by clicking the LastPass icon (as of this writing, it looks like a button with an ellipsis: ...).

5. Your initial, empty vault should look something like Figure 4-1.

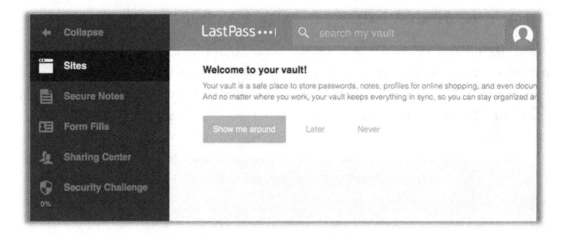

Figure 4-1. *LastPass password vault*

6.   I *strongly* recommend taking the tour and watching the tutorials.
     LastPass does tons of cool stuff, and the tutorials are the best
     way to understand how it all works. Please, just do this right now
     before you go any further. You can find them under More Options
     and then the Help menu.

Note   If you have a ton of saved passwords in your browser, you can jump
through some hoops to import them into LastPass. It's not as easy as it used to
be (which is actually good because the browsers are locking this down more). You
may have to first export the saved passwords from your browser's vault to a file
and then import that file's contents into LastPass. But if all those passwords are
crappy... you're frankly going to want to reset them to something better anyway
(covered later in this chapter).

Tip 4-3. Install the LastPass App on Your Smartphone

I would go ahead and install the LastPass app for your mobile phone using either the
App Store (iPhone) or the Google Play Store (Android). You may not think you'll need it,
but I'll bet you will, and it's part of the free service, so why not?

Once you have installed the application, launch it and sign in. If you have a phone with a fingerprint scanner (like Apple's Touch ID), you may be asked whether you want to allow the password vault to be opened using your fingerprint. I'm not a lawyer... but as of the writing of this book, it appears that law enforcement can force you to unlock things with a fingerprint but not with a password/PIN. If you care about that, don't use fingerprints for unlocking your password vault.

Tip 4-4. Enable Two-Factor Authentication

This is *strongly* recommended. You're going to be putting all of your passwords in a single place—all your eggs will be in one digital basket. You should protect it *well*. Hackers are going to start focusing their efforts on breaking into password managers, so having some "defense in depth" here is very smart. Note that once you enable two-factor authentication, you must have your cell phone with you whenever you want to log into LastPass on an untrusted computer. I know that sounds like a pain, but you honestly get used to it pretty quickly. And most of us keep our cell phones with us all the time.

Note that LastPass has its own authenticator app, and that app has some advantages for LastPass itself. However, I recommend using Google Authenticator instead. It's more versatile, is easy to use, and is supported by many, many services.

1. Download and install the Google Authenticator app on your smartphone. Launch the app. You will probably have to set it up first, so follow the instructions carefully. This may involve sending a text message to your phone.

2. Using your computer's web browser, click the LastPass icon in the toolbar and open your LastPass vault. Open Account Settings.

3. Click the "Multifactor options" tab. Find Google Authenticator and click the pencil icon to enable this service.

4. On the next screen (Figure 4-2), you'll want to enable Google Authenticator.

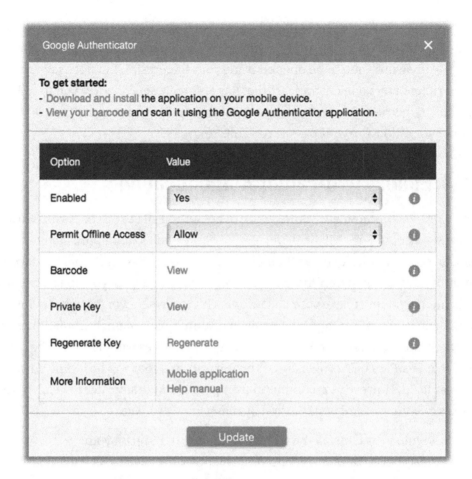

Figure 4-2. *Google Authenticator setup for LastPass*

5. If your smartphone has a camera, then use the Barcode option.
    Click the View link to reveal your barcode. You should see a
    square QR code like Figure 4-3.

Figure 4-3. *Sample QR code for initializing Google Authenticator*

6. Open the Google Authenticator app on your phone. Click the plus sign to add a new account.

7. Click the "scan barcode" button. Hold the phone up to the QR code on your computer screen until it scans. You should then start seeing the 30-second PIN codes on your screen.

8. If your phone doesn't have a built-in scanner, you can click the Private Key link to get a manual code. Then select "enter manually" on the Google Authenticator app to enter this code.

9. At this point you will need to enter one of your six-digit codes to verify that it works.

Note that this is exactly the process you'll use when adding other accounts to Google Authenticator.

Tip 4-5. Disallow LastPass Login from Foreign Countries

This is another nice feature of LastPass—preventing anyone from logging in to your LastPass vault from outside your home country. Now, there are ways to fool this (i.e., appearing to be within the United States when you're not), but it can't hurt to turn this on. (Just be *sure* to change this setting if you happen to be traveling abroad, before you leave!)

- Open your LastPass vault, as before. Open Account Settings.

- Under the General tab, first click the Show Advanced Settings at the bottom. Then you should see an area for "only allow login from selected countries." Check this box and then check off all the countries from which you might log in.

Tip 4-6. Create Some One-Time Passwords

LastPass has a feature that will let you create a list of passwords that will work only one time (once you use a password from this list, it will no longer work). This can be useful when logging into your LastPass account via the web browser on a completely untrusted computer (cybercafe, hotel computer, library, etc.). In addition to keeping a few of these in your wallet, you should consider printing up a handful of these and putting them in your safety deposit box or giving them to your lawyer or something—in case you have an untimely death, you may want a spouse or relative to be able to access all your accounts.

- While logged into LastPass browser plugin, go to this web site: https://lastpass.com/otp.php.

- If this fails, log in to the LastPass web site, and go to More Options at the lower left and then One Time Passwords.

- You can generate as many one-time passwords as you like. A half-dozen is probably sufficient.

- When you're done, you can print the passwords and put them in a safe place. If you put them in your wallet, don't label what they are!

Tip 4-7. Disable Password Saving on Your Browser

How you do this will differ depending on which browser you use. If you have multiple browsers, you should disable this on all of them. It also depends on which version of the browser you're using—but if you followed the instructions in the previous chapter, you should be running the latest version, right? Even so, browsers change constantly, so the instructions here may already be stale. If so, search for *disable password saving* *<browser>*, where *<browser>* is your particular web browsing application.

Internet Explorer:

1. Open the gear icon and select "Internet options."

2. Select the Content tab.

3. Click the button labeled Settings under AutoComplete.

4. Uncheck the box next to "user names and passwords."

5. At the bottom of this same dialog box, click "Delete AutoComplete history."

6. Select "passwords." (You can deselect the others, if you want.) Then click Delete.

Safari:

1. Select Preferences from the Safari menu.

2. Click the Passwords tab. If necessary, enter your Mac password.

3. Uncheck the box for autofilling passwords.

4. If there are any saved passwords listed, select them and delete them.

Firefox:

1. Select Preferences (Mac) or Options (Windows) from the Firefox menu (usually a little icon at the upper right).

2. Click the Privacy & Security tab.

3. Uncheck the box "remember logins and passwords for sites."

4. Click the "Saved logins" button.

5. Click "Remove all."

Chrome:

1. Select Settings from the Chrome menu.

2. At the top, search for *manage passwords*, and select the setting to change it.

3.   Turn this feature to "off" along with the Auto Sign-In option.

4.   If there are any passwords listed under Saved Passwords, delete them. Unfortunately, it appears you have to do them one at a time.

Edge:

1.   Select Settings from the Edge menu.

2.   Select "View advanced settings" from the bottom of the Menu list.

3.   Turn off "Save passwords" under "Autofill settings."

Tip 4-8. Perform a Security Check in LastPass

This is one of the really handy features of LastPass. It will analyze all your passwords to see which ones are bad and also help you find web sites that were hacked (meaning you should probably change those passwords). In many cases, it can also automate the process of changing weak/old passwords for you with a single click!

Note that if you haven't imported any passwords yet (or had the opportunity to add your passwords), then there won't be much info here for LastPass to work with. You might want to return to this step once you have your vault populated with your main account passwords.

1.   From your web browser, open your LastPass vault using the icon on the toolbar.

2.   At the left, click Security Challenge.

3.   Click Show My Score on the security challenge page. It will decrypt your vault and analyze all your passwords.

4.   On the e-mail page, click Continue. LastPass will check to see if any of your e-mail addresses have been associated with a hacked server.

5.   Heed any warnings you're given here and follow the instructions to fix any serious problems.

6.   Review your passwords and see how strong your passwords are.

7.   Run this check periodically and do what you can to improve your score!

Tip 4-9. Generate Strong Passwords for Key Accounts

You will eventually want to do this for *all* of your online accounts, which may be time-consuming. At first, focus on the critical ones: your e-mail, social media, and financial accounts, plus any web sites that have your credit card information on file. You can use the output of your security check to find and change the passwords for these sites. Just click the "Visit site" button next to the entry in the list. (LastPass can actually automatically change passwords on some sites! Use this option where you can to save yourself some time and effort. Otherwise, follow these instructions to manually change them.)

1. Go to the web site for which you'd like to change your password.

2. If this web site is already in your LastPass vault, it should automatically fill in your username and password. You'll know it's LastPass doing this because the form boxes will have a little LastPass ellipsis icon at the far-right end (see Figure 4-4). If you see an icon there with a little number on it, that means that LastPass thinks it may know multiple logins for this page. In either case, click the icon to select your login.

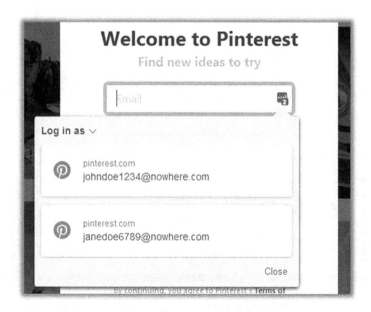

Figure 4-4. *LastPass form fill option list*

3. If this web site is not already known by LastPass, you will need to log in manually. If you had to enter your ID and password by hand, once you click the button to log in, LastPass should ask you if you want to save this password—say yes!

4. Every web site is different here. You'll need to figure out how you change your password for each site. It's usually in your "account" or "profile" or "security" settings. Click whatever links/buttons you need to bring up the form for entering a new password.

5. In the new password form fields, you should see another little icon at the right side like a lock with a circular arrow around it. This is the button that will ask LastPass to generate a kick-butt random password for you. When you click this icon, it will pop up the "Generate password" dialog box. If you click the More Options button, you will see something that looks like Figure 4-5.

Figure 4-5. *LastPass password generator for web form/account*

6. For most web sites, I recommend a password of at least 12 characters, but since you'll never have to type this yourself, why not go to 15 or 20? If you are unlucky enough to be on a web site that does not allow certain types of characters or passwords of a certain length, you can make adjustments using the setting. LastPass will remember these settings as your defaults, so be sure to change them to back to better settings the next time you change a password. That's why I always like to show the expanded options.

Note   If this password is something you know you will have to sometimes enter by hand, either on a smartphone or worse yet something like an Apple TV, Roku, smart TV, or some other device without a full keyboard, you might want to consider unchecking that last box for symbols—they can be a real pain to get to on smartphone keyboards or using a remote control. You might even want to remove capital letters. If you do this, you should increase the length of the password to offset the loss of special characters.

---

7. If you changed any settings, the password should automatically regenerate. But if not or if for some reason you want to create a different one, just click the little circular arrow button. Do this as many times as you want.

8. When ready, click Fill. This should automatically fill the new password into the form field(s) on the page (many password change forms have a "new password" box and a "confirm new password" box; LastPass should fill both).

9. LastPass should then pop up a little banner at the top of the web page to ask if you want to save this password; obviously, say yes.

10. Note that at any time you can edit this login information directly in your LastPass vault. You can see your password history, too, in case for some reason the change didn't "take" or if you just want to see what your previous passwords were. You can also add handy little notes to a site in your LastPass vault (see the next item).

Tip 4-10. Use LastPass to Store Secure Notes

For passwords that are not for online/web accounts, passwords that you will always need to enter by hand, you still need a way to remember them. LastPass has a "secure note" feature that is perfect for this. You can also store other important but sensitive info this way: passport info, Social Security numbers, driver's license numbers, credit card info, computer login credentials, PIN numbers, etc.

- Click the LastPass icon on your web browser and select Secure Notes (Figure 4-6).

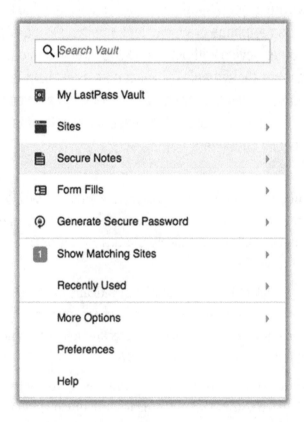

Figure 4-6. *LastPass create secure note*

- In the next screen, click Add Note at the bottom. That should bring up a screen something like Figure 4-7 (with some sample info filled in).

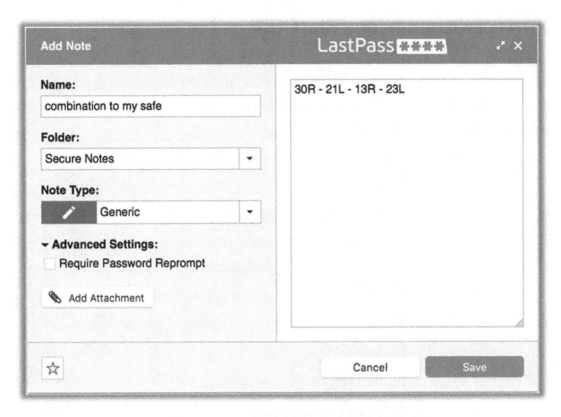

Figure 4-7. *LastPass secure note example*

- If you want, give this note a category. It will provide you with addition form fields to help you organize the data. For example, if you select "passport," it will give you a form where you can enter your name, birth date, passport number, expiration date, etc. Otherwise, leave it as "generic."

- Give this note a name that will help you find it quickly. Fill in your info and save the note. If this note is somehow particularly sensitive, you can check the box for "require password reprompt," which is under the advanced settings. This will require that you to re-enter your master password before showing you the contents.

Tip 4-11. Generate and Store Offline Passwords

There will be some situations where you need to generate a strong, random password for things besides web sites. We'll have such a situation in the checklist of the next chapter, in fact. So, you need to know how to generate and save passwords without having a corresponding web password form to fill out.

1. To do this, click the LastPass icon and select Generate Secure Password. See Figure 4-8.

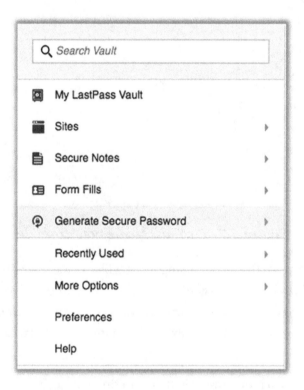

Figure 4-8. LastPass generates secure passwords for any purpose

2. Set the advanced options appropriately for your situation (Figure 4-9). If there are no restrictions, the settings shown in the figure are good defaults. Once it's generated, you'll want to select the text and copy it to your computer clipboard. You can then just click Cancel. You're not going to use this password on the web page; you're going to store it in a secure note.

Figure 4-9. *LastPass secure password generation settings*

3. Using the process from the previous step, create a new secure note
    in LastPass (Figure 4-10). There is no "password" note type, so just
    use "generic." The password was saved by your computer in the
    previous step, so just paste it in the big open space. Give the note
    a descriptive name and feel free to add more info in the note with
    the password; you want to be *sure* you know what this is for, and
    you also want to make it easy to search for.

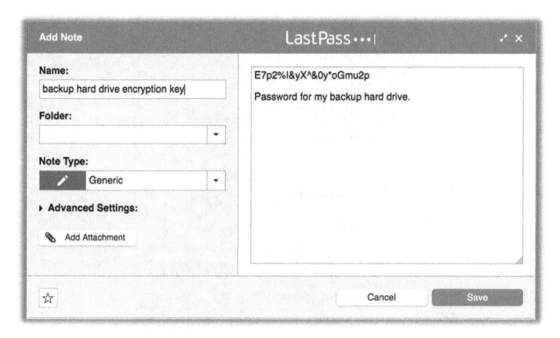

Figure 4-10. Saving generated passwords in a LastPass secure note

Tip 4-12. Use Throwaway Accounts

Many web sites ask you to create a free account just to access their content. Big newspapers and magazines are notorious for this. You go to read an article, but they won't show it to you unless you create an account. This is extremely annoying, especially if you intend to use the site only once. Use one of the following web sites to look for public accounts that someone created for everyone to use, so you don't have to create your own. They don't always work, but it's worth a shot.

- http://bugmenot.com/
- http://login2.me/

You can also create a throwaway account by using a throwaway e-mail address. (We'll cover this later in the book!)

CHAPTER 5

Computer Security

Now it's time to really get into the meat of the book—computer security! This chapter covers the topics that most people probably associate most with security: Macs versus PCs, antivirus software, and operating system security settings. This chapter will cover those topics and more, with a slew of top-notch tips to make sure your desktop or laptop is locked down tight.

Macs Are Safer Than PCs

Let's start this chapter by stirring up some controversy: Macs are safer than PCs. That's right, I said it. However, I had to seriously resist the urge to put "air quotes" around the word *safer*. So, let me be a little more specific. Macs are "safer" than PCs...because most people who write malware are looking for the largest market, and that would be Windows. Despite the recent resurgence in popularity of Macintosh computers, they still make up only a small percentage of the computers on the Internet. According to NetMarketshare, Macs account for just under 9 percent of all desktop operating systems as of March 2018, while Windows holds about 89 percent. If you were going to try to design some sort of computer virus, which operating system would you focus on?[1]

This is a form of what we call *security through obscurity*, which I mentioned in Chapter 2. Macs are more "secure" because they are more "obscure." Security through obscurity means that you try to lie low and not draw attention. If they don't see you, they won't attack you. As a security practice, it's horrible. It's sorta like hiding the key to your house under your door mat. Sure, your house is technically locked, but if someone goes to the trouble of looking around for a key, then it may as well not be locked.

---

[1]If you're in the market for a new computer, you might check out this web site: `https://www.howtoreplaceyourpc.com/`.

© Carey Parker 2018
C. Parker, *Firewalls Don't Stop Dragons*, https://doi.org/10.1007/978-1-4842-3852-3_5

Modern operating systems have included lots of great security features over the last decade or so, and I think you'd be hard-pressed to argue that the latest Mac OS is significantly more secure than the latest Windows OS. However, there are a lot more PCs out there running very old versions of Windows than there are Macs running really old versions of Mac OS. Again, according to NetMarketshare, almost half of Windows PCs are still running Windows 7, which was released in 2009 and was cut off from support in 2015 (other than a few critical security patches). Despite a period where Microsoft offered free updates to Windows 10, that version of the OS is on less than 40 percent of all PCs after two years on the market.

In 2013, Apple shifted to a policy of free upgrades for its operating system, which is a huge plus for Mac users and their security (and removes any excuse for not upgrading). As of March 2018, more than half of Mac users are using the latest Mac OS despite being released only six months ago.

So, on some level, you're marginally safer with a Mac than with a PC. But I'm not going to leave that to chance. Let's talk about the things you can do to really make yourself safer, regardless of what operating system you're running.

Nonadmin Accounts

One of the basic principles of security is the practice of *least privilege*. This is sorta like the "need to know" that we're familiar with in our spy novels and movies (and of course, it's a real thing in security agencies). Benjamin Franklin once said, "Three can keep a secret, if two of them are dead." The idea here is that the fewer people who have access to the truly important stuff, the more likely it is that the important stuff will remain safe.

Let's look at the castle analogy again. You might give everyone on your guard the keys to the front gate, but you would give the keys to the castle only to your special castle guard. Why? Because the guard at the front gate doesn't need access to the castle. Likewise, the king might keep the keys to the gold vault on his person, not even trusting the castle guard with that level of access, because at the end of the day, the only person who really needs to access the coffers is the king. If every member of your castle guard had a copy of the castle and vault keys, then what happens when one of the guards is knocked over the head and his keys are stolen? All of a sudden, your most precious items are at risk. Guards don't have any need to access the gold in the vault to do their job. They just need to protect it. So, guards don't get that key.

Who has a key to your house? Probably everyone in your family. Maybe you will give a key to a house sitter or pet sitter while you're away because for that limited period of time, they actually need to be able to get into your house. When you get back, you take back your keys. Who has keys to your safe deposit box, though? Probably just you. You would probably never lend that key to anyone else, at any time, because the only person who *needs* to get in there is you.

The principle of least privilege says that people should be allowed to access only those things they need to access to do the things they're supposed to do, and no more. If necessary, you can grant temporary access and revoke it later.

You may already know that your computer allows you to set up multiple user accounts. You've probably never used it, but you probably know that it's possible. What you may not know is that each of these user accounts can have different levels of privilege. That is, you can restrict the level of access—the power to make important changes—for each account. At first you might think that this feature is mainly for parental control, preventing kids from doing stuff they shouldn't be doing. Actually, it's for all users—even you! But wait... surely if you can trust anyone, you can trust yourself! Turns out you can't. It's not about trusting yourself, it's about preventing malware that gains access to your account from acting on your behalf. If you accidentally click a bad link, download a virus, or hit a web site with a malicious Java app, then whatever you are allowed to do, *the malware can also do.*

Let me drive this home with some chilling statistics. According to a 2017 report by a company called Avecto, 80 percent of all Windows security vulnerabilities that were considered "critical" could have been prevented or significantly mitigated if the user had not had full administrator (*admin*) privileges. Furthermore, removing admin rights could have mitigated 95 percent of the critical vulnerabilities in Edge (the new Microsoft browser).

Great. Now I can't even trust myself! Now what?

The solution to this problem is to always create at least two accounts on your computer: an admin account, which you use only when necessary, and a regular, nonadmin account for everyday use. When you first pull your shiny new computer out of the box, you're going to need that admin account to install your software and tweak all your security settings. But after that, you need to create and use a more restrictive account for day-to-day stuff.

I would go further, however. I believe strongly that each person in the household should have their own account. It's easy to set up, and there's really no excuse for not doing this. It's not about keeping secrets—everyone deserves their own space, their own settings and preferences, and some basic privacy. It lets everyone express their individuality and also compartmentalizes any risks. This will also allow you to use parental controls to restrict access for young children, without affecting your ability to...uh...do parent things. And if something goes horribly wrong with one of the user accounts, you can just delete it and create a new one without affecting anyone else or having to completely wipe and reinstall everything on your computer.

There are other interesting reasons to have multiple accounts. If you're a hard-core gamer or have some other intense application that requires some system tweaks to be efficient, you can create a second account for this purpose. This other account will be stripped down and dedicated to the special task at hand.

If you regularly give presentations for work using your computer, you can log into a special account for when you're presenting. You can have a special desktop picture, avoid sharing your cluttered desktop, and also avoid annoying pop-up notifications from all your personal accounts.

You can also set up a special guest account so that when someone just wants to check their mail or look something up on your computer, you don't have to worry about giving them access to your personal stuff (including your password vault).

Microsoft has announced a new feature called "Controlled folder access" (available in Windows 10) whose purpose is to restrict access to your personal files to only a few authorized applications. You select the files as well as the approved applications. While this may seem odd, it's really just another form of least privilege. If configured properly (and I'll walk you through this later in the checklist for this chapter), this tool would prevent ransomware from encrypting your irreplaceable files and demanding money to unlock them.

I expect that we'll see more and more features like this as time goes on from both Apple and Microsoft. As things get worse out there, the balance between security and convenience will necessarily move in the direction of security.

iCloud and Microsoft Accounts

Get ready for a big dose of "good news, bad news." In the old days (like 2004), your computer was more likely to access the Internet via dial-up modem than always-on broadband. Around this same time, smartphones came on the scene, and suddenly people had not one but two devices that were always connected to the Internet. It was only a matter of time before people wanted their address book, web bookmarks, calendars, and to-do lists to be the kept in sync across their various devices.

Apple and Microsoft heard the call and launched services to meet this growing need. The current versions of these services are iCloud and OneDrive,[2] respectively. While these services offer limited Internet-based file storage and sharing, in this chapter I'm focusing on the data synchronization aspects. You can't argue with the convenience factor here. When you update your vagabond sister's home address for the umpteenth time or add little Johnnie's complete Little League spring schedule to your PCs calendar, it's really nice to have those changes automagically appear on your smartphone and your work computer. Oh, and you can probably also access all of this info from the Web by logging into your cloud account, even from a computer or device you don't own. Finally, you can use these same services to share this information with the rest of your family. What's not to like?

Well, that was the good news—arguably great news. It's a killer feature. Here's the bad news: you're not just sharing that all that juicy information with all your devices and your family members, you're also sharing it with Apple or Microsoft. Here's the worse news: you're probably sharing that information with many other companies, too. Apple and Microsoft will argue that this is a feature, not a bug—they're giving you the opportunity to access this information from within other applications, saving you the trouble of having to manually transfer things like contacts and calendar events to some third party. But you need to stop and think about what all that data is revealing about you. Your address book probably contains more than friends and family. It may also contain embarrassing contact information—maybe your AA sponsor, herpes doctor, or mistress. And if you're like most other people I know, you put lots of other info in your address book like Social Security numbers, PINs and passcodes, account numbers, and who knows what else.

That said, it's almost impossible to avoid signing up for these services today. Both Apple and Microsoft have deeply embedded these services into their products to the point where many key features simply won't function without them. Furthermore, you pretty much need to have one account for each person in your family, not just one shared account. These services are not just about synchronizing data across your devices, it's about personalization of the experience on these devices for each individual.

---

[2]These marketing names change all the time. Apple's service used to be called Me.com and MobileMe. OneDrive used to be called SkyDrive. No matter what they're called, these are Apple and Microsoft accounts.

For example, it allows parents to control what each of their children can access—what's right for your elementary school son is different than what's right for your teenage daughter.

Of course, all of these hyper-personalized settings are a gold mine for marketers. If you dig around in the end user license agreements (EULAs) you "sign" by clicking that I Agree button, I'm sure you'll find references to how you consent to sharing some of your information with "partners." I guarantee you'll find language about how Apple and Microsoft will hand over this information to law enforcement authorities "in accordance with the law," too. That may or may not require a warrant, by the way.

This is the world we live in now. We're offered enticing and often very valuable services, usually at no (monetary) cost—we just have to sign away our privacy. And this is increasingly becoming unavoidable as these services are tightly integrated with our computer and mobile operating systems. For most of this book, I try to avoid using these accounts. However, in Chapter 9, I'll show you how to enhance the privacy settings for these accounts.

Built-in Security Features

Computers are meant to make our lives easier and richer by offering all sorts of valuable functions, taking over the drudgery of tedious tasks, helping us to organize our increasingly complex lives, and giving us powerful tools to create documents, presentations, greeting cards, images, and so on. In the early days, before the advent of the Internet, computers were wide open—they were ready and willing to accept instructions from other computers on the home or work network. Our operating systems and software applications were happy and naive, gladly offering their help to anyone who asked. Then came the Internet. It was like transporting Mary Ann from Gilligan's Island to the Island of Dr. Moreau. The cheerful eagerness to help without question went from being an asset to a serious security liability.

Modern computers have lots of built-in security features, though until recent years, many features were not enabled by default. Security is frequently at odds with convenience, and both Microsoft and Apple want to avoid causing their customers undue grief. Thankfully, however, as computer security has become more important, computer and software makers are finally enabling these features right out of the box.

One of the most important features in modern home computer networks is the *firewall*. Firewalls keep out unsolicited connections from outside your network but allow you to initiate connections from inside your home to the broader Internet. They also allow you to set up specific rules that explicitly allow certain types of connections from outside your home. It's sort of like a phone that can only call out by default but will let you give it a list of people who you allow to call you. (Why no one sells such a phone is beyond me. I'd buy it in a heartbeat.) You probably have multiple firewalls in your network. Your ISP's modem might have a built-in firewall. If you have a Wi-Fi router, it almost surely has a firewall function, enabled by default. Finally, your operating system also has a built-in firewall. These firewalls do an excellent job of protecting your computer.

Another aspect of your Wi-Fi router that helps protect you is a feature called Network Address Translation (NAT). As we discussed earlier in the book, communication with the Internet is like mailing letters: the information you send is chopped up into a letter-sized payload, stuffed in an envelope called a *packet*, and shipped out with a destination and return address written on it. But to the outside world, every smart device on your home Wi-Fi network looks the same—that is, all the communications appear to come from the same address. This is because your router acts as a sort of local mail delivery system. Think of a large company. When you send a package to someone in that company, you probably just address it to the person at the general company address. You don't know the specific building and/or mail slot within the company; you just trust the company's internal delivery service to find them. This also means that the company can filter incoming packages. Your router performs a similar function. This means computers outside your home network have no direct way to contact an individual entity (computer, smartphone, or other Internet-connected device) within your home, even if there was no firewall in place. This is one form of security through obscurity that actually benefits you.

These features may sound nice on paper, but you'd be surprised how well they work—all by themselves—to thwart Internet attackers. Because unprotected computers are so vulnerable, hackers and other bad guys are constantly scanning the Internet for computers without these basic protections. Multiple studies[3] have shown that unprotected computers (particularly older models without these modern, built-in protections) connected directly to the Internet are routinely and easily taken over. In fact, if you connect an older, unprotected Windows machine directly to the Internet, it will be subverted, on average, *within ten minutes*. Before this computer can even download

---

[3]Such as this one: `https://isc.sans.edu/survivaltime.html`

the system updates that would probably protect it, it will be hacked[4] by some automated bot. The firewall and NAT functions serve as an excellent first line of defense, and luckily these features are standard in home networks now.

So far we've talked only about features that are already in place and working for you right now, and these features tend to be enabled by default. But there are other built-in security features in modern operating systems that are just sitting there, waiting to be used.

Full hard drive encryption is a feature that's been built into recent versions of Mac OS and Windows. While Apple's drive encryption utility (FileVault) is available on all of its recent OS variants, Microsoft's encryption utility (BitLocker) is available only on the Pro, Ultimate, and Enterprise versions of Windows. Encrypting your entire hard drive might seem like overkill, but it's so easy to do; there's just no reason not to do it. As a user, you won't even notice it. The operating system takes care of decrypting all the files (and applications and even the OS itself) on the fly and in the background. What this means is that if someone were to have physical access to your hard drive, they would be unable to read any of the data, unless they were somehow able to guess your encryption password. While this may not be that important for desktop computers that stay inside your house, it can be important for laptops and other devices that you carry around with you— particularly if you travel to foreign countries[5] with these devices. If your laptop were to be lost or stolen, you'll be happy to know that your data is perfectly safe, even if they were to pry open the case and attempt to directly access the hard drive.

One last free feature deserves special mention: Apple's Find My *Device* service, where *Device* is Mac, iPhone, or iPad. Offered with Apple's iCloud service, this feature allows a person to track the location of all their devices and control them from afar. When you register your device with the Find My *Device* service, Apple uses the various wireless technologies (mainly Wi-Fi and cellular signals) on the device to help you communicate with the lost device, send remote control commands to it, and, as a last resort, remotely erase the data from the device. It's truly a marvelous feature, and everyone with an Apple product should take advantage of it.

---

[4]Hackers refer to this as "being p0wned." It rhymes with *owned,* and the meaning is that the computer has been hacked and subverted to the hacker's will. Hackers often use numbers in place of letters, like the zero here in place of the letter *O.* Hackers refer to this as *leetspeak* or just *leet,* usually spelled with numbers as l33t or even 1337.

[5]By the way, the danger here for U.S. citizens is at the U.S. border crossing. U.S. law currently allows law enforcement to inspect and even seize your electronics for any reason. See https://www.eff.org/issues/know-your-rights#5.

Let me demonstrate the usefulness of this feature with personal story. My family and I went to Los Angeles last year for a big family vacation, and part of our trip included Universal Studios. I normally carry my iPhone in my shirt pocket, and I do *not* normally ride theme park rides. However, on this day, we rode several—and at one point when I went to pull my iPhone out to take some pictures, I realized it was gone. It must have fallen out, but I had no idea where. This park is massive, and it could be anywhere. I alerted our tour guide, and she said she would put in a call to their lost-and-found department but that they probably wouldn't be able to look for it until after the park closed at 10 p.m. We got home around 9 p.m., and I jumped on my laptop to check Find My iPhone on iCloud...and there it was, in the Jurassic Park ride building! As it hit 10 p.m., I was able to actually send signals to my iPhone to make alerting noises and post a message on the main screen with contact information. As I watched the map update, I finally saw it move! Someone had found it! It stopped moving at the building where the lost-and-found office was. I went first thing the next morning and retrieved it!

The Pros and Cons of Antivirus Software

When people think of computer security, they invariably think of antivirus (AV) software. That's no accident. Companies that make this software spend lots of money marketing their wares and convincing you that you'd be foolish not to buy them. Most Windows PCs come preloaded with all sorts of trial software that claims to protect you from the big bad Internet—for just a small (ongoing, hard-to-quit) service fee! This is a perfect example of what we call FUD, which stands for "fear, uncertainty, and doubt." Computer malware is a very real problem—don't get me wrong—but in many cases today, the cure can be worse than the disease. Let me explain...

In simpler times, AV software was essential did a good job at finding malware on your computer. Generally speaking, the core function of AV software is to recognize known malware and automatically quarantine the offending software. Some AV software is smart enough to use heuristic algorithms to recognize malware that is similar to the stuff it already knows is bad or recognize suspicious behavior in general and flag it as potentially harmful. A popular new feature for a lot of AV software is to monitor your web traffic directly, trying to prevent you from going to malicious web sites or from downloading harmful software.

That all sounds good, but the devil (as always) is in the details. First, in the ever-connected world of the Internet, malicious software is produced so frequently and is modified so quickly that it's really hard for AV software to keep a relevant list of known viruses. Also, the bad guys have moved to other techniques like phishing and fake or hacked web sites to get your information, attacking the true weakest link: *you*. AV software just isn't as effective as it used to be.

But the problem is much worse than that. In many cases, the AV software *itself* is providing bugs for hackers to exploit. Not long ago, Symantec/Norton products were found to have horrendous security flaws[6] (which it claims to have since fixed). Increasingly, AV products are offering to monitor your web traffic directly, but this means inserting themselves into all of your encrypted (HTTPS) communications, which has all sorts of ugly security and privacy implications.

So, I strongly believe you don't need to pay for an antivirus service today. That is, I don't personally believe that the benefits of the various for-pay services warrant their cost for most people. There are totally free alternatives from the operating system creators that do a good job (which I will be helping you install later in this chapter). Furthermore, if you just do the things I outline in this book, you will significantly reduce your risk. It's like debating the value of buying a bulletproof vest. While walking around in a bulletproof vest is inarguably safer than walking around without one, it's actually more important to just avoid war zones and disputed gang turf.

How to Properly Delete a File

Did you ever wonder what happens when you delete a file on your computer? On Windows and Mac OS, this is represented by dragging the file or folder to the trashcan icon. Most of you probably realize that the file isn't actually deleted until you "empty the trash." What you may not realize is that even then, the data associated with that file is not really gone. It's still there on your hard drive. While your file system no longer shows it to you, the actual bits and bytes are still there, and special software can be used to recover that information.

This is sort of like the difference between throwing away a document and shredding it. Just because you threw your old legal will into the garbage and the trash collector took it away doesn't mean that it can't be salvaged and read. You can't see it anymore, but it still exists in a landfill somewhere. It will slowly decay over time, but until then, someone could dig around and find it. This is why document shredders were invented. When your operating system "deletes" a file on your hard drive, all it really does is forget about it. It treats that part of the hard drive as if it were empty. When you want to save a new file, the operating system will put that file in the space on your hard drive that is marked as

---

[6]https://www.us-cert.gov/ncas/alerts/TA16-187A

empty. Someday it will eventually overwrite part or all of your old "deleted" file, but until that day, the data is actually still there and capable of being read by special tools.

So, if you really want to delete a file from your computer, you need to digitally "shred" it. I'll show you how to do this in the checklist for this chapter.

Summary

- Macs are targeted less often than PCs by hackers and malware makers, mostly because Windows is a lot more common than Mac OS. Apple computers are also much more likely to be running the latest version of the operating system than their Windows counterparts, largely because Apple has been giving away all updates to its OS for years. Because major security features are added with each OS release, Macs tend to be more secure because they are more likely to be running an OS that has these new features.

- Modern computers come with firewalls built in and turned on by default. Likewise, modern Wi-Fi routers come with Network Address Translation (NAT) turned on by default. These two features alone are very good at protecting your computer from evildoers on the Internet.

- Having a separate nonadmin account on your computer can significantly reduce the damage done by malware, particularly on PCs. It also makes sense to have separate user accounts for each person in the family—to provide a personalized space for everyone and also to compartmentalize exposure to malware.

- Cloud-based storage and data synchronization services have become ubiquitous and nearly impossible to avoid. It's important to understand what information you're sharing and do what you can to reduce your exposure.

- While there are many for-pay services and software tools out there to protect your computer from malware, they're probably not worth the money. There are free alternatives that do a very good job, especially if you follow the other tips in this book.

- To truly delete a file, you need to do more than just "empty the trash/recycle bin." You need to digitally "shred" it.

Checklist

This chapter covers some key things you can do on your computer to reduce your "attack surface" and practice the policy of "least privilege." That is, you need to reduce unnecessary risks, turn off features you don't need that might be exploited, and set up some reasonable boundaries on who can do what on your computer.

Note   Many of the items in this checklist will require you to choose a password. In some cases, you will need a really strong password; in others, you will just need something moderately strong. I will make a recommendation in each case. But I want to be clear what I mean by "strong" and "moderate."

Strong password   Use LastPass to generate a crazy, random password. It should be at least 12 characters long and include all the various types of characters. These passwords are used to protect really important things, specifically things that might be subject to a computerized (offline) attack.

Moderate password   Use the techniques described in Chapter 4 for master passwords to come up with something at least eight to ten characters long that you can easily remember. These passwords will be used to protect your computer login and less important things and/or things that will require a human to sit there and guess them by hand.

If you have the option to specify a "password hint," just use the phrase *LastPass* or even *LP*. All of these passwords should be stored there, even the "moderately strong" ones that you should be able to memorize. You don't actually want to give someone a hint that might allow them to make educated guesses.

Tip 5-1. Choose a New Computer: Think Different

If you are a PC user, you might want to at least consider switching to a Mac the next time you upgrade your computer. While it's debatable whether Macs are inherently more secure than PCs, it's a fact that Macs are targeted by hackers less often than PCs—mostly because there are way more PCs out there than Macs. If you just use your computer for e-mail and web browsing, you would probably not notice the difference. If you're a hard-core gamer or if you have some very specific applications you use that run only on Windows, then you're probably stuck with a PC.

If all you do on a computer is surf the Web and check e-mail and you like the portability of a laptop, you might want to seriously consider getting a Chromebook. A Chromebook is essentially a laptop that runs only Google Chrome (web browser) and some Google Play apps. They're affordable and not nearly as susceptible to malware. The downside is that Google pretty much knows everything you do on it.

Tip 5-2. Require Passwords for Computer Accounts

I know this will seem like overkill, especially for desktop computers in your own home, but you should require a password to log in. If you live alone and never have other people in your house, I suppose you can let this slide. But if you have kids, guests, maids, contractors, or any other visitors, you should set your computer to require a password to unlock your computer.

Note   Some newer computers may have the option to sign in with a fingerprint scan or face recognition. This is better than not having any authentication at all and can be very convenient. However, I personally feel that a password is still the most secure way to go. For one thing, unlike passwords, if someone somehow manages to copy or steal your biometric information, then you're screwed for life—these things don't change. Once that information is digitized, it has to be stored somewhere... and if they make a mistake in the software that keeps it secure, then bad guys can pull it out. However, if you choose to use biometrics for convenience, it's definitely better than having nothing at all.

Tip 5-2a. Microsoft Windows 7

1. Open the Control Panel and search for *password* (Figure 5-1).
    If you have not already set a password for your account, select
    "Create or remove your account password." (If you already have a
    password set, skip ahead to the screen saver part.)

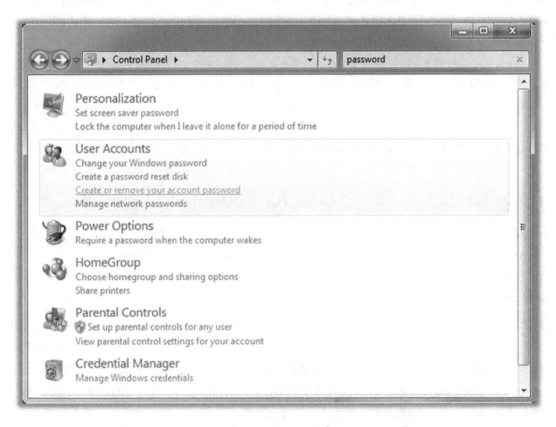

Figure 5-1. *Windows 7 Search for password*

2. On the next screen, click "Create a password for your account"
    (Figure 5-2).

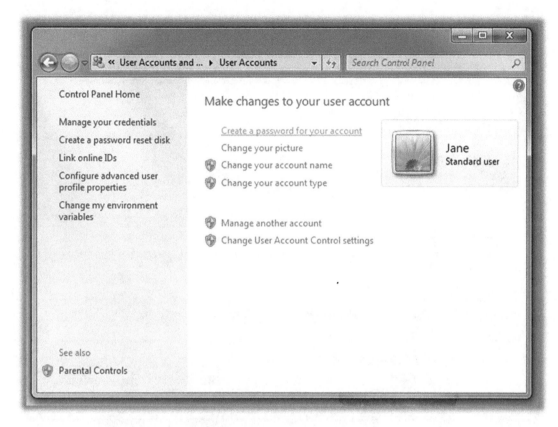

Figure 5-2. *Windows 7 user account settings*

3.   Choose a moderately secure password that you can remember.
      This password does not have to be crazy strong like Internet
      account passwords. Nevertheless, I recommend saving this
      password in LastPass, in case you forget it. I usually put *LastPass*
      as my hint, so I know that I saved it there. Click "Create password"
      (Figure 5-3).

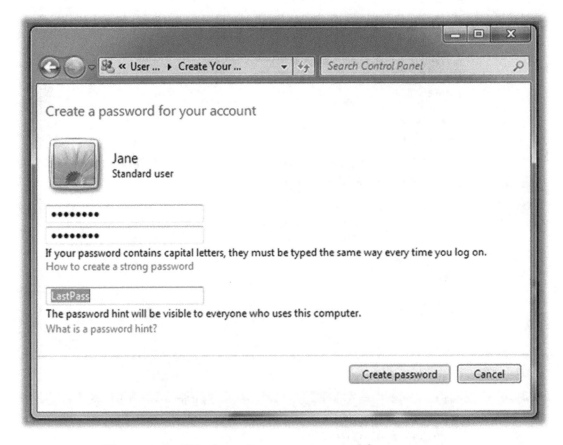

Figure 5-3. *Windows 7 create password for account*

4. Now search in the Control Panel again for *password*. This time, click "Lock the computer when I leave it alone..." (Figure 5-4).

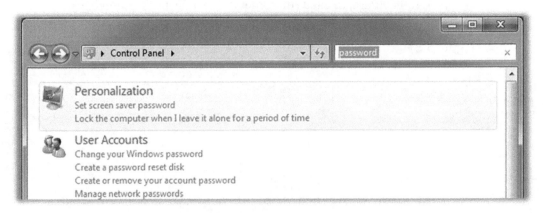

Figure 5-4. *Windows 7 Search for password*

5. Select a screen saver, if you want. Select "On resume, display logon screen." You can set the timeout to a higher value, if you want, but I wouldn't go too high or it will defeat the purpose. For a home computer in a secure location, you might go as high as an hour. But for a laptop, I would make it very short (like 1 minute), as shown in Figure 5-5.

Figure 5-5. *Windows 7 screen saver settings*

Tip 5-2b. Microsoft Windows 8.1

1. Open the Control Panel and search for *accounts* (Figure 5-6).
   If you have not already set a password for your account, select
   "Create or remove your account password." (If you already have a
   password set, skip ahead to the screen saver part.)

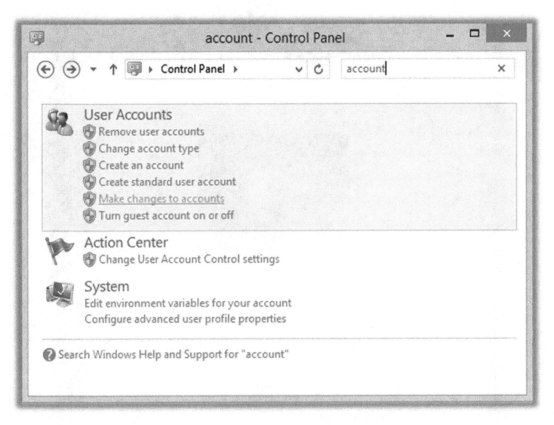

Figure 5-6. Windows 8.1 Search for account

2. Click the account you want to change (Figure 5-7).

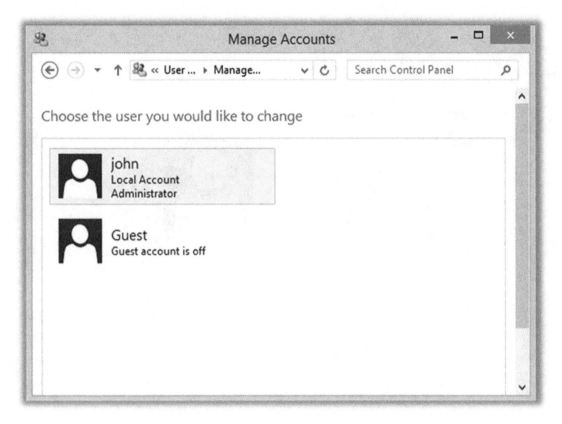

Figure 5-7. *Windows 8.1 manage accounts settings*

3.   Select "Create a password" (Figure 5-8). (Again, if you already have a password set, you can skip down to the screen saver part.)

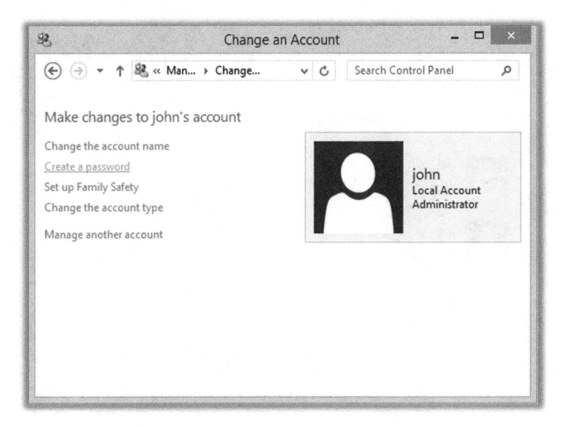

Figure 5-8. *Windows 8.1 change account settings*

4. Choose a moderately secure password that you can remember.
    This password does not have to be crazy strong like Internet
    account passwords. Nevertheless, I recommend saving this
    password in LastPass, in case you forget it. I usually put *LastPass*
    as my hint, so I know that I saved it there. Click "Create password"
    (Figure 5-9).

Figure 5-9. *Windows 8.1 create password settings*

5.   Now search in the Control Panel again for *lock* (Figure 5-10). This
      time, click "Lock the computer when I leave it alone...."

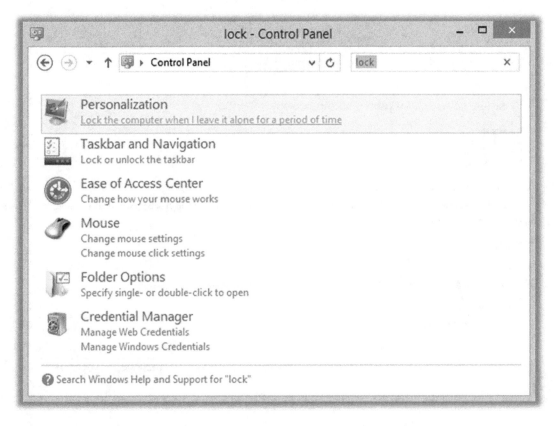

Figure 5-10. *Windows 8.1 personalization settings*

6. Select a screen saver, if you want. Select "On resume, display logon screen." You can set the timeout to a higher value, if you want, but I wouldn't go too high or it will defeat the purpose. For a home computer in a secure location, you might go as high as an hour. But for a laptop, I would make it very short (like 1 minute), as shown in Figure 5-11.

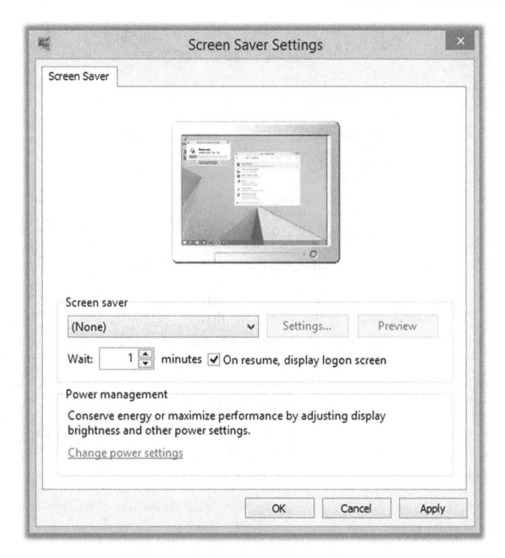

Figure 5-11. *Windows 8.1 screen saver settings*

Tip 5-2c. Microsoft Windows 10

The following settings will force your PC to lock after a fixed amount of time. There's a nifty feature in Windows 10 called Dynamic Lock that will allow you to automatically lock your PC when you walk away from it—if you pair a device to your PC. It's a little beyond the scope of this book, but if you're interested, check the "Learn more" link under Dynamic Lock in these settings.

1.   Open Settings and search for *sign-in* (Figure 5-12). Select "Sign-in options."

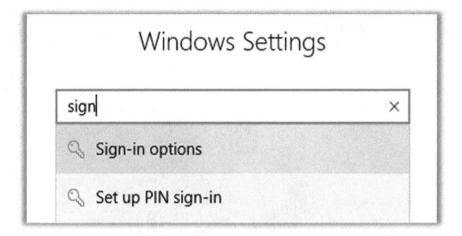

Figure 5-12. *Windows 10 sign-in options search*

2.   Click Add under Password (Figure 5-13). (If you don't see the red warning about adding a password, then you already have a password, and you can skip ahead to the screen saver part.)

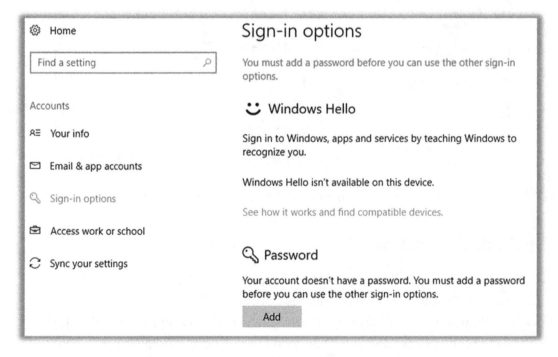

Figure 5-13. *Windows 10 sign-in options settings*

3. Choose a moderately secure password that you can remember. This password does not have to be crazy strong like Internet account passwords. Nevertheless, I recommend saving this password in LastPass, in case you forget it. I usually put *LastPass* as my hint, so I know that I saved it there. Click Finish on the next screen (Figure 5-14).

Figure 5-14. *Windows 10 create password settings*

4. Return to Settings, but now search for *lock*. Select "Lock screen settings" (Figure 5-15).

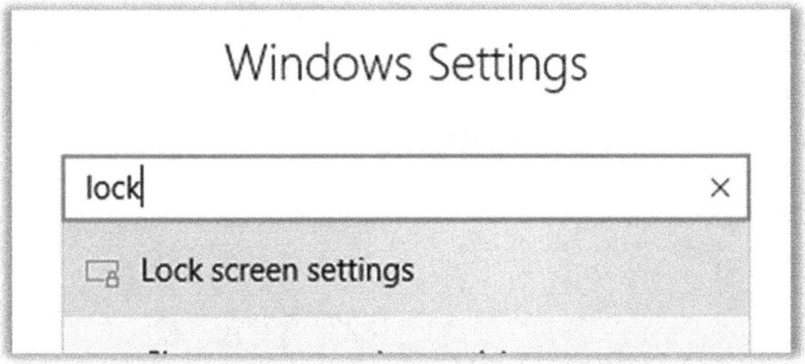

Figure 5-15. *Windows 10 lock screen settings search*

5. At the bottom of the Lock Screen Settings screen (you may have to scroll down), select "Screen saver settings." This should bring up a window like the one in Figure 5-16. Select "On resume, display login screen." You can set the timeout to a higher value, if you want, but I wouldn't go too high, or it will defeat the purpose. For a home computer in a secure location, you might go as high as an hour. But for a laptop, I would make it very short (like 1 minute), as shown in Figure 5-16.

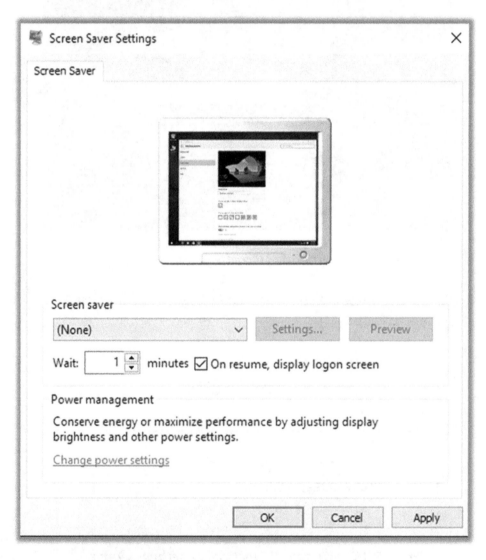

Figure 5-16. *Windows 10 screen saver settings*

Tip 5-2d. Mac OS

The screenshots for Mac OS 10.11, 10.12, and 10.13 are all similar. In this section I show you the view of macOS 10.13 (High Sierra).

Mac OS requires passwords by default in most cases. If you can log in to your Mac without a password, follow the steps here to require a password (and disable automatic login):

1.   Open System Preferences.

2.   Select Users & Groups at the lower left (Figure 5-17).

Figure 5-17. *Mac OS users and groups preferences*

3.   If the lock icon at the lower left is locked, click the icon and enter your password to unlock these settings.

4.   Select Login Options at the lower left, just above the lock icon. Make sure that "Automatic login" is set to Off (Figure 5-18).

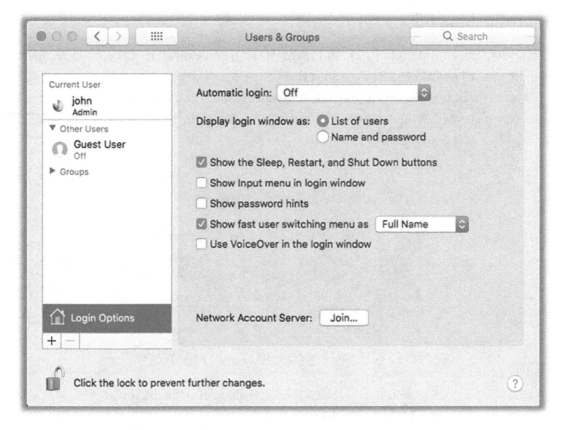

Figure 5-18. Mac OS users and groups settings

Tip 5-3. Create a Separate Admin Account

One of the best ways to limit the damage that can be done by malware is to limit yourself. Malware running on your computer can do whatever you can do. More accurately, malware running on your account will have the same permissions as you do. Therefore, it's best to have at least two accounts on your computer: an admin account for installing software and making system changes and a nonadmin account for regular, day-to-day stuff.

We're going to assume that you have only one account on your computer. (If you already have multiple accounts, then you just need to make sure that the special admin account is the only one with administrator privileges.) What we're going to do here is create a new admin account and then downgrade the level of your current account to normal (nonadmin). After you make these changes, you will need to enter the admin credentials whenever you install software or make certain system changes. The key here is that malware will not be able to use your nonadmin privileges to do anything really nasty.

These accounts will require you to choose a password. While you could use LastPass to generate a strong password, you really need something you can easily remember. So, you should generate a moderately strong password here using the techniques we discussed in the previous chapter. If this computer is a desktop computer that be used only within your home, you really don't need a crazy long password here—eight characters is probably enough. If this is a laptop or if for some reason many strangers might have easy physical access to this computer, then you should make it 10 to 12 characters. Note that for almost all of my "password hints," I just use *LastPass* or even just *LP*—because I store all these passwords as secure notes in my LastPass vault.

Tip 5-3a. Microsoft Windows 7

1. Open your Control Panel and search for *admin account*. Click "Create administrator account" (Figure 5-19).

Figure 5-19. *Windows 7 Search for admin account*

2. You need to create an account name. I personally prefer *admin*— short and to the point (Figure 5-20).

Figure 5-20. *Windows 7 create account dialog*

3. Once the account is created, you will need to set a password.
    Choose a moderately strong password. As always, create a secure
    note in LastPass so you won't forget it. Click Create Password to
    finish (Figure 5-21).

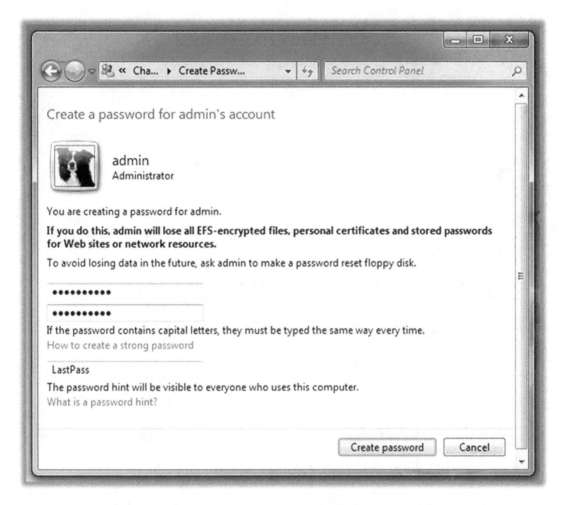

Figure 5-21. *Windows 7 create password dialog*

4. Now we need to remove admin privileges from your regular account. Click "Manage another account" and select your regular account.

5. Click "Change account type." Select Standard User and then Change Account Type (Figure 5-22).

Figure 5-22. *Windows 7 change account type dialog*

6. You should set a password for your regular account, as well. It's just good practice. Use the same steps as earlier to do this now.

7. If you have other family members or people in your household, you should take this opportunity to create accounts for each of them, using the same steps as shown earlier—just be sure to only give them Standard User accounts (not Administrator). Also, be sure that whatever backup utility you chose is set up for every account (see Chapter 3).

8. Log off and log back in for these changes to take full effect. You can do this from the Start menu (Figure 5-23).

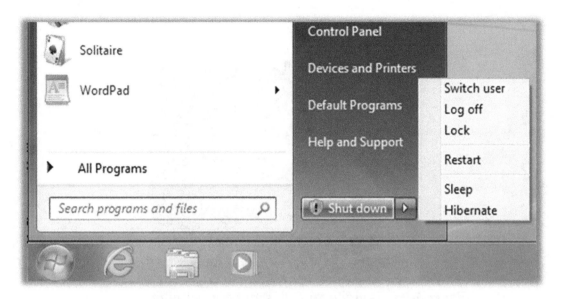

Figure 5-23. *Windows 7 logoff menu*

Tip 5-3b. Microsoft Windows 8.1

1. As of Windows 8, Microsoft introduced accounts that are tied to a Microsoft online account via an e-mail address. For an admin user, we want a local account.

2. Open "Change PC settings" from the right-side menu (Figure 5-24).

Figure 5-24. *Windows 8.1 change PC settings menu*

3.   Select Accounts (Figure 5-25).

Figure 5-25. *Windows 8.1 PC settings account menu*

4.   Select "Other accounts" and then click "Add an account" (Figure 5-26).

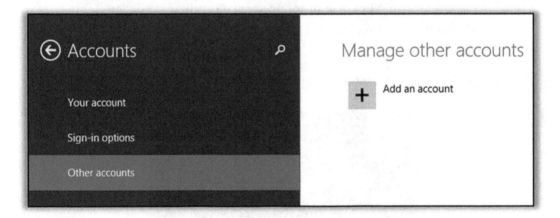

Figure 5-26. *Windows 8.1 add account settings*

5.   Ignore the stuff about creating an e-mail address. Find the link at the bottom called "Sign in without Microsoft account (not recommended)," as shown in Figure 5-27.

Figure 5-27. *Windows 8.1 sign-in without Microsoft account option*

6. On the next page, click the "Local account" button.

7. Create your account name. I personally prefer *admin*—short and
    to the point. Choose a moderately strong password and create a
    secure note in LastPass so you won't forget it. Click Next on this
    window and Finish on the following window to complete the
    process (Figure 5-28).

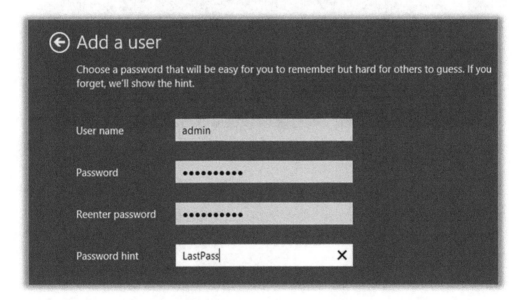

Figure 5-28. *Windows 8.1 add user dialog*

8. You need to now enable admin privileges for this account. Once
    again, select "Other accounts" and then click the new admin
    account (Figure 5-29).

Figure 5-29. Windows 8.1 manage other accounts settings

9. Click Edit. Change the account type to Administrator. Click OK. (Figure 5-30).

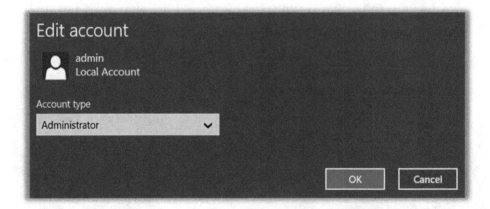

Figure 5-30. Windows 8.1 change account type settings

10. Log out of your regular account, and log back in to your new admin account. This may take a little time while the new account is set up the first time (Figure 5-31).

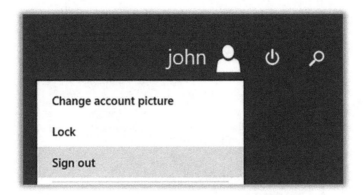

Figure 5-31. *Windows 8.1 sign-out menu*

11.   Using the same sequence as earlier, open the Accounts settings
      and click "Other accounts." Click your regular account, change the
      account type to Standard User, and save these changes.

12.   You can now log out of the admin account and log back in under
      your regular account.

13.   If you haven't done so already, you should set a password for your
      regular user account. Using the same procedure as earlier, re-open
      the PC Config settings and go to the Accounts page.

Tip 5-3c. Microsoft Windows 10

As of Windows 8, Microsoft introduced accounts that are tied to a Microsoft online
account via an e-mail address. For an admin user, we want a local account.

1.   Open Settings and click Accounts (Figure 5-32).

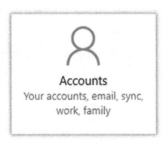

Figure 5-32. *Windows 10 Accounts button*

2. At the left, click "Family & other people" (Figure 5-33).

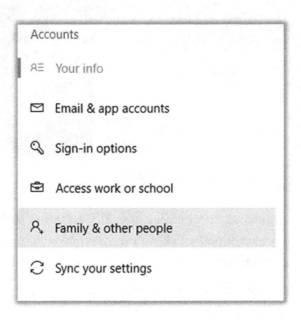

Figure 5-33. *Windows 10 Accounts menu*

3. Click the plus sign next to "Add someone else to this PC."

4. They make it hard to add a purely local account. Click the link at the bottom that says "I don't have this person's sign-in information."

5. At the bottom of the next page, click "Add a user without a Microsoft account."

6. Create your account name. I personally prefer *admin*—short and to the point. Choose a moderately strong password and create a secure note in LastPass, so you won't forget it. Click Next on this window and Finish on the following window to complete the process (Figure 5-34).

Create an account for this PC

If you want to use a password, choose something that will be easy for you to remember but hard for others to guess.

Who's going to use this PC?

```
admin
```

Make it secure.

```
••••••••••
```

```
••••••••••
```

```
LastPass|                                              ×
```

| Back | Next |

Figure 5-34. *Windows 10 create account dialog*

7. You need to now enable admin privileges for this account. Once again, select "Family & other users" and then click the new admin account. When you click it, you should see the options as in Figure 5-35.

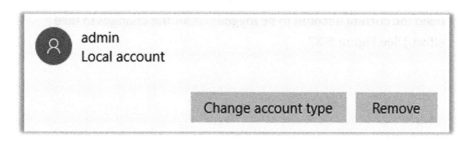

admin
Local account

Change account type   Remove

Figure 5-35. *Windows 10 change account type dialog*

Figure 5-38. *Windows 10 login screen*

12. You'll have to sit through some welcome messages while your new
    account is set up. When this completes, open Settings and go to
    Accounts and then "Family & other users" (as we did earlier). This
    time click your personal account ("john" in our example). Then
    click "Change account type" (Figure 5-39).

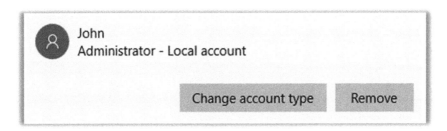

Figure 5-39. *Windows 10 change account type dialog*

13. Change the account type to Standard User (Figure 5-40).

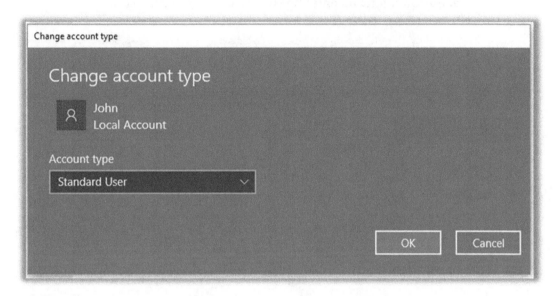

Figure 5-40. *Windows 10 change account type to standard user dialog*

14. Repeat the logout and login procedure, switching back to your regular account. This account is now restricted, which will prevent malware that gets by your defenses from doing too much harm. If you run into a situation where you need admin privileges, you can log into your admin account.

Tip 5-3d. Mac OS

1. From the Apple menu, open System Preferences. Select Users & Groups at the lower left (Figure 5-41).

Figure 5-41. *Mac OS Users & Groups preferences*

2. If necessary, unlock the account preferences by clicking the lock icon at the lower left and entering your password (Figure 5-42).

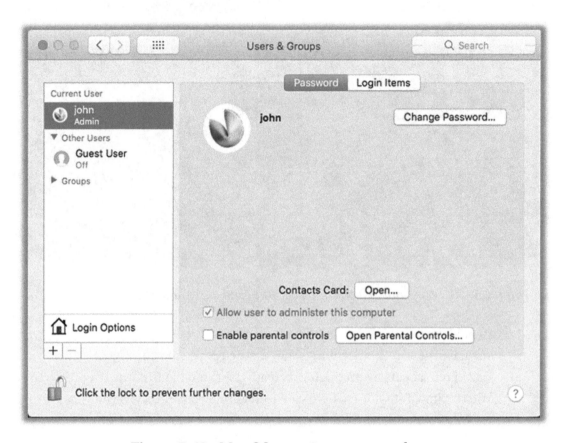

Figure 5-42. *Mac OS users & groups panel*

3. Click the little + (plus) sign under the list of accounts to create a new account. Choose an account name. I personally prefer *admin*—short and to the point. (In some versions of Mac OS, there's an option called "Use iCloud password"—don't use this; instead, choose "Use separate password.") You can add a password hint. I usually just use *LastPass* because that's where I'll store a copy of this info for future reference. Click Create User to finish (Figure 5-43).

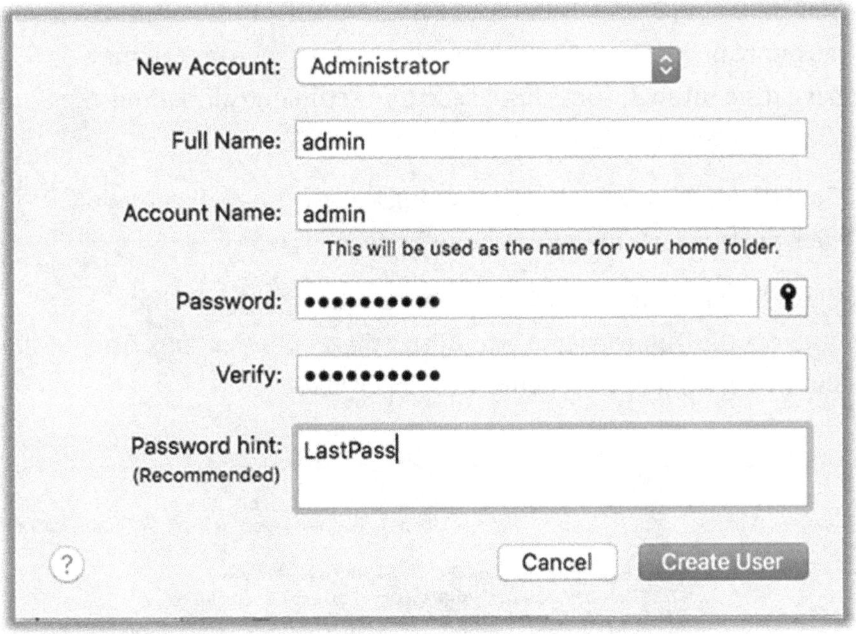

Figure 5-43. *Mac OS administrator password dialog*

4. Now we need to remove admin privileges from your regular account. To do this, you need to log out of your current account and log back in as the admin account. In the Apple menu, select Log Out <user>. (Figure 5-44).

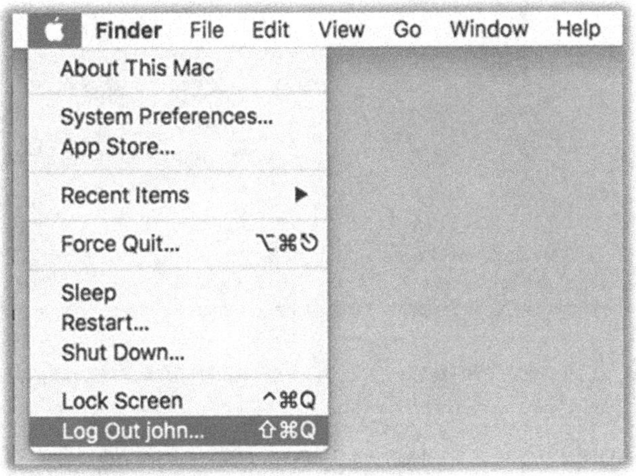

Figure 5-44. *Mac OS logout menu*

5. You should now see a list of your accounts. Select your admin
    account and log in using the password you just chose. You may
    have to go through some initial account setup questions. You can
    skip these for now ("setup later").

6. Go back to the Users & Groups settings, as we did earlier. Again,
    click the lock icon to unlock the settings.

7. Click the entry for your original Mac account at the left. Then
    uncheck the "Allow user to administer this computer" box. You
    should get a dialog like Figure 5-45. Click OK.

Figure 5-45. Mac OS remove administrator confirmation dialog

8. From the Apple menu, restart your computer to make the changes
    take full effect. You can then log back in as your original user
    ("john" in our example). See Figure 5-46.

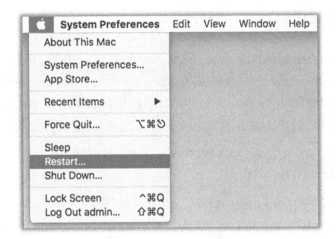

Figure 5-46. *Mac OS restart menu*

Tip 5-4. Install Free Antivirus Software

Antivirus (AV) software used to be a must for any computer owner. But lately, the effectiveness of AV software has become questionable. Furthermore, many AV products have become rather over-zealous in their protection schemes by embedding themselves deeply into your operating system so that they can monitor network traffic and inspect all files. However, in doing this, they often do more harm than good—in some cases, it's been shown that AV software itself is either causing problems or creating new vulnerabilities for hackers to exploit.

For these reasons, I feel that most people should forego expensive antivirus software products. You'll do a better job protecting yourself using all the other tips in this book. However, there are good and totally free software utilities for protecting your computer that I can recommend, if you feel you'd like to have something installed. If you have a teenager in the house, it's probably best to have AV software installed at least for their account.

Note   If you already have another antivirus program installed, you should disable and remove it before installing something new.

Tip 5-4a. Microsoft Windows 7

1. Go to this web site to download Microsoft Security Essentials
    (MSE). If for some reason this link fails, try going to Microsoft.com
    directly and find the search button (magnifying glass). Search for
    Microsoft security essentials windows 7.

    ```
    https://support.microsoft.com/en-us/help/14210/security-
    essentials-download
    ```

2. Last I looked at this page, it was a confusing list of options—by
    language and computer type. Start with the 64-bit version. If you
    need the 32-bit version, the installer should tell you this, and you
    can come back for the other version (Figure 5-47).

| English | English | Windows Vista/Windows 7 32-bit |
| | | Windows Vista/Windows 7 64-bit |

Figure 5-47. *Windows 7 Microsoft Security Essentials download*

3. Download and run the installer. Click the default buttons on the
    installer as you go. When you reach this part of the installer, make
    sure that both of these boxes are checked (Figure 5-48).

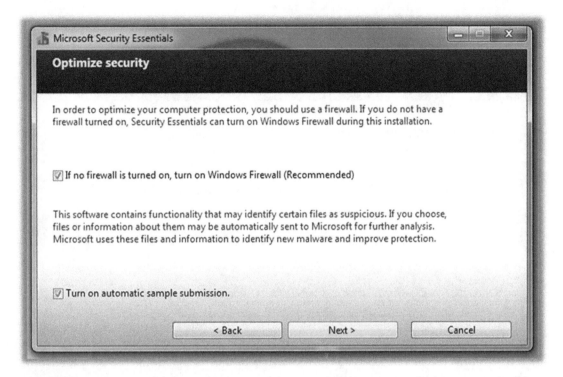

Figure 5-48. Windows 7 Microsoft Security Essentials security options

4. Click the Next buttons and eventually the Install button. When the installer is finished, check the box "Scan my computer" and click Finish. This will automatically launch MSE and update the virus/spyware definitions, and then it will perform a scan. Let this continue until finished (Figure 5-49).

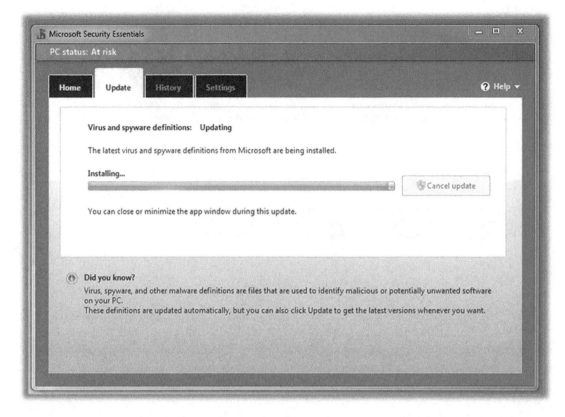

Figure 5-49. *Windows 7 Microsoft Security Essentials update progress*

5.   The default settings should be good. If you'd like to check them, you can look at the next section on Windows Defender—they are nearly identical.

Tip 5-4b. Microsoft Windows 8.1

Windows 8.1 comes with Windows Defender[7] pre-installed. You just need to verify that it is enabled and configured properly.

1.   Open your Control Panel and search for *defender* (Figure 5-50). Click Windows Defender.

---

[7]This used to be called Microsoft Security Essentials.

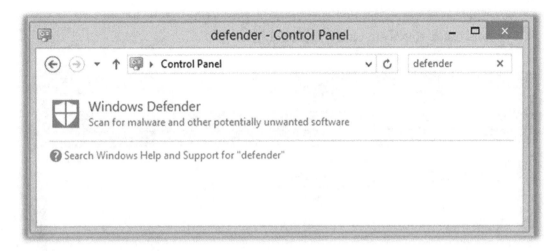

Figure 5-50. *Windows 8.1 Search for defender*

2. You should see a dialog box like Figure 5-51.

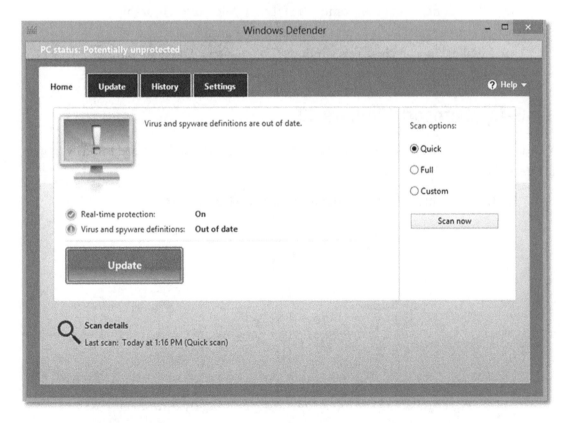

Figure 5-51. *Windows 8.1 Windows Defender home dialog*

3. Click the Settings tab. Select "Real-time protection" at the left and make sure this is enabled (Figure 5-52).

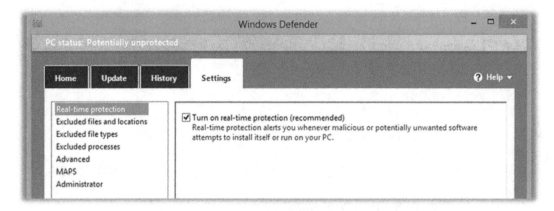

Figure 5-52. *Windows 8.1 Windows Defender settings*

4. When done, select the Home tab. If the Update button is orange, go ahead and click it to update your virus scanner. This may take a while. You can close this window, though—it will do it all in the background.

Tip 5-4c. Microsoft Windows 10

Windows 10 comes with Windows Defender[8] pre-installed. You just need to verify that it is enabled and configured properly.

1. Open Settings and click Update & Security (Figure 5-53).

Figure 5-53. *Windows 10 Update & Security button*

---

[8]This used to be called Microsoft Security Essentials.

2. Click Windows Defender at the left. Then click Open Windows Defender Security Center (Figure 5-54).

Windows Defender

Windows Defender Antivirus protects your computer against viruses, spyware, and other malicious software. Open Windows Defender Security Center to use it.

Open Windows Defender Security Center

Figure 5-54. *Windows 10 Windows Defender Security Center button*

3. You want to see green check marks on all of these, as shown in Figure 5-55. In particular, right now we're concerned with "Virus & threat protection." If this item doesn't have a green check mark, click it and check the settings.

Virus & threat protection
No action needed.

Device performance & health
No action needed.

Firewall & network protection
No action needed.

App & browser control
No action needed.

Figure 5-55. *Windows 10 Windows Defender status*

4. Under "Virus & threat protection," click "Virus & threat protection settings." Make sure the top three items are on, as shown in Figure 5-56. (We'll talk about "Controlled folder access" in the next tip.)

Figure 5-56. *Windows 10 Windows Defender virus and threat protection settings*

Tip 5-4d. Mac OS

Modern Mac computers come with some basic anti-malware protection built into the operating system, but it's not on the same level as Windows Defender. There are a few decent, free antivirus applications for Mac. Unfortunately, the capabilities and efficacy of these applications change constantly. These third-party programs are often adding features that break your encrypted Internet connections in an attempt to see everything you're doing. These techniques are dangerous and can lead to some severe vulnerabilities. Honestly, I've personally decided not to install AV software at all on my Macs.

If you'd feel better with some type of AV software installed, I recommend a simple and free application like Sophos Home. If you find that Sophos isn't working for you, you might try Avira's free Mac product.

1. Go to the Sophos web site and download the free version for Mac.

    `https://home.sophos.com/download-mac-anti-virus`

2. It will ask you to create an account. I know…it's a pain. But go ahead and sign up. They will send you an e-mail confirmation with a button—click that button to complete your sign up and log in to your new account. It should then offer you a download button. There will also be a link at the bottom of the page—if you have other computers in your house that you'd like to protect with Sophos, use this link to e-mail yourself the download link.

3. Download and run the installer.

4. You may see a scary pop-up dialog about a system extension being blocked. It's just Mac OS trying to protect you from malware, which is a good thing! But in this case, we want to allow it, so click Open Security Preferences.

5. In Security Preferences, unlock the lock with your password and then click the Allow button for Sophos (Figure 5-57).

Figure 5-57. *Mac OS security extension warning dialog*

Tip 5-5. Enable Controlled Folder Access (Windows 10 Only)

As of Windows 10 2017 Fall Creators Update (Microsoft has weird names for its Windows 10 updates), you can turn on some really powerful protection for your files called "Controlled folder access." This feature will restrict the ability for applications to add, change, or delete user and system files by creating a "white list" of approved apps.

Microsoft already adds the most common, trusted applications to this list for you, but you can add other apps if you want. But the point is that malicious apps will not be able to mess with any of the protected files or folders without explicit permission. This feature is primary aimed at fending off ransomware, which will attempt to lock up (encrypt) all of your files and hold them for ransom—that is, demand a payment before giving you the key to unlock (decrypt) them. By restricting which applications can modify your files, you're preventing malware and other rogue applications from being able to alter or delete these files (including encrypting them).

To enable this feature, go to the same Windows Defender Security Center area we went to in the last tip, under "Virus & threat protection settings." Just scroll down and enable the feature.

1. Enable "Controlled folder access" (Figure 5-58).

Figure 5-58. Windows 10 "Controlled folder access" setting

2. You can see what folders are protected and add other folders by clicking "Protected folders."

3. Most well-known apps will already be allowed to change files from these folders, but if you run into a case where a particular application you want use isn't on Microsoft's list of known-safe apps, you can add the app using the "Allow an app through Controlled folder access" here.

Tip 5-6. Turn On Disk Encryption (Mac OS Only)

Turning on full disk encryption is an easy step to protecting your precious data, and you won't even notice it. The process itself can take quite a long time, but you can use your computer while the encryption is going on in the background.

Some versions of Windows have a built-in tool called BitLocker that will encrypt your hard drive. Unfortunately, BitLocker is not available in the Home or regular versions of Windows. You need a Pro or Enterprise version. While there are other alternatives, for non-technical folks I think built-in solutions from the OS maker are best. However, if you really want to do this on Windows, check out VeraCrypt (free).

```
https://www.veracrypt.fr/
```

Tip 5-6a. Mac OS

1. Open System Preferences. Select Security & Privacy (Figure 5-59).

Figure 5-59. *Mac OS Security & Privacy preferences*

2. If necessary, unlock this preference pane by clicking the lock icon at the lower left. Then select the FileVault tab (Figure 5-60).

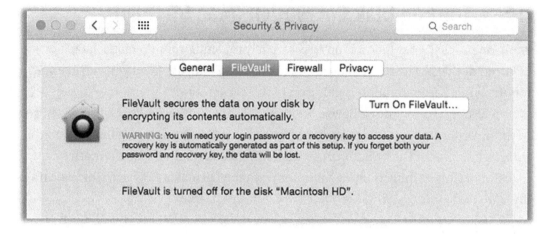

Figure 5-60. *Mac OS Security & Privacy FileVault settings*

3. Click the button Turn On FileVault. You will then be asked where you want to store your recovery key. You can elect to store this with your iCloud account, but personally I prefer to save it myself—in LastPass (Figure 5-61).

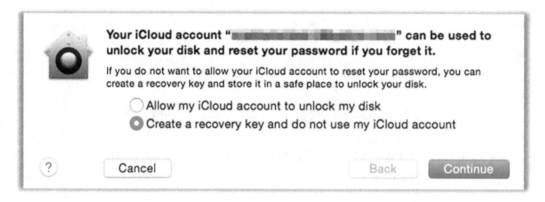

Figure 5-61. *Mac OS recovery key location options*

4. Once you click Continue, you will be shown your recover key. *This step is absolutely crucial!* If you lose this key, you will not be able to recover any of your files if there's some problem with your computer down the road. Carefully select the text from the screen and copy it and then paste it to a secure note in LastPass (see the previous chapter for instructions). You might want to also paste

this key into a text file and print it off and then save it somewhere very safe (like a safe deposit box). Triple-check it to be certain you copied the entire key faithfully. Then click Continue (Figure 5-62).

Figure 5-62. *Mac OS recovery key*

5. You will need to enter the passwords for every user on your system before you proceed. Click each Enable User button and enter the proper passwords (Figure 5-63).

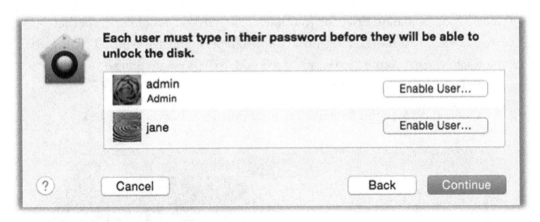

Figure 5-63. *Mac OS FileVault account enable dialog*

6. Once you've entered all the passwords, click Continue again. You will be asked to restart your Mac. As the message says, you will be able to use your Mac while the encrypting happens (which is pretty amazing, if you ask me). You can check the progress by going back to the FileVault preference pane. It will give you an estimate of the remaining time. It will probably be many hours, perhaps more than a day, if you have a large hard drive (Figure 5-64).

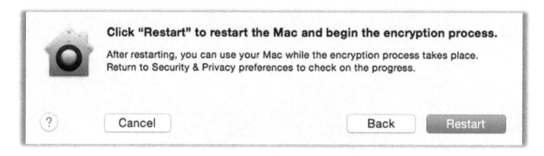

Figure 5-64. *Mac OS restart dialog*

Tip 5-7. Encrypt Your Backups (Mac OS Only)

If you used an external hard drive for your backups, then you should encrypt that hard drive, as well. When we set this up a couple chapters ago, we skipped setting up encryption—because I wanted to be sure you had LastPass set up first so you could generate and store the backup password.

1. Open Time Machine Preferences from the menu bar (Figure 5-65).

Figure 5-65. *Mac OS Time Machine preferences menu*

2. Click the Select Disk button (Figure 5-66).

Figure 5-66. *Mac OS Time Machine preferences*

3. Select your disk in the "Available disks" list and then check the "Encrypt backups" box at the bottom. Click Use Disk (Figure 5-67).

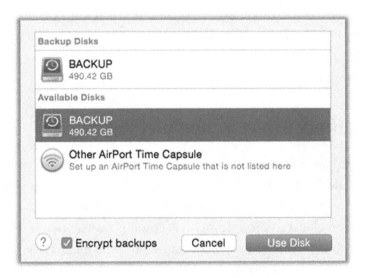

Figure 5-67. *Mac OS Time Machine disk selection dialog*

4. You will be asked to enter a password and a hint. Use the steps in the previous chapter to generate a kick-butt password and save it in a secure note in LastPass. Then paste that password here (twice). For the password hint, you can just use LastPass so that you know where you've saved this password (Figure 5-68).

Figure 5-68. *Mac OS Time Machine backup password dialog*

5. Now you can click the Encrypt Disk button. Once you've started this, it will take a long time, possibly more than a day. Just let it go. You don't have to wait for it to complete, it will happen in the background.

Tip 5-8. Securely Erase Sensitive Files

If you want to throw away a sensitive file, you need to do more than simply put it in the virtual Trash bin and "empty" it. As discussed in this chapter, when the operating system "deletes" a file, it doesn't actually erase the bits and bytes; it just forgets about it. That means that it's technically still there, until it's eventually overwritten by new files. With the right software tools, these files are recoverable. So if you really want sensitive files to be erased, you have to take some extra precautions.

There's one gotcha, though... modern computers that use solid-state drive (SSD) technology for their hard drive don't really have a way to properly delete a file. Because of the way SSD drives work, your files are actually moved around constantly to improve performance and balance the usage of the memory sectors. That means there are potentially several places on the drive where copies of your file's bits and bytes may be lying around, waiting to be overwritten. So in this case, your best protection is just encrypting your entire drive (the previous tip). Even if there are remnants of the file floating around the disk, they're not readable by someone who's not logged into the computer.

Note that if you're getting ready to sell, donate, or recycle a computer, you should absolutely wipe the entire drive first. This is covered in the next tip.

Tip 5-8a. Microsoft Windows

Windows does not have a "secure delete" feature built into the operating system, at least as of this writing. If you feel the need to securely erase some files, you can try one of these two free utilities:

- *Eraser*: http://eraser.heidi.ie/download.php

- *Freeraser*: https://www.pendriveapps.com/freeraser-portable-file-shredder/

Tip 5-8b. Mac OS

The Secure Empty Trash option was removed in OS X version 10.11. In true Apple fashion, since Apple felt this feature would give users a false sense of security, the company simply removed it.

However, the feature is still available if you're willing to get really geeky and use the command-line interface. That's honestly beyond the skills of most people likely to read this book, but if you're determined, you can do the following:

1. Put your file in the Trash.

2. Empty the Trash by right-clicking the trashcan icon and selecting Empty Trash.

3. Now you need to securely erase the "free space" on your hard drive. To do this, open the Terminal application and find the drive volume for your main hard drive. By default, this would be Macintosh HD.

4. At the prompt, type the following (assuming your main drive is Macintosh HD):

```
diskutil secureErase freespace 0 /Volumes/Macintosh\ HD
```

5. You can try higher levels of security by increasing the 0 to 1 or 2.

Tip 5-9. Prepare a Computer for Sale/Donation/Recycle

Your computer probably contains a lot of juicy information about you. Before you get rid of it (sell, give, or even recycle), you should make sure that no one else can get to your data. Now, if you've fully encrypted your hard drive like I've recommended, then you don't need to bother trying to erase everything. Your data is completely inaccessible—total gibberish, even to the NSA. All you need to do is delete your accounts. (If you really want to be sure, look at the final chapter of the book for tips on how to securely wipe any hard drive.)

Tip 5-9a. Microsoft Windows

Here's how to prepare a Windows computer for selling or donation. Obviously, before you do this, you're probably going to want to back up any and all files first. Once you follow these steps, all that data will be *gone*. So, make *sure* you've backed everything up before you do this!

Do the following steps for every nonadmin account on your PC:

1. If you have an iTunes account, sign out of iTunes and deauthorize this computer. Within iTunes, select the Store menu and then Deauthorize this Computer.... Follow the instructions.

2. Sign out of your Microsoft account and any other cloud accounts tied to this computer.

When you have completed these steps for all the accounts on your computer, log in to your admin account and perform the following steps:

1. Repeat the previous steps.

2. Open the Control Panel and search for *remove*. Select "Remove user accounts" and delete all the other accounts on the computer.

3. The easiest step at this point is to create another admin account (using the steps I showed you before) and then delete this admin account. The new admin account will be fresh and have zero data. You can give the password of the new admin account to the next owner. If you want to be super-thorough, though, you should probably completely reinstall the operating system. That's beyond the scope of this book, but you can search on the Web for *Reinstall Windows* for help. If you still have the Windows installation disk that came with your computer, you'll use that to reinstall the OS.

Tip 5-9b. Mac OS

Here's how to prepare an Apple computer for selling or donation. Obviously, before you do this, you're probably going to want a full backup of your computer. If you use the Time Machine method, you can easily use this back up to transfer all your data to your new computer. But once you follow these steps, all that data will be *gone*. So, make *sure* you've backed everything up first!

Do the following steps for every nonadmin account on your Mac:

1. Sign out of iTunes and deauthorize this computer. Within iTunes, select the Store menu and then Deauthorize this Computer…. Follow the instructions.

2. Sign out of iCloud. Go the System Preferences and find the iCloud settings. Click the Sign Out button at the lower right.

3. Sign out of Messages. Within the Messages app, go to Preferences and then Accounts. Select your Messages account and sign out.

4. If you have any other cloud service accounts tied to this computer (like Dropbox, Backblaze, Google Drive, etc.), be sure to sign out of them, as well.

When you have completed these steps for all the nonadmin accounts on your Mac, log in to your admin account and perform the following steps:

1. Repeat the previous steps.

2. Open System Preferences and select Accounts.

3. Delete all the other accounts on the computer.

4. The easiest step at this point is to create another admin account (using the steps I showed you before) and then delete this admin account. The new admin account will be fresh and have zero data. You can give the password of the new admin account to the next owner. If you want to be super-thorough, though, you should probably completely reinstall the operating system. That's beyond the scope of this book, but you can search the Web for *Reinstall OS X from Recovery* to find detailed instructions from Apple on how to do this.

Tip 5-10. Buy a Paper Shredder

Okay, so this isn't really a computer tip—but it's hard to talk about securely deleting computer files and securely wiping your computers before selling them without thinking about physical file security, too. Many people don't realize this, but once you throw something away, it's fair game for anyone to take. Legally, once you "abandon" your trash and place it off your property (at the curb), you give up any expectation of privacy.

At a high level, you want to shred anything that's private and personal. That would include financial, medical, and legal papers. That probably seems obvious, but I'll bet you still throw away a lot of stuff that you should be shredding.

You're going to want to buy a decent shredder for this work. The main feature you want is `cross-cutting`. Strip-cutting shredders that just cut paper into long, thin strips are not good enough. Even cross-cut paper can be painstakingly re-assembled, but it's a lot harder—especially if it's mixed up with a bunch of other shredded documents.

You can also buy shredders that can handle credit cards and optical disks (CDs and DVDs) in addition to paper, which is handy. We don't use CDs and DVDs much anymore to store data—which is possibly why you might be throwing them away. When you get rid of old credit cards or when some company sends you a "starter card" as part of a mailed offer, you definitely want to shred them before you throw them out.

The last thing to consider is the size of the output bin. I would just get yourself the biggest one that fits your needs—it means having to empty it less often and mixes a lot more stuff up together. You can find shredders at office supply stores or from Amazon online.

Tip 5-11. Set Up Find My Mac (Mac OS Only)

This is a very nice feature for laptops, which are portable and can be lost or stolen. When this feature is enabled, you will be able to track your Mac, send messages to the screen, and even remotely lock or erase it, if you believe it was stolen. You will need to sign up for a free iCloud account, if you haven't already. I will not cover this process here, but I'll get you started.

1. Open System Preferences on your laptop (the computer that you want to be able to find).

2. Open the iCloud preferences.

3. If you have not signed up for an iCloud account, you can do it here. Click the little "create Apple ID" link under the first text box. Follow the instructions there; it's very simple. Be sure to do three things, though.

4. First, give them a "rescue e-mail" account, if you have a second e-mail account.

5. Second, be sure to check the box to enable Find My Mac.

6. Finally, when it asks you if you would like to allow Find My Mac to use your Mac's location, click Allow—otherwise it defeats the whole purpose (Figure 5-69).

Figure 5-69. Mac OS iCloud sign-in dialog

7. Once you've signed into iCloud, you should be able to see a list of iCloud features. Scroll to the bottom and check Find My Mac. You will be asked if it's okay to use location information—select Allow.

8. You can now use your iCloud account (in a web browser on another computer, or using the Find My Mac app on an iPhone or iPad) to locate this Mac if it's lost or stolen.

Tip 5-12. Don't Trust Other Computers

Whenever you're using a computer that is not your own, you need to be careful what you do. Sometimes bad guys will install software on public computers that can record every single keystroke from the keyboard—these are called *key loggers*. So, everything you type is saved off somewhere. If you're just doing some web searches and accessing web sites that don't require you to log in, then you don't need to really worry because you're not typing in anything really valuable. However, you should avoid ever entering sensitive data like passwords, Social Security numbers, credit card numbers, and so on. It doesn't matter if the web site is secure; the information is being captured before it even gets to the form on the web page.

If you simply *have* to use a public computer to log into a web site that requires a password, you can try these techniques to protect yourself:

1. If you need to use one of your crazy, random LastPass passwords, you can't just install the browser plugin or look it up on your iPhone and type it in. Log into your LastPass vault via the web browser (`https://www.lastpass.com`) using one of your one-time passwords (*never* use your actual master password on a public computer!). Cross off this one-time password on your list since it will no longer work. Find the site you need and view the password. You can copy the password from your vault and paste it into the web site's login form. (Do *not* simply type in the password you see in your vault—you *must* copy and paste it!) After you paste the password, you should make a point to copy some other nonsense text from somewhere to clear out the contents of the copy clipboard.

2. You can also try to confuse the key logger. This is a pain in the butt. Start typing your password, one letter at a time. Between each letter, go to some other place—search text box, text document, something—and type some other random characters. The key logger will record all of these keystrokes, in order, and will have no idea which characters are part of your password and which ones are just junk you're typing somewhere else.

3. Be sure to log out of all your web sites when you're done, especially LastPass!

4. If you're using a computer at a friend's house, you might ask if they have a guest login account you can use. If so, use this account and log out when you're done.

Tip 5-13. Avoid Foreign/Unknown USB Devices

We don't think much about all the USB peripherals we attach to our computers...mice, keyboards, printers, webcams, thumb drives, and so on. These devices seem simple enough, but *every* USB device can contain software—and often, our computers will automatically read and run that software when the device is first plugged in. The point of this is for these devices to have built-in driver software, allowing most devices to "just work" when we plug them in.

To save money, many manufacturers will make this software updatable after manufacture. That is, instead of making this software read-only, they give themselves the option to retroactively change the software—so that if there's a problem with it, they can simply change the software without having to throw away the hardware and start over.

The bottom line is that it's possible to install malware on a USB device. Therefore, you should be suspect of any USB device you plug into your computer. Think of it as like having unprotected computer sex. Believe it or not, you can buy a "USB condom" for this exact purpose! It works only for charging devices—it explicitly blocks the data and allows only the power to go through. This can be helpful when traveling and you need to charge your phone on a public USB port (airports, airplanes, coffee shops, etc.).

While spreading malware via infected USB devices is not that common, you should still be aware that it's possible. Here are some things you can do to avoid catching a virus from a bad USB device or plug.

1. Never pick up a USB flash drive that you find lying around and plug it into your computer. This is probably the number-one way this technique is used by hackers.

2. Get your USB devices from a reputable retailer. Make sure they're new and unopened.

3. Don't buy used USB devices.

4. Don't use USB devices from other people.

5. Use "power only" USB cables (no data) or buy a "USB condom" for charging your phone and tablets on public USB ports.

6. Set your computer screen to lock right away and require a password to unlock. Don't leave it alone with others present while it's unlocked. It's already been shown that bad guys can completely hack your computer in less than a minute by plugging in a bad USB device. You'll never even know they were there.

Tip 5-14. Don't Use Adobe Reader to Read PDF Files

Adobe Flash isn't the only popular program that's notoriously insecure and buggy. The popular PDF[9] viewing app called Reader is also known for its share of problems. This isn't an issue with Mac OS since Apple provides an excellent PDF viewer called Preview (though some Adobe products will still install Reader). On Windows, however, you should consider downloading and installing a new PDF reader app.

- Most web browsers can open PDF files now. So, you can try opening the file with Microsoft Explorer or Edge (or better yet, Firefox!).

- If you just want a simple, quick application for reading PDF files, try Sumatra PDF reader.

  `http://blog.kowalczyk.info/software/sumatrapdf/free-pdf-reader.html`

- If you would like a full-featured PDF reader that will also let you create PDFs, try Nitro PDF reader.

  `https://www.gonitro.com/pdf-reader`

Tip 5-15. Unplug or Cover Webcams When Not in Use

This is going to sound paranoid, but it's for real. It's actually possible to remotely enable some webcams and watch what people are doing, in some cases even without turning on the little light that indicates that the webcam is active. This would usually require that your computer has already been compromised with malware—which is to say that if you have this problem, you probably have others, too. Nonetheless, I would unplug webcams if you're not using them or put a sticky note over the lens if the webcam is built-in. (Mark Zuckerberg, CEO of Facebook, was famously seen doing this.)

---

[9]Portable Document Format (PDF) is a popular format for creating documents that can be read on a variety of devices and operating systems.

Tip 5-16. Beware Cold Calls for Computer Support

If someone calls you out of the blue and tells you that your computer is having problems and offers to remotely debug your computer for you, just hang up. Real computer support companies will never do this. While this company may actually offer computer support services (at a low, low subscription cost of $199/year), you probably don't need them.

Likewise, if you're getting a weird pop-up on your computer warning you that you're infected or your computer's performance could be optimized or even that some scanner has detected illegal materials on your hard drive, just close the window without doing anything. This is almost surely a scam.

If the pop-up messages continue or you're just worried that something really is wrong, contact a tech-savvy friend or relative and get their advice. If that's not an option, call a reputable computer store or call your computer's support line (even if you're out of warranty).

CHAPTER 6

LAN Sweet LAN

In this chapter, we're going to discuss your home network. Even if you have only one computer connected to the Internet, you still technically have a network. A network is something that allows two or more devices to communicate and share resources. The Internet is the most famous network; it's the network that connects us to computers and services all over the globe. But most of us also have an intranet within our homes, and how we allow our personal network to communicate with the public network is crucial to our security and privacy.

Network Overview

Let's start by identifying the parts of your home network—called a *local area network* (LAN). For your computer to connect to the Internet (referred to as a *wide area network* [WAN]), you first need to have Internet service—often called *broadband* or *high-speed Internet* service. For most people, this is provided by their cable or phone company.[1] In rural areas, you might get your Internet service from a satellite company. In many metropolitan areas, you can get Internet service over fiber-optic cable. But regardless of the specific way in which you connect to the Internet, the company that provides you with this service is called your *Internet service provider* (ISP). Somewhere in your house you will have a box that this company provided to you that allows you to connect your computer. This box is usually called a *modem* (which is short for "modulator-demodulator"). A typical modem looks something like Figure 6-1.

---

[1]Service from your cable company uses technology called Data Over Cable Service Interface Specification (DOCSIS); service from the phone company usually uses technology called Digital Subscriber Line (DSL) or Asymmetric DSL (ADSL).

© Carey Parker 2018
C. Parker, *Firewalls Don't Stop Dragons*, https://doi.org/10.1007/978-1-4842-3852-3_6

Figure 6-1. *Cable modem*

The modem converts the common Internet Protocol (that your computer understands) to some sort of special protocol that allows the communication to flow over the phone lines, cable line, fiber-optic cable, or satellite link. This device is assigned an Internet Protocol (IP) address, and like the address on your house, it's associated specifically with you (or your account). When your computer talks to the Internet, the return address on all its packets is your IP address.

In the simplest case, you just connect your computer directly to this modem and you're done. That's your entire network. But many of us today have more than one device in our homes that wants to access the Internet, and in that case you need another piece of equipment called a *router*. Your ISP gives you only one IP address. If you have multiple devices, then you need some way to give those devices their own addresses—at least within your home—so that each one of those devices can carry on their own conversations with other things on the Internet. (We discussed how this works in previous chapters.)

It's important to note that if you have multiple devices on your home network, they often talk to each other, as well. That is, they send information between themselves that's not meant to leave your house. Maybe you're streaming some music from your computer to your home theater system or printing a document from your laptop to a network printer. In this case, all the info is completely within your network. It's like someone in marketing sending a package to the sales department via internal company mail. The U.S. Postal Service never sees or knows about this; it's completely internal and private. We'll see why this is important in the next section.

Most routers today are wireless routers. This is a little box that often has one or more little antennas on it and is directly connected to your modem via a cable called an *Ethernet cable*. It will look something like Figure 6-2.

Figure 6-2. *A sample Wi-Fi router*

Ethernet cables are like phone cables—they usually have little clippy things on the end that snap into place. Ethernet cables are the most common cords that are used to connect things to a network directly. The router box is then connected to all the other devices in your house that need to access the Internet—either hardwired with an Ethernet cable or connected virtually over the air, wirelessly. The wireless connection is called *Wi-Fi* or sometimes by its technical spec name, 802.11. Networks created by Wi-Fi routers are commonly referred to as *wireless LANs* (WLANs). (I know... couldn't they come up with something a little less confusing? LAN, WAN, WLAN—really? Don't shoot the messenger, folks.) There are many versions of Wi-Fi—over the years they improved things and gave the spec different names like 802.11b, 802.11n, and 802.11ac. But all you really need to know is that the router acts like an internal, private mail room—the router allows all the devices in your house to have private addresses inside your home to talk with each other and to share a single public Internet address for communications with the outside world. Many businesses (hotels, cafes, restaurants, airports, libraries) often provide free Wi-Fi Internet access for customers. These locations are referred to as *Wi-Fi hotspots*.

That's pretty much your home network in a nutshell. You have a modem, a router, and a bunch of devices that are connected to that router (either wired or wirelessly). Those devices include desktop computers, laptops, smartphones, printers, and tablets. We're now also seeing other "smart" devices connecting, as well: TVs, streaming boxes (like Apple TV, Fire TV, or Roku), DVRs, home appliances, thermostats, and even light bulbs.

Now that we know the pieces to the home network puzzle, let's take a look at the security and privacy issues associated with your home network and how to deal with them.

Modem

The modem provided to you by your Internet service provider is generally something you cannot control, and that makes a security- and privacy-conscious person nervous. Many ISPs are now providing a combo product: a modem and Wi-Fi router all in one—how convenient! That's even worse. Why? Because what's best for your ISP is not the same as what's best for you.[2] Your network router is doing two crucial things: it's a wall between your network and the rest of the wild, woolly Internet, and it's the hub for all the data traffic within your home network. There's just no reason to trust your ISP to perform those critical functions. While ISPs will usually try to protect your home network from bad actors on the Internet, they have no reason whatsoever to protect your privacy or to insulate you from their own meddling. Furthermore, you want to have full control over the configuration of your Wi-Fi router, and your ISP may not give you that access. For these reasons alone, I strongly suggest you always insert your own router between your computer and your ISP's modem. Basic models are pretty cheap, and this book can help you get it set up.

Here's an interesting story that will help to illustrate my point. A few years ago, Comcast (the largest ISP in the United States) began rolling out a service for its customers called Xfinity Wi-Fi. This service allows Comcast customers to use "millions" of free Wi-Fi hotspots around the world. Sounds great, right? What's not to like? Well, the company accomplished this by turning people's private cable boxes into public hotspots—that is, Comcast enabled this feature on your home combo modem/Wi-Fi box so that its customers near (or in) your home could connect to the Internet using your equipment. While I'm sure Comcast customers somehow implicitly gave Comcast permission to do this somewhere in their licensing agreement, I'm willing to bet most people had no idea they were doing this. Your modem is, after all, Comcast's equipment—not yours. It provides you with a service, and that contract surely allows Comcast to offer other services using its equipment.

---

[2]According to the 2017 American Customer Satisfaction Index (ACSI) survey, cable companies and Internet service providers are tied for last place in the United States, well below even health insurance companies and airlines.

When this became widely understood, people rightly had serious questions about this service. Won't this slow down my Internet connection (having to share it with others)? Will this give strangers access to my home network? What if someone uses my Internet connection to do illegal things—won't that appear as if I did those things? Comcast has some partial answers for these concerns, and there does exist a way to opt out of this program by changing your account preferences online. But the real question is: do you trust your ISP to do what's best for you (as opposed to what's best for them)? If Comcast changes its strategy or decides to offer another feature like this in the future, how likely are you to be properly informed of this? And will you be given the choice to opt out? (Two customers in San Francisco filed a class action lawsuit against Comcast over this, but it was thrown out because all Comcast customers agreed to settle disputes via arbitration in their terms of service.)

The simplest solution to this is to just use your own router. If your ISP provided you with a combo modem and Wi-Fi router, I would call them up and ask them to disable the Wi-Fi service entirely. If you're a Comcast customer, I would also opt out of the Xfinity public/shared Wi-Fi program, if possible.

Since your modem is usually provided to you by your ISP, there's usually not much else you can do here. However, sometimes you can get your own modem—see the tips at the end of this chapter.

Wi-Fi Router

Your Wi-Fi router is arguably the most important part of your network in terms of your overall Internet security. It's also probably the most complicated one because it performs a wide variety of important functions. Understanding how to properly configure a Wi-Fi router is not easy, but that's why you bought this book! I'll walk you through the primary settings you need to worry about and show you how to configure them properly. Before we get to the specifics, let's discuss the key functions of your Wi-Fi router.

As I mentioned in earlier sections, one of the primary functions of your router is to serve as a barrier between your private, home network and the wider, public Internet. Regardless of how many devices you have inside your house, the external world sees all your packets as coming from a single address—your public IP address. Your router takes care of delivering all inbound traffic to the proper device inside your home. This function is called Network Address Translation (NAT), and we discussed it earlier. However, your router does a lot more than that. Let's break it down.

The primary function of a router is to act as a boundary between your private home network and the public Internet. Again, it's like an internal mail service within your house, allowing all the devices on your network to talk to each other and, when necessary, establishing connections between your internal devices and external, public servers and services. In fact, your router is actually in charge of assigning mailing addresses (that is, IP addresses) for all the devices in your network. It does this using Dynamic Host Control Protocol (DHCP). When you plug a device into the network or allow a new device to connect wirelessly, that device needs to have an IP address to communicate with anything else on the network—and your router is in charge of handing out those addresses.

As we've discussed, most routers come with a built-in firewall function that specifically prevents external entities from prying into your private home network, unless you explicitly allow it or something inside your home initiates the conversation. Routers also act as a sort of traffic cop, directing traffic in the network. The router can allow some traffic to have a higher priority than others—for example, allowing live video streams to flow freely while sending Google queries to the back of the line. Packets of audio and video information are very time-sensitive—if those packets are delayed or lost, you will have glitches in your music or your streaming movies. However, things like querying Google for local restaurants or checking your e-mail can wait a bit, if necessary (and by "a bit" I'm talking fractions of a second). This is referred to as *quality of service* (QoS); some network packets are more "important" than others. Some routers will automatically detect important traffic and prioritize it, while others need to be configured for this feature. The quality of service flag on these packets is not required to be honored, it's more of a suggestion—but it's a mechanism that can be used to improve the performance of time-sensitive network traffic.

Wi-Fi routers allow you to connect to your home network wirelessly. This feature, while extremely handy, brings with it a lot of security issues. Instead of having to physically plug an Ethernet cable into your router to get onto your network, you can now connect your laptop or other smart device through the ether simply by changing a setting. Instead of having to be physically inside your house, with Wi-Fi you only have to be *near* your house—like next door or parked outside on the street. To protect your network, Wi-Fi has some security options that will restrict access to your network. These include adding encryption, authentication, and even some good ol' security by obscurity. However, there are also a lot of add-on features for convenience that have exposed some weaknesses. All of these will be discussed at length in the checklist at the end of this chapter.

The Internet of Things

The *Internet of Things* (IoT) refers to the current tech trend of making all of our dumb devices smart—that is, connecting them to the Internet (which I'm not sure necessarily makes anything or anyone "smart"). What good is your refrigerator if you can't query its contents from the office before you come home? Who wants a dumb thermostat that you can't change from halfway around the globe? Who needs a Bluetooth speaker that won't respond when you ask it for today's weather? We're already spoiled by our smart devices, and this whole trend is just getting started.

The problem with adding smarts to cheap devices like light bulbs, baby monitors, thermostats, and appliances is that it adds cost—in some cases, significant cost (compared to the equivalent "dumb" version). People pay for features they can see and experience—and they tend not to pay for other stuff, like security. Security in particular can cost a lot of time and money to develop and build into your products, especially if you're going to do it right. And so many companies don't do it right or at all. We like to say that the *S* in IoT is for security...meaning there is none. So, as we're bringing all these wonderful, connected devices into our homes, we also need to be very cognizant of the risks involved.

What does that mean, exactly? There are two primary reasons that bad guys might want to target your weak IoT devices: to establish a beachhead inside your LAN to get at other devices or to conscript your devices to serve in a zombie computer army (I'm not kidding). Let's take these one at a time.

If a hacker wanted to try to spy on you or score some personal data, they need to get onto your home network, meaning they need to get past your router's firewall. The best way to do that is to have an "man on the inside," and usually the easiest target is a vulnerable IoT device. Each of these devices contains a tiny computer. If the hacker can take over that computer with malware by exploiting the weak security, it can now roam around your home network at will. Maybe they'll try to infect other devices, including your computers. They could turn on microphones or cameras to spy on you or root around your files for sensitive information. While you might wonder why anyone would target you for this, you have to realize that many of these hacking programs are automated. It's like robotic burglars roaming around neighborhoods looking for unlocked doors and windows and taking stuff that looks valuable.

But once they've compromised your devices, the more likely scenario is to use these devices to do nefarious things. We call these groups of hacked computers and devices a *botnet*. They listen for instructions from remote command-and-control computers and

225

do their bidding. This may be attacking other, higher-value computers or simply mining Bitcoin to make their masters some money. But once conscripted into this zombie army, they can be called upon to do anything at any time.

This might sound silly, but it's a real problem, and it's already being exploited. Remember the Target credit card breach in 2014? Hackers got into Target's payment system by first hacking the heating and air conditioning system. The system was on the same network as the credit card database. In another story, the CEO of cybersecurity company Darktrace revealed that a casino's high-roller data was exfiltrated by first compromising a smart aquarium thermostat in the casino's lobby.

Botnets are even more serious. When done well, a thousand compromised devices can bring down an entire web site. The Mirai botnet was responsible for crippling Internet service of much of the United States and parts of Europe in 2016 by taking down the DynDNS service.

The Internet of Things has a lot of promise, and at this point its spread is pretty much unstoppable. But device manufacturers have to step up their game, and governments need to start requiring these devices to meet minimum security and privacy standards, including the ability to be remotely and automatically upgraded to fix bugs as they're found.

Virtual Private Network

Another important tool in the network security arsenal is the *virtual private network* (VPN). If you've heard this term before, it's probably because you've worked at a large company. The most common use of a VPN is to allow traveling or telecommuting workers to access the big corporate network no matter where they are, as if they were located at the main office. That is, it allows remote workers to access e-mail, files, and internal web sites (resources that are normally blocked to all outside access) as if they were in the main office, plugged into a local network port or connected to the in-building Wi-Fi. The VPN extends the private corporate network (or LAN) outside the boundaries of the company. This creates a *virtual* private network—it's not hardwired, but it acts as if it is. It allows someone connected to the public Internet, from any location, to appear as if they are connected to the private, internal corporate network. Furthermore, this connection is completely hidden from the other people on the public Internet, even though the packets of information are flowing freely between the mobile computer and the corporate network back at headquarters.

It's sort of like having a private, opaque pipeline from your computer to the office. In fact, VPN connections are often referred to as *tunnels* for this reason. Let's say you were locked in your castle, with an invading army at your gates laying siege to your stronghold. You would like to be able to send communications to your allies on the outside, perhaps send for help. You can't just send a messenger out the front gate, can you? But what if you had a secret tunnel under the castle wall that ran two miles to a neighboring keep? Then you could send messengers out and even allow messengers to come in, and the army surrounding would have no idea it was happening. Actually, even if they knew it was happening, there's nothing they could really do, unless they could somehow figure out where the tunnel was buried. If the tunnel was wide enough, your people could come and go as they pleased. That's sort of the analogy for a corporate VLAN (virtual LAN).

But VPNs have other very interesting uses outside the corporate world, and they're starting to become more popular with regular, everyday Internet users. Let's look at our analogy again. A VPN is like setting up a tunnel between you and another network. This tunnel is essentially 100 percent impregnable and opaque to outside viewers. They may know it's there, but even if they do, they don't know where it goes. For the purposes of this analogy, it's really almost like a magic portal: when you step through it, you are instantly transported to another place. How might we use such a thing?

Well, let's say you're traveling internationally for some reason—business or pleasure, it doesn't matter. But you want to be able to access stuff on your home computer, maybe music or movies or files. You can create a VPN tunnel that will connect your laptop or tablet through the public Internet, halfway around the globe, back to your home network—as if you were sitting in your living room. (Okay, there is going to be some delay if you're really far away, but you will still have full access to your stuff.)

But what if you want to access some of your favorite web services while you're traveling, like Netflix or Pandora or Spotify? All three of those services are restricted; they usually work only if you're accessing them from within your home country or region. With a VPN service, you can create a tunnel or portal from wherever you are back to your home country and appear to these services as if you're inside the country. All of your network traffic goes through this tunnel and comes out wherever you choose (most VPN services offer you multiple "exit point" locales). For example, you might be in Italy for the summer, but as far as Netflix can tell, you're really in Seattle, Washington, because the return IP address on all your network packets is located in Seattle, Washington. That's because there's a VPN server in that area that is the other end of your tunnel. (Note that these companies have begun blocking access from known VPN service addresses, so this technique doesn't always work.)

As you might guess, the other great use for a VPN is for privacy. You may buy your Internet service from Spectrum or Comcast, but maybe you don't want them snooping around on what you're doing.[3] Better yet, if you're in some place with free, open Wi-Fi, you don't want all the people around you being able to sniff the packets you're sending and receiving. Oh, yes…they can do that. It's wireless. You're broadcasting your data indiscriminately to everyone within a few dozen feet. Now, if your connections are encrypted (HTTPS instead of HTTP), then the traffic to and from those specific sites can't be sniffed in the open air… but not all web sites use encryption, though in the last year it's gotten a lot better. As of 2014, according to SSL Pulse,[4] only about 24 percent of the most popular web sites use HTTPS. Now they estimate that nearly 65 percent of today's web sites have adequate HTTPS support. Industry and government initiatives have made it much easier to adopt HTTPS, but we've still got a way to go. So, if you're using public Wi-Fi hotspots often, you should seriously consider signing up for a VPN service.

Summary

- We reviewed the key parts of a home network and defined some common networking terms like *modem*, *router*, *Wi-Fi*, *LAN*, *WAN*, *WLAN*, and *VPN*.

- We discussed important aspects of networks that provide security like firewalls and Network Address Translation (NAT).

- The Internet of Things (IoT) promises some amazing advances in connecting all of our electronic devices, but many of them are severely lacking in cybersecurity. This is already leading to threats from vast botnets and providing beachheads for cybercrime in otherwise well-protected networks.

- We explain how virtual private networks are becoming more important for home users, providing security and privacy, as well as access to some region-restricted services like Netflix.

---

[3]Unfortunately, with the U.S. privacy regulations being gutted in 2017, ISPs can legally track everything you do and sell that information to others.
[4]https://www.trustworthyInternet.org/ssl-pulse/

Checklist

One quick note before we start the checklist. If you have trouble with your home network or if you change some settings and all of a sudden you can't connect to anything on the Internet, you might want to reset your equipment. The proper way to reset your equipment is as follows:

1. Turn your equipment off including your modem, your router, and any other hardware devices like network switches, set-top boxes used for streaming music and movies, Internet telephony equipment (like Vonage or Ooma), etc. (Computers and smartphones can probably be left on; they will usually sort themselves out on their own.) You can turn off these devices by unplugging them from the wall, or sometimes you can unplug the power cord from the back of the device itself. Give this about 30 seconds.

2. Turn the equipment back on starting at the point furthest "upstream." In most cases, that will be your modem (the device you got from your ISP). Wait for your modem to come up completely. This usually means there are three to four solid lights and one rapidly flashing light.

3. Follow the chain downstream. The next device is probably your router (which is probably a Wi-Fi router). Power it back up and give it a few seconds to get itself up and running.

4. At this point, the next level downstream is probably the devices on your network. Turn them all back on.

5. If your computer or smartphone still can't connect, you might try restarting them, as well.

Many of the configuration items in this checklist require you to log in to your router. Unfortunately, every router is different—even routers from the same maker can have different configuration screens. There's really no way I can cover them all in this book, so you're going to probably have to do some searching around. Your best source is the manual that came with your router. If you can't find your manual, search the Web for it. Type in your router's make and model plus the word *manual*—that will usually find it. You can find your router's model info on a sticker on the router.

While you can use special software "wizards" to configure your router, you should also be able to access a web page on your router that has the full configuration. In most home routers, there is a special IP address assigned to your router for this purpose. Once you get to this web page, you'll usually be asked to log in using the default administrator credentials. Again, this will be in your router's manual.

If you can't find the manual, you try Table 6-1 for some common router info. If these fail, see the web sites after the table. (In the table, [blank] means enter nothing.)

Table 6-1. *Common Router IP Addresses and Admin Credentials*

Router Make	Admin IP Address	Default Admin ID/Password
Linksys	192.168.1.1	admin/admin
Belkin	192.168.2.1	admin/[blank], admin/Admin, admin/password
Netgear	192.168.0.1, 10.0.0.1	admin/password
D-Link	192.168.0.1	admin/[blank], admin/admin
Asus	192.168.1.1	admin/admin

For a longer list of router default IP addresses, try this:

```
https://www.techspot.com/guides/287-default-router-ip-addresses/
```

For more default passwords, try this:

```
https://www.routerpasswords.com/
```

Once you find this admin web page, spend some time looking around. Most of these special admin web pages will have helpful information right there to tell you what all the settings are for. Don't let it overwhelm you, though—we will be tweaking only a few of these options.

Note   Whenever you change administrative settings on your router, be sure to "save" and "apply" those changes. That is, sometimes you can change a setting, but nothing will actually happen until you save and apply the changes. Some changes may require your router to restart, which is fine—but you will lose Internet service for maybe a minute or two while the router comes back online.

Without further ado, here's the checklist for this chapter.

Tip 6-1. Get Your Own Modem

Internet service providers will usually install their own modem for you to use, and that modem is often a combination modem and Wi-Fi router. They will also likely charge you a monthly fee to rent this modem for $10 a month, which can be expensive over time. However, in many cases, you can buy your own modem for as little as $70 to $90—it's often the same make and model that the ISP gives you.

Note that ISPs don't like this and sometimes will find ways to make this difficult. Be sure to check with them first to make sure they'll let you hook up your own router without any weird service charges or fees. You should also ask them which makes and models they support.

Tip 6-2. Get Your Own Router

If you haven't done this already, you should buy your own home router. Even if the modem given to you by your Internet service provider has a built-in Wi-Fi router, for privacy and security reasons, you should not use it. Even if you have only one computer, you should insert your own router between it and your modem.

- There are many good brands to choose from. I would go with something like Linksys, Netgear, Belkin, D-Link, or Asus.

- I would definitely get a Wi-Fi router—there are just too many cool things out there that require Wi-Fi connections, and your friends and family will appreciate having free, secure Internet access within your home. You can always disable the Wi-Fi part when you don't need it, if you want to be super paranoid.

- Wi-Fi routers are pretty easy to set up these days. However, you should *avoid using Wireless Protected Setup (WPS)*. While this technique is convenient, it's also fraught with security bugs. Just use the "old-school" method of setting a password on the router and entering this password on the Wi-Fi devices that you want to connect to the network.

Tip 6-3. Lock Down Your Wi-Fi

Always set a password for accessing your Wi-Fi network. (Your router admin page might call it a *key*, a *shared key*, or *passphrase*.) This password should be fairly strong, but it doesn't have to be crazy. People still need to be within Wi-Fi range to try to hack it, so that limits the number of attackers. I would say use a short phrase that's easy to say and remember, maybe 12 to 15 characters long.

Tip 6-4. Use WPA2 (or WPA3, When Available)

Use Wireless Protected Access version 2 (WPA2) for your Wi-Fi encryption. Absolutely do not use Wired Equivalent Privacy (WEP)—this is old technology that was cracked a long time ago and is not secure. WPA is okay, but WPA2 is better. If there's an option of WPA Personal or WPA Enterprise, you should use WPA Personal.

The Wi-Fi Alliance announced plans for WPA3 in early 2018, which will replace WPA2 and comes with some much-needed security updates. When this becomes available and is supported by your devices, you should use it.

Tip 6-5. Set a Strong Password for Your Router Admin Page

Your router will come with a default user ID and password to configure the router itself through the admin web page (usually something of the form 192.168.x.x). (Note that this ID and password is totally different from the Wi-Fi network password from the earlier tip!) You should change this password as soon as possible. Malware will often try to log into your router using these well-known default passwords, and if they get in, they can get up to all sorts of nasty business. You want to lock them out by changing the password to something the bad guys can't guess.

Generate a password using LastPass and save it there. Since it's a web page, LastPass should fill it in for you, so it can be a truly strong random password. Don't be afraid to write this password down—you can even tape it to your router, if you want. The bad guys won't be in your house; they'll be trying to guess this password from some remote location.

Tip 6-6. Change Your Default SSID

Your router will come with some default network name that it broadcasts. When you whip out your smart device and look at the available Wi-Fi networks, the names you see listed there are the service set identifiers (SSIDs) of all the Wi-Fi routers near you. Having a default name can be confusing, especially if your neighbors have similar names. I would change your SSID to be something more unique but also not easy to associate with you or your home (like your name or street address).

   If you really want to get paranoid, you can prevent your router from broadcasting the name at all. This might be some helpful security through obscurity if there are a lot of people near you, like in an apartment complex. Basically, you tell your router not to broadcast your network name SSID so that when people nearby scan for available networks, they won't see anything. To join your network, you will have to manually set up a connection by specifying the network name (SSID).

Tip 6-7. Disable External Admin

Some routers allow you to log into their admin pages from outside your network—that is, from the public Internet or WAN. This is almost never necessary and extremely risky. If you find this feature on your router, disable it.

Tip 6-8. Disable External Services

Some routers also have services like Universal Plug and Play (uPNP) and telnet enabled on the *outside* of your network, the WAN side. Again, this is almost never needed and just gives hackers another place to prod for weaknesses. If you have any of these services enabled on the WAN side, be sure to disable them.

Tip 6-9. Enable and Use the Guest Network

If your router supports a guest Wi-Fi network, you should enable that. This allows people who visit your house to have access to the Internet, but not to your regular home network. You might think: but I trust these people! But you never know what devices people are bringing into your home or where they've been.

Be sure to set a password for the guest network, as well. You can put this password on your fridge or something so your guests can easily see it and copy it to their smartphone or whatever.

Tip 6-10. Put "Internet of Things" Devices on the Guest Net

If you have smart devices in your home like thermostats, refrigerators, smart TVs, Wi-Fi digital picture frames, light bulbs, toasters, whatever...put them on your guest Wi-Fi network, not your regular Wi-Fi network. If these devices only need to talk to something on the Internet or to each other, then there's no reason to give them access to anything else within your home.

Note, however, that if you're not using the "smart" features, then don't bother connecting the device to the network at all. For example, if you're only using your TV for regular TV functions, then there's no need to connect it to the Internet at all.

Tip 6-11. Register Your Devices

We all hate junk mail—electronic or otherwise. And we all know that when you register the products you purchase and give them your address, you can expect to increase your level of spam. However, for any product you have that connects to the Internet—including smart devices like TVs, thermostats, light bulbs, web cams, and also your Wi-Fi router—you want to make sure the manufacturer can contact you about potential security issues and remedies. For this reason, you should suck it up and register these devices online if you haven't already. Some of these devices will require manual software updates to fix security bugs; others may require outright replacement. But if you don't know about the bugs, they will just sit there, waiting to be hacked.

When you register online (using your make and model number or perhaps the serial number), you should get a confirmation e-mail of some sort. Make sure that it didn't go to your junk mail or spam folder. If you see it there, you can usually mark is as "not junk," which should tell your e-mail service to not hide e-mails from this source in the future. If you want to be doubly sure, you can add the "from" e-mail address to your e-mail's contact list.

Tip 6-12. Update Your Router's Firmware

Your Wi-Fi router, in particular, is important to keep up-to-date. Using Table 6-1, you should log into your router's admin interface and find the tab/page that lists the current version of the software installed (on appliances like this, the software is sometimes referred to as *firmware*). If you're lucky, this page will have a link or button to check for updates and install them if found. If not, you will need to go to your device's manufacturer web site to see whether you're up-to-date. In either case, you may be asked to download a file and then upload it to your router for installation.

If you've registered your router with the manufacturer, you should be notified of important software updates via e-mail.

Tip 6-13. Disable Auto-connect to Wi-Fi

Many laptops, tablets, and smartphones will automatically connect to public Wi-Fi when available. Some will automatically re-connect to Wi-Fi networks that you've been on before. Both of these are bad. You should tell your devices to always ask you before connecting to any Wi-Fi network. If you've given your home Wi-Fi a unique name, then you can automatically connect to this network. But in general, you should always be notified first. Bad guys will often create fake networks with common names like "Linksys" or "Starbucks" in an effort to attack or spy on devices that auto-connect.

If you use a VPN service that automatically enables for untrusted networks, this can protect you in situations like this, too.

Tip 6-14. Turn Off Your ISP's Wi-Fi

If your ISP's modem comes with Wi-Fi built in, call your ISP and ask them to disable it. Assuming you have your own Wi-Fi router (explained earlier), you have no need for the ISP's Wi-Fi, and there's no reason to leave it on—it's just another way someone can try to get into your home network.

If Comcast is your ISP, call Comcast and tell them you want to opt out of the Xfinity Wi-Fi service (1-800-XFINITY). You can supposedly disable this yourself, if you want to try. According to Comcast, do the following:

1. Visit My Account at `https://customer.comcast.com/`.

2. Click Users & Preferences.

3. Then select Manage XFINITY Wi-Fi.

Tip 6-15. Use ShieldsUp to Check for Vulnerabilities

One of my favorite security guys, Steve Gibson, has a web site that will help you check to see whether your router or modem has any obvious weaknesses. It's a service called ShieldsUp (in reference to the Star Trek Enterprise).

1. Go to this web site: `https://www.grc.com/x/ne.dll?bh0bkyd2`.

2. Read the little blurb in the box and then click Proceed.

3. The next few pages are a little hard to follow. First click the big yellow Instant UPnP Exposure Test button. This should verify that you've disabled external UPnP access (see earlier).

4. Then, in the funny table below, click the silver "Common ports" button... or if you want to go full tilt, click the All Service Ports button. It will scan your system to see whether any of these ports are accepting requests from outside, which they shouldn't be. If your report is anything but green, you should use the web site to dig further. You may have to go back to your router's admin pages to turn more things off on the WAN side.

Tip 6-16. Use a VPN

As we discussed in the chapter, if you commonly use Wi-Fi hotspots in airports, restaurants, cafes, etc., you should seriously consider signing up for a VPN service. Sometimes your device or laptop will automatically connect to these networks, and quite often you will have smartphone apps or background computer apps that automatically send and receive information whenever they're connected. Also, VPNs can be handy for international travelers who want to access services that are restricted to their home region (like Netflix).

VPN services are hard to evaluate and recommend because they change all the time and different people have different priorities for their secure connections. However, here are a few options that are solid to consider. However, in general, I would avoid services that are primarily free—that is, that don't have an obvious revenue model. If they show you ads or push "pro" services all the time, I would worry about their trustworthiness. If you're going to use a VPN, it's usually safest to pay for it.

- NordVPN

- ExpressVPN

- ProtonVPN

- TunnelBear

CHAPTER 7

Practice Safe Surfing

It's hard to believe that the World Wide Web is more than 25 years old. While technically launched in 1991 by Tim Berners-Lee, most people didn't really know about it until the mid-1990s. The Web as we know it today really took off in the late 1990s with the "dot-com" boom and subsequent bust. We've come a long way since the early days of Mosaic and Netscape Navigator (the first popular web browsers). Web pages have gone from simple blocks of text and hyperlinks to amazingly powerful and complex web sites that can do just about anything. Many of the tasks that were relegated to heavyweight software applications like Photoshop and Microsoft Office are now moving into "the cloud." With high-speed Internet connections and powerful new web technologies, there's so much you can now do within the confines of your web browser. In fact, Google has a whole operating system called Chrome OS that is essentially a web browser that acts as a full-fledged desktop operating system. (This OS is the basis for the popular and inexpensive Chromebook laptops.)

Much of what we do today on our computers is surfing the Web. (I must admit I never understood that phrase...wouldn't you be *crawling* a web? Or even getting stuck in a web? But surfing? I guess it makes as much sense as "channel surfing," which is probably where we got the term.) So, in this chapter we're going to learn about how to surf safely.

The way we access the Internet directly is usually with a web browser. Therefore, we need to find a good one—and by "good" I mean safe, not just full of whiz-bang features. Microsoft and Apple each have their own browsers that come with their operating systems: Internet Explorer or Edge on Windows and Safari on Mac OS. And because most people take the path of least resistance, these default web browsers tend to be popular on their respective platforms.[1] However, there are better choices out there, and in this chapter I will help you choose the one that's best for you.

---

[1]The term *platform* here refers to the type of computer and operating system you're using. So, if you hear the term *platform-independent*, it just means that it will work on all the major computer and operating system varieties.

© Carey Parker 2018
C. Parker, *Firewalls Don't Stop Dragons*, https://doi.org/10.1007/978-1-4842-3852-3_7

Because web browsers have become the portal to the Internet, the bad guys have focused a lot of time and attention on finding ways to track, scam, and even infect you via this magical gateway. The functionality of a web browser can be extended in many ways, including plugins, extensions, and add-ons. I will help you figure out which of these are good, which are bad, and which are just plain ugly.

Before we get into those specifics, let's dig a little deeper into how security works on the Web. This is going to sound rather technical, but it's important to understand the basics at a high level. Don't worry too much about the acronyms in this chapter—you don't need to memorize them. But I want to get the terms out there in case you've seen them before or run into them in the future. The real key thing to take away here is the general "web of trust" concept that forms the basis for our current Internet security scheme.

Recall that all your computer communications (in both directions) are chopped up into small packets and shipped out over a massive web of interconnected computers. The packets will take many hops before they reach their destination, and each packet could take a slightly different path—it doesn't really matter, as long as they all reach their destination. Previously in this book, we discussed the basic issues that we need to address when trying to communicate securely over the Internet. First, we need to somehow ensure that the person or web site we're communicating with is actually who they say they are. Second, we would like our communications to be completely private—that is, we don't want anyone between us and our intended recipient to be able to read what we're saying or what data we're exchanging. Finally, we would also like to know that the messages haven't been tampered with along the way (you don't have to be able to read something in order to alter it).

The way we secure Internet communications and authenticate third parties is using a technology called Transport Layer Security (TLS).[2] TLS is used all over the place today to secure all sorts of communication, including digital phone calls, file transfers with cloud storage providers, and, of course, web surfing. When TLS is added to regular web communications via a browser, we move from "HTTP" to "HTTPS"—the added *S* stands for "secure." When you are connected to a web site via HTTPS, you should see a little lock icon to the left of the web address that indicates that the connection is secure. Most of this happens automatically behind the scenes. Your web browser and the server at the far end do some quick negotiation, and when both sides are capable of using TLS, they establish a secure connection.

---

[2]It used to be called Secure Sockets Layer (SSL). Some tech people use TLS and SSL interchangeably, but TLS is the proper term for the current technology. While SSL still exists in the wild, it is being supplanted by TLS.

But how does that really work? How do we really know that we're talking to Amazon. com or Bank of America? TLS trust is based on the concept of a certificate. There are special agencies called *certificate authorities* (CAs) that are in charge of verifying entities and issuing these special certificates that are digitally "signed" by the CA verifying its authenticity. These certificates are good for a certain amount of time, usually one to two years. When that time is up, the company or person who owns the certificate must re-apply. If you click the lock icon in your browser (or perhaps right-click), you can dig down and see the nitty-gritty certificate information. Figure 7-1 shows a sample for Amazon.com, issued by the certificate authority Symantec. Again, you don't need to know this stuff, I'm just showing you what it looks like.

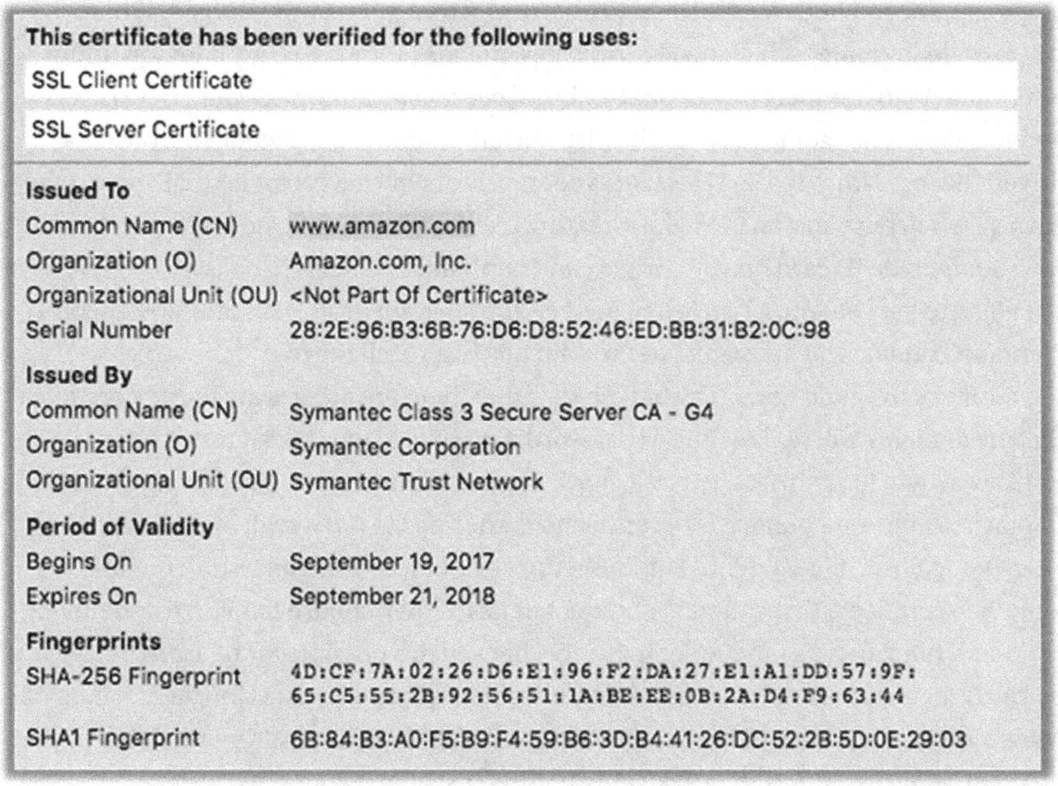

This certificate has been verified for the following uses:

SSL Client Certificate

SSL Server Certificate

Issued To

Common Name (CN)	www.amazon.com
Organization (O)	Amazon.com, Inc.
Organizational Unit (OU)	<Not Part Of Certificate>
Serial Number	28:2E:96:B3:6B:76:D6:D8:52:46:ED:BB:31:B2:0C:98

Issued By

Common Name (CN)	Symantec Class 3 Secure Server CA - G4
Organization (O)	Symantec Corporation
Organizational Unit (OU)	Symantec Trust Network

Period of Validity

Begins On	September 19, 2017
Expires On	September 21, 2018

Fingerprints

SHA-256 Fingerprint	4D:CF:7A:02:26:D6:E1:96:F2:DA:27:E1:A1:DD:57:9F: 65:C5:55:2B:92:56:51:1A:BE:EE:0B:2A:D4:F9:63:44
SHA1 Fingerprint	6B:84:B3:A0:F5:B9:F4:59:B6:3D:B4:41:26:DC:52:2B:5D:0E:29:03

Figure 7-1. *Sample certificate*

There are three levels of certification and therefore three types of certificates: domain validation (DV), organization validation (OV), and extended validation (EV). The EV certificate (or *cert*) is the Cadillac model. As you might expect, the requirements to obtain an EV cert are more stringent, which generally means that you can trust them more than regular domain and organizational certs.

Once the CA issues a cert to the owner of the web site, the web site provides the cert as proof of identity when establishing a secure connection. This is like showing your driver's license when buying booze to prove that you are who you say you are and that you're old enough to buy alcoholic beverages. (An EV cert might be more like a passport.)

But wait... driver's licenses can be faked. What about certificates? Well, I've got good news, and I've got bad news. The good news is that because certificates use solid cryptographic methods for creation, CA-backed certs can't really be forged. While it's possible to create "self-signed" certificates, no one is going to trust it for anything important. Web browsers have a built-in list of certificate authorities that they trust, and Joe Blow is not going to be on that list—just like liquor shops would only accept driver's licenses from the 50 U.S. states and they probably have a folder that shows what each state's license should look like. Creating a self-signed certificate is like printing up a homemade ID card on your printer and laminating it. Sure, it looks nice, but it's not going to get you into a bar. Self-signed certificates *can* be used to properly encrypt communications; you just can't be sure who it is you're talking to.

So, that's the good news. The bad news is that there are other ways to get a certificate that are arguably worse. Creating a trustworthy certificate is a crucial task, so you'd think we would limit this job to a select few organizations that we can all agree to trust. In practice, there are hundreds of certificate authorities in the world, including the Hong Kong Post Office (I'm not kidding). Any one of these CAs can issue a completely authentic certificate that contains nothing but lies, if they choose to. We trust them not to do this, but if they "go rogue" or if they get hacked, it's possible for bad guys to get perfectly legitimate certificates that will allow them to impersonate Google or Yahoo or whoever they want. It would be like getting your "fake ID" directly from the Department of Motor Vehicles... it would be fake only in the sense that it contained wrong information, but it's a perfectly valid driver's license that would pass any examination.

As bad as this sounds, in practice this is not easy to do. You're not worried about average teenager hackers in this situation; you're worried about highly skilled and well-funded attackers, probably backed by a government or a big corporation. The target in this case would mostly be information (espionage). Also, there are other safeguards in place that mitigate the risk of being duped by one of these bad certs. For one thing, even if the bad guys get their hands on one of these mendacious certs, they still have to somehow get between you and your target server. This is a "man-in-the-middle" attack, which we discussed earlier—they insert themselves in the communication channel and pretend to be the other side to each end. That is, you establish communications with them, and then they turn around and establish communications with Amazon.com, let's say. To you, they appear to be Amazon.com; to Amazon.com, they appear to be you. To do this, they need to somehow redirect you to the false web site instead of the real one. When you type *amazon. com* into your web browser, it uses the Domain Name Service (DNS) to figure out where your request really needs to go on the Internet—that is, the IP address of Amazon's web server. Unless you can somehow also intercept that DNS lookup and provide a hacked reply, then the user will still be connected to the real Amazon web site. Also, there are new technologies coming online that will make this even more difficult in the near future (like Google's Certificate Transparency[3] project). So, while there are definite problems with the current CA-based system, it still works very well for the vast majority of web surfers, and other safeguards are being put in place to make it much harder to thwart or subvert.

So, if we can assume that the certificate system works (which is, as we've said, a significant "if"), then we can assume that when we establish an HTTPS connection to another web site that a) we can believe they are who they say they are and b) no one else can eavesdrop on our communications.

There's one last—but crucial—point here. When you see that lock symbol on your web browser, that means your traffic is encrypted and that the certificate used by the web site is valid. That's all. It doesn't mean you can trust the web site. You can now get free domain validation certificates thanks to an effort by a large consortium of companies called Let's Encrypt. That's great—it makes it much easier for mom-and-pop companies to offer secure communications to their web site. But the bad guys can also use this free service to obtain a valid certificate for a malicious web site. So, the lock icon doesn't mean the web site you're on is trustworthy; it only means that no one else can spy on your communications with them.

Again, don't worry about remembering all the technical details. All you really need to remember here is that HTTPS connections are secure. Many web sites are moving to HTTPS for all communications, which is a good thing, because everything we do on the Internet should be safe from prying eyes, even simple stuff. In the next section, we'll take a look at just how pervasive web tracking has become.

---

[3]https://www.certificate-transparency.org/

Tracking Tech

While secure communications are vitally important, we have to also address the elephant in the room: web tracking. The amount of information you divulge every time you use a web browser is absolutely staggering: what web sites you visit, how long you stay on a given web site, how you got to that web site (i.e., which site you just came from), whether you bought something on a given web site, what ads you saw, what links you clicked, and even how much you spent while there. There has been a lot of debate on the value of this "metadata," but the proof is in the pudding, as they say. These companies wouldn't be bending over backward to get this info if it wasn't making them money. And just in case you think it's only retailers that are trying to find the right way to hook you into buying that spiffy new TV or anti-aging cream, you should also know that the politicians are using this data to find sympathetic potential voters and even to identify voters who might be convinced to switch sides. The recent scandal involving Facebook and Cambridge Analytica is a shining example.

This data is often used to specifically tailor a web site just for you—and not in a good way. For example, if the retailer happens to know that you're wealthy or that you're a heavy online shopper, they can actually make sure to show you the more expensive products first—in fact, they may even raise the prices[4]—if not based on your information specifically, perhaps based on whether you appear to be from a wealthy area.

The Webs We Weave

Most people just don't realize how wide and vast this tracking network really is. The best way I know to explain the pervasiveness of web tracking to you is to use a nifty little web tool called Lightbeam.[5] When you go to a web site, the content you see is often provided by multiple different companies. In addition to the first-party site (the web site you actually intended to visit), there are often many other third-party web sites that provide ads and other images—and also track what you're doing. To see these third-party relationships, Lightbeam draws a graph that shows you all the third-party sites that are associated with the first party site you visited. (I know, all this "party" stuff sounds like legalese. It sorta makes your brain want to tune it out. But bear with me here.)

---

[4]http://lifehacker.com/5973689/how-web-sites-vary-prices-based-on-your-information-and-what-you-can-do-about-it

[5]Currently available only for Firefox: https://addons.mozilla.org/en-US/firefox/addon/lightbeam/

Let's try a real-life example and graph the relationships behind some popular web sites and their hidden third parties. We'll start our browsing with Wikipedia (Figure 7-2).

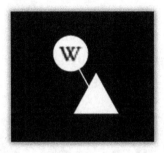

Figure 7-2. *Wikipedia graph*

In Figure 7-2, you'll see the first-party site as a circle—in this case, the one with a *W* in it, which is wikipedia.org. The little white triangle next to that is a third-party web site that is associated with the site we visited. However, in this case, the third-party site is just wikimedia.org, which is directly associated with Wikipedia (that is, it's not a third-party advertising or tracking site). It's not uncommon for the third-party sites to just be extensions of the first-party site, and it's also not uncommon for the third-party sites to be perfectly normal other web sites that provide things like web tools, images, and other harmless content. However, many of them are marketing firms and other "Big Data" companies whose sole purpose is to build a portfolio on you.

Now, let's go to Yahoo.com (Figure 7-3).

Figure 7-3. *Wikipedia + Yahoo graph*

Our little graph (Figure 7-3) has now grown substantially. While Yahoo.com was our primary target (the white circle with the *Y* in it), we can see that we've also triggered five other sites, only two of which are associated with Yahoo itself. The others are all tracking sites, including doubleclick.net and agkn.com. Note that there is no intersection here—no common third parties. Wikipedia—since it doesn't track you—is actually pretty boring in this regard, so from here on, we'll just cut them out of our picture.

Now let's move to Amazon.com (Figure 7-4).

Figure 7-4. *Yahoo + Amazon graph*

You can see in Figure 7-4 that loading Amazon's web site also caused you to communicate with eight other third-party web sites. At least three of those sites were associated directly with Amazon (even though there's no *A* logo on them like in the circle). Note that two of the third-party sites were also associated with Yahoo. Those are tracking sites. And they now know that you went to Yahoo and then to Amazon, and they quite likely know a lot about what you did there. Starting to get the idea?

Let's go for the jugular now...let's go to Dictionary.com (Figure 7-5).

Figure 7-5. *Yahoo + Amazon + Dictionary graph*

The graph in Figure 7-5 is so crowded now that you can't really even read it. It's hard to tell, but there are 100 third-party web sites there. You've visited just four web sites so far. The triangles that have multiple connections are the tracking sites.

So, just exactly how is it that they track you? The details would make your eyes glaze over. It's very technical, and the techniques are legion and myriad. But essentially it boils down to somehow marking you in a way that can later be recognized if they (or someone they know) see you again. These markers come in many forms. One of the most popular tracking devices is called a *cookie*. A cookie is a small bit of data that web sites give to your computer, asking your browser to save it off and then repeat it back to them later when they ask for it. This is sort of like a medical chart—the information is kept on you, and when you interact with another party, they look at it to refresh their memories of you. These cookies were originally used by the first-party web site to help keep track of your login, your personal preferences, your shopping cart contents, etc. However, third parties have used them to mark people as they move around to different web sites, tracking all sorts of stuff about you. That's the key point here... first-party cookies are between you and the site you *intended* to visit, which tends to be mutually beneficial; third-party cookies are things you generally didn't ask for and may not even be aware of, and it's almost completely for the benefit of the third party.

Let's try an analogy to explain how this works. Let's assume that your local mall wants to gather information on the people who shop there, and all the merchants agree to participate in the program. It's time for you to go Christmas shopping, so you park your car and walk in via the Macy's door. As you walk through the door, a silent little blowgun shoots a sticky dart that attaches to your back. This dart contains a little homing beacon that puts out a unique identifier, specific to you. They don't know who you are (yet), but they want to be able to distinguish you from all the other people wandering the mall. This ID is logged in a special computer system, along with a little note: "Customer 4372 entered mall via Macy's East door on first floor." This entry in the log automatically notes the time and date, as well. You walk through Macy's and into the mall proper. As you do, you walk by another sensor that detects your tag: "Customer 4372 left Macy's without buying anything." Since the time of entry and time of departure were so close, they could probably also conclude that you didn't even look at anything.

Now you walk into a jewelry store. You look around, find the perfect gift—a diamond tennis bracelet—and go to the register to buy it. Your entry to the store was of course logged, but now you've also made a purchase. They now know quite a bit more about you. If the store is trying to be nice, they may only log that you are a white male in his mid-50s who lives nearby (based on your credit card billing address) and that you bought an expensive piece of jewelry. From this, other retailers in the mall (who can see all of this information) may well assume that you are married and have an above-average income level.

You leave the jewelry store and head down to Victoria's Secret, where you make a very different purchase on a rarely used credit card. Marketing data analysis may suggest that you have not just a wife but also a mistress. You now walk into an electronics store. The store personnel can see from your records that you're in a buying mood today and you have plenty to spend, so they ignore other customers who show less promise and focus on you. They steer you to higher-end equipment, and given that you probably have a wife, they test your interest in kitchen appliances and push hard for you to get a store credit card.

This is all just from a single trip to the mall. Think about all the other places you've been and purchases you've made—what could they tell about you? How detailed would your profile be? And would you want that profile to be shared with every store you walk into?

The key here is that all the stores have contracted with the same tracking company. They have a common set of sensors that are all networked together, creating a central place to log your activity. While you might think it's entirely reasonable for a given store to keep information on previous buying and shopping activity, how do you feel knowing that information is being shared with many other retailers (and credit bureaus, potential employers, insurance companies, and so on)? It may be that this tracking company hordes the juiciest bits of information and gives only partial information to each store owner (depending on what level of service they've paid for). But it's important to realize that even with the best of intentions, the fact of the matter is that that information exists somewhere—and therefore it can be stolen, abused, or even compelled by the government.

Enter the Panopticon

But we're just getting started! There are several other tracking mechanisms, as well. People have gotten wise to the third-party cookie tracking method and have learned how to block them, so marketing companies have come up with other ways to track you—ways that can be difficult to avoid. Installing things like toolbars and social media extensions in your browser can give them access to all sorts of info. Even those social media buttons such as Facebook's Like, Pinterest's Pin It, and Twitter's Tweet can be used to track you—*even if you don't click them*! Sometimes they use tiny little one-pixel images with unique names... when you load that image, they know you've been there. Sometimes they use invisible web form fields. The list goes on and on, and the exact techniques change all the time.

Some really clever folks have figured out ways to "fingerprint" your web browser. To help web sites present themselves optimally, your web browser gives up all sorts of general information about your computer and web browser configuration: what plugins you have installed (even if they're disabled), all the fonts you have on your computer, computer screen dimensions, what type of operating system you're running, and what type of browser you have. The idea behind browser fingerprinting is that few people will have the same combination of these items.

Not convinced? The Electronic Frontier Foundation (EFF) has a web site you can visit that will tell you just how unique your configuration really is. Take a minute to click that link and see just how recognizable you are.

```
https://panopticlick.eff.org/
```

Unlike regular cookies and other forms of tracking, there is no way to know that browser fingerprinting is happening to you, and it's very hard to prevent. It's just not easy to disguise yourself as you traverse the Internet. In this case, your best defense would be to look like everyone else—blend into the crowd. Unfortunately, many of the measures you might take to increase your online security and protect your privacy also tend to make you stand out because so few of us take the time to install these tools. Finally, this is just one technique—if you combine this technique with others (even just looking at your IP address), it becomes difficult to hide your tracks.

By the way, the name Panopticlick is based on an 18th century surveillance and behavioral conformance concept dubbed a *Panopticon*. An English philosopher by the name of Jeremy Bentham pioneered the design of an institution in the shape of a circle. The residents would be in cells on the rim, facing in, and the guards would be in a watchtower in the center, with a view into all the cells. The genius of this design was that the watchees couldn't see the watchers, and therefore they could never know for sure when they were being monitored. Even though a handful of watchmen couldn't actually observe everyone at once, each inmate had to *assume* that they were being watched at any given moment. This effectively forced all inmates into constant compliance.

AUTOMATED LICENSE PLATE READERS

You're being tracked much more often in the physical world now, too. Several companies are now marketing systems that will use high-resolution video cameras to scan a scene to find all the license plate numbers it can see. The system records each plate number along with the time and place it was seen. These cameras are being mounted on utility poles, traffic lights, overpasses, and even police squad cars as they patrol. This information is hoovered up and shared with other agencies, creating a massive database of millions of cars. The timestamp and location information can be used to track where you go, identify your travel patterns, and even (potentially) track who you associate with. While this could obviously be useful finding who was near the scene of a crime and where those people live and work, it could just as easily be used to track an ex-wife, patrons of a gun show or a Planned Parenthood, or people attending a political protest. Now think about what happens when they upgrade from recognizing license plates to recognizing faces.

I know it sounds far-fetched, folks, but we are truly heading into an era of constant, global surveillance. Our "institution" is the Internet, and the watchmen are numerous. Unlike the 18th century, we have the computing power to actively monitor a large swath of the populace in real time. And with massive data storage facilities, like the one built by the NSA in Utah, our watchmen can record massive quantities of our Internet and cell phone activity, review it later at their leisure, and store it effectively forever.

Many people feel that their e-mails, texts, and web habits aren't that important, that they're not worthy of surveillance. Or perhaps they feel that only "bad" people have something to hide. Edward Snowden once said:

Arguing that you don't care about privacy because you have nothing to hide is no different than saying you don't care about free speech because you have nothing to say.[6]

We all have aspects to our lives that are private. Why are there doors on bathrooms? Why do people sing in the shower? Why do we have bumper stickers that say "dance like no one is watching"? Privacy is a basic human right and is fundamental to any healthy society. We act differently when we're watched—not because we're doing anything wrong but because we all need safe spaces to express ourselves. Glenn Greenwald explains this very eloquently is this TED talk. Whether or not you agree with this, it's worth watching.

https://www.ted.com/talks/glenn_greenwald_why_privacy_matters

On the Ethics of Ad Blocking

The business model for most of the Internet revolves around advertising, which in and of itself is not a bad thing. It may be an annoying thing, but passive advertising isn't actually harmful. Passive advertising is placing ads where people can see them. And savvy marketers will place their ads in places where their target audiences tend to spend their time. If you're targeting middle-aged men, you might buy ad space on fantasy football or car racing web sites, for example. If you're targeting tween girls, you might buy ad space on any site that might feature something about Taylor Swift or Ed Sheeran. And if it stopped there, I don't think many of us would object—or at least have solid grounds for objection. After all, this advertising is paying for the content we're consuming. Producing the content costs money, so someone has to pay for it or the content goes away.

Unfortunately, online marketing didn't stop there. On the Web, competition for your limited attention has gotten fierce. With multiple ads on a single page, marketers need you to somehow focus on their ad over the others. And being on the Internet (and not a printed page), advertisers are able to do a lot more to grab your attention. Instead

---

[6]Reddit comment, May 21, 2015

of simple pictures, ads can pop up, pop under, flash, move around, or float over the articles you're trying to read. Worse yet, ad companies want to be able to prove to their customers that they were reaching the right people and that those people were buying their product because this makes their ad services far more valuable, meaning they can charge more for the ads.

Enter the era of "active advertising." Today, you're not just watching ads—those ads are now watching you back. The code that displays these ads is tracking where you go and what you buy, building up profiles on you and selling those profiles to marketers without your consent. Furthermore, those ads use precious data on cell phones and take a lot of extra time to download regardless of what type of device you use. And if that weren't bad enough, ad software has become so powerful, and ad networks so ubiquitous and commoditized, that bad guys are now using ad networks to distribute malware. It's even spawned a new term: *malvertising*.

Over the years, browsers have given users the tools they need to tame some of these abuses, either directly in the browser or via add-ons. It's been a cat-and-mouse game: when users find a way to avoid one tactic, advertisers switch to a new one. The popular modern tool in this toolbox is the ad blocker. These plugins allow the user to completely block most web ads. Unfortunately, there's really no way for ad blockers to sort out "good" advertising from "bad" advertising. AdBlock Plus (one of the most popular ad-blockers) has attempted to address this with their "acceptable ads" policy, but it's still not perfect.

But many web content providers need that ad revenue to stay afloat. Many web sites are now detecting ad blockers and either nicely asking people to "whitelist" the web site (allowing them to show you ads) or in some cases actually blocking the content unless they view their ads. In a few cases, you have the option to subscribe (i.e., pay them money directly).

So... what's the answer here? As always, it's not black and white. I fully understand that web sites need revenue to pay their bills. However, the business model they have chosen is ad-supported content, and unfortunately the ad industry has gotten over-zealous in the competition for eyeballs. In the process of seeking to make more money and differentiate their services, they're killing the golden goose. Given the abusive and annoying advertising practices, the relentless and surreptitious tracking of our web habits, the buying and selling of our profiles without our consent, and the lax policing that allows malware into ads, I believe that the ad industry only has itself to blame here. We have every reason to mistrust them and every right to protect ourselves. Therefore, I think that people are fully justified in the use of ad blockers—and I wholeheartedly recommend that you use them.

That said, web sites also have the right to refuse to let us see their content if we refuse to either view their ads or pay them money. However, I think in the end they will find that people will just stop coming to their web sites if they do this. (It's worth noting that some sites do survive with voluntary donations, like Wikipedia.) Therefore, something has to change here. Ideally, the ad industry will realize that they've gone too far and that they must stop tracking our online pursuits and stop trafficking in highly personal information without our consent.

The bottom line is that the ad industry has itself to blame here. They've alienated users, and they're going to kill the business model for most of the Internet. They must earn back our trust, and that won't be easy. Until they do, I think it's perfectly ethical (and frankly safer) to use ad-blocking and anti-tracking tools.

Information Leakage

As you can see, it's hard to hide your tracks as you surf the Web. But there are even more ways in which your web surfing is tattling on you.

As we've discussed in early chapters, when you enter a web address into your browser like amazon.com, your computer must actually convert that human-friendly host name to a computer-friendly IP address. This is done via the Domain Name Service (DNS). Your computer is usually given its DNS provider automatically when it's connected to your home network at the same time that your computer obtains its local IP address. Your home router is in charge of this, and it all happens behind the scenes without you having to do anything. Your router usually gets its DNS service from your Internet service provider, in much the same manner. So, when your computer asks the router to convert "amazon.com" to an IP address, your router turns around and asks your ISP to do it.

Unfortunately, unlike much of our regular communication now on the Internet, DNS queries are not encrypted. And because we have rolled back regulations on what your ISP can track, they are more than happy to keep information about every web site you visit.

To fix this, you need to choose another DNS provider—preferably one that supports encrypted DNS queries so that your ISP can't see what hostnames you're looking up. The best way to do this is to just alter the DNS provider on your router—change the default to something better. This means every device in your home network will inherit this setting. However, if you have a laptop, you'll want to change this setting on your computer, as well, so that when you go out and about, it will still use your DNS provider of choice.

There's another obscure way that your computer rats you out, and it's actually part of the most basic part of the Internet: HyperText Transfer Protocol (HTTP). It's just trying to be helpful really, but in doing so, it's over-sharing. When you enter a web address (http://something.com), your web browser hands over lots of potentially helpful information to the web site you visit including the web site you just came from. This data is passed to the new web site through the Referer header (yes, it's misspelled... a classic Internet-ism). Why? Well, sometimes web sites work together, so it's helpful for them to know where you came from. It's also a way to pass data on to the next site. But if the web site isn't careful, it can share too much information (TMI).

Here's an actual example of a Referer header from the U.S. government web site everyone loves to hate, healthcare.gov:

```
Referer:https://www.healthcare.gov/see-plans/85601/results/?
county=04019&age=40&smoker=1&pregnant=1&zip=85601&state=AZ&inco
me=35000
```

Take a close look at the info contained in there. Those are parameters that the user had submitted to the web site, probably in a form page. As a quick-and-dirty way to pass that data around to other pages on the healthcare.gov site, it simply included the form values in the web address, which would show up in the Referer header. But as soon as you leave healthcare.gov and go to amazon.com, let's say, Amazon would get all that info, as well—and you wouldn't know it. This bug was fixed, but who knows what other web sites might be oversharing like this? Luckily, at least one browser maker is automatically cleaning up this for you. We'll discuss that shortly.

Speaking of web forms, I need to let you in on another dirty little web site data-slurping secret. How often have you started filling in a web form—maybe to sign up for an account or to answer a survey—and then changed your mind because you felt it was getting too personal or something? So you closed the page without hitting Enter or Submit. No harm done, right? Maybe not. Some web sites are now recording all the data you enter, even if you never submit the form. Web technology that can be used to make sure that you entered good data (for example, a valid telephone number or e-mail address) can just as easily be used to save that data. It feels really slimy, but it's actually being done on some sites. So, just be aware.

Choose Your Weapon

Your primary interface to the wild and woolly Internet is the venerable web browser. For many people, the web browser *is* the Internet. So, it stands to reason that you would want to pick the safest browser to do your web surfing.

There are at least two primary aspects to safety when it comes to web browsing: security and privacy. A secure browser will do whatever it can to prevent you from visiting bad web sites, warn you against entering sensitive information on insecure pages, identify sites that aren't encrypted, and strictly enforce policies that prevent malvertising and other malicious web exploits. A privacy-protecting browser will help protect your privacy by severely limiting the ability of web sites and marketers to track you.

According to NetMarketshare, the most popular browsers as of this writing are Chrome (60 percent), Internet Explorer/Edge (20 percent), Firefox (13 percent), and Safari (4 percent). Internet Explorer and Edge are the default browsers on Windows PCs, and Safari is the default browser on Apple Macintosh computers. Firefox (which rose from the ashes of Netscape Navigator) is the only browser in the top four that is open source (meaning the source code is freely available for inspection). Firefox is made by the nonprofit Mozilla Foundation, which is funded primarily by search royalties (accepting money to set a particular search engine as the default). Despite very different aesthetics, at the end of the day, all four of these browsers do basically the same thing: they show you web pages. So, how do you know which is safest?

Most Secure Browser

Let's just get this out of the way now: it's almost impossible to know which browser is the most secure. This is largely because all of these browsers are constantly rolling out new security-related features, fixing security-related bugs, and generally trying to claim the title of "most secure." That's a good thing—they're competing to be the best, so we all win. There are dedicated hacking contests to reveal bugs in browsers, but it's hard to say whether the number of bugs found in these contests really reflects the security of the browser. How likely were bad guys to find these bugs? How severe were the bugs? What about the bugs they didn't find? These hack-a-thons also don't address factors like how quickly the browser maker fixes their bugs and whether the browser is smart enough to self-update (because if you don't have the latest version, you don't have the bug fixes). It's really hard to compare the relative security of web browsers.

However, if I had to pick a winner here, I'd probably have to choose Chrome. Google is doing some fantastic work in the realm of computer and web security. That said, I think Firefox and Safari are also fairly secure browsers. And you could argue that because Firefox is open source, it can actually be audited by cybersecurity experts—unlike the other three major browsers. Ideally, this vetting leads to less bugs.

Most Private Browser

Unlike security, there are significant and important differences between the four major browsers when it comes to privacy. And this (to me) is the real deciding factor.

While Google has been a true leader in terms of security, it's pretty much the worst in terms of privacy. Its whole business model revolves around advertising (Google makes about 90 percent of its money from ads[7]). And that leads to an enormous conflict of interest when it comes to protecting your personal data and web surfing habits. Apple has gone out of its way to basically be the anti-Google, making it a point of pride to collect as little data on their users as possible (and causing a collective freak-out by advertisers because of technology that limits tracking). But Firefox is also doing some great work in this area.

So, who's the winner in terms of privacy? Today, I'd say it's a toss-up between Firefox and Safari, with Chrome being dead last. Internet Explorer and Edge are somewhere in between, but with Microsoft's recent penchant for collecting user data, I would put it closer to Chrome. Chrome has been trying to tame obnoxious ads with a built-in ad-blocking technology, but it's important to note that it does nothing, really, to prevent tracking.

And the Winner Is...

Based on everything I've found in my research, I personally choose Firefox as my go-to browser. No browser is 100 percent secure, and it's hard for even the most erstwhile browser to completely protect your privacy. But I think Firefox, on balance, is the best of the bunch. That said, there is at least one reason to *also* have Chrome installed on your system. And we'll talk about that in the checklist at the end of the chapter.

Beyond the Big Four

There are actually several other web browsers you might want to consider, but I'll just mention three.

---

[7]https://www.investopedia.com/articles/investing/020515/business-google.asp

The fifth most popular browser is Opera, and many people enjoy using it. If you're not satisfied with any of the big four, you might give it a try. Opera is fast and works on both Mac and PC.

The Brave browser is a new, open source browser built for privacy, with built-in ad blocking and tracking protection. However, in a move to try to acknowledge the need for ad-based revenue, it also has a mechanism to insert its own ads, which opens up a lot of issues. I would wait and see on this one.

Lastly, the Tor Browser is all about privacy. In fact, it tries to achieve true anonymity (though that is extremely difficult to do in practice). It's based on Firefox and builds in several kick-butt privacy tools that are too technical to sum up here. But if you really need to surf privately, you should give the Tor Browser a serious look.

Summary

- Surfing the Web is one of the main ways in which we interact with our computer and the Internet, and as such, it's one of the most important things that we need to secure.

- Our web security system is based on special digital certificates that are used to a) prove that you're talking to who you think you are and to b) encrypt the communications between you and the other end. While the certificate authority system has flaws, it's the best we have right now, and it's good enough for most things.

- We've learned why and how your actions are tracked via the Web. Simple things like web cookies and nearly invisible images can be used to track everywhere you go, reporting the information back to central locations run by marketing companies. Worse yet, the configuration information your browser provides to every web site can be used to recognize you.

- We also saw how your browser leaks information about you in several other ways: DNS lookups, Referer headers, and web forms.

- When choosing a web browser, you need to consider both security and privacy. While all browsers attempt to be secure, one a few are really trying to protect your privacy.

Checklist

I have to give one caveat here. Many security and privacy tools can cause some web sites to act strangely or even fail to work at all. This is an unfortunate side effect of trying to protect yourself. When you come to a web site that no longer seems to work properly, you may need to try adding a special exception for that web site or disable some security plugins temporarily. I realize this is painful. As with all security choices, you need to weigh safety against convenience. I would try to be safe by default and make security exceptions only when necessary.

Note   Browsers change their screen layouts all the time. These screenshots were accurate at the time of this writing, but you may find them a little different. Use the search feature within the browser's settings/preferences window to find these settings if they move around.

Tip 7-1. Install Firefox and Chrome

Choosing a good web browser is important. For me, the current choice to maximize consistency, flexibility, security, and privacy is clear: Firefox. Chrome is good at all of those, too, except privacy. Google potentially has access to everything you do in that browser, and that creeps me out. Google already knows way too much about me. However... Google's Chrome browser comes packaged with a copy of Adobe's Flash Player built in, and Chrome makes sure that Flash Player stays up-to-date. So, my recommendation is that you install both Firefox and Chrome. I would use Firefox most of the time, but when you run across an archaic web site that won't function without Flash, then (and only then) use Chrome.

Note   You do *not* need to sign up for a Firefox or Google account to use these browsers. Just bypass/close the sign-up screens, if you're presented with any.

- Mozilla Firefox: `https://www.mozilla.org/en-US/firefox/new/`

- Google Chrome: `https://www.google.com/intl/en/chrome/browser/`

- When asked, you will probably want to go ahead and import bookmarks, favorites, etc., from your current web browser. However, do *not* import passwords.

Tip 7-2. Configure the Security and Privacy Settings on Browser

To get the best protection, you need to change some default settings. If you already have Firefox or Chrome installed, double-check these options. Note that the Do Not Track feature is often ignored. That's okay. Register your desire not to be tracked anyway.

Tip 7-2a. Firefox

1. Open the Firefox menu at the upper right. Click Preferences (Mac) or Options (Windows) (Figure 7-6).

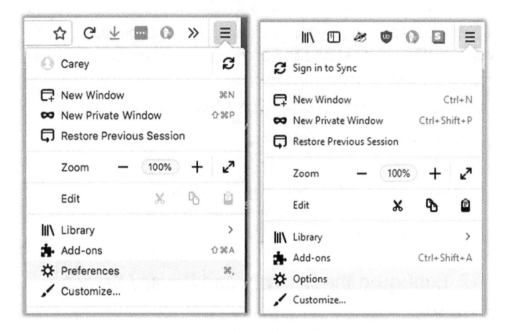

Figure 7-6. *Firefox preferences (left: Mac, right: Windows)*

2. Select the Privacy & Security tab at the left. Under Forms &
    Passwords, be sure to uncheck "Remember logins and
    passwords"—we'll be using LastPass for this. And if there are any
    saved passwords under Saved Logins... be sure to remove them all
    (Figure 7-7).

Figure 7-7. *Firefox Forms & Passwords settings*

3. Find Cookies and Site Data (Figure 7-8). Set "Accept third-party cookies and site data" to Never. The first option of "Accept cookies..." is for first-party cookies, and that's fine as is.

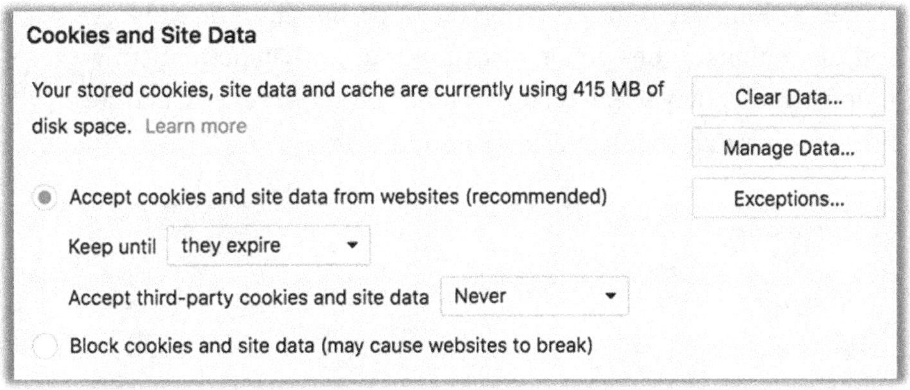

Cookies and Site Data

Your stored cookies, site data and cache are currently using 415 MB of disk space. Learn more

[Clear Data...]

[Manage Data...]

(●) Accept cookies and site data from websites (recommended)

[Exceptions...]

Keep until [they expire ▼]

Accept third-party cookies and site data [Never ▼]

( ) Block cookies and site data (may cause websites to break)

Figure 7-8. *Firefox Cookies and Site Data settings*

4. Next, find Tracking Protection (Figure 7-9). Set it be always on. Turning on Do Not Track is just a suggestion to the web site, but still you should tell everyone that will listen that you don't like being tracked.

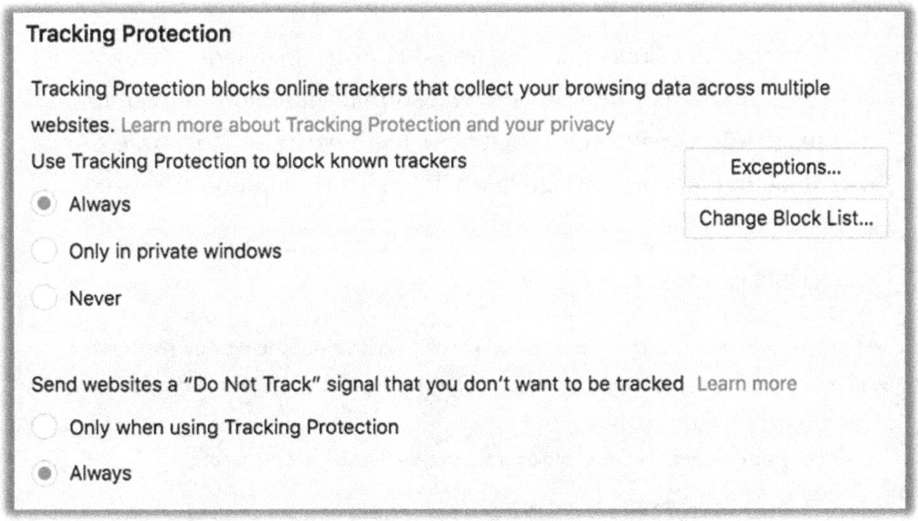

Tracking Protection

Tracking Protection blocks online trackers that collect your browsing data across multiple websites. Learn more about Tracking Protection and your privacy

Use Tracking Protection to block known trackers

[Exceptions...]

(●) Always

[Change Block List...]

( ) Only in private windows

( ) Never

Send websites a "Do Not Track" signal that you don't want to be tracked Learn more

( ) Only when using Tracking Protection

(●) Always

Figure 7-9. *Firefox Tracking Protection settings*

5. Next, find Permissions (Figure 7-10). There are several settings here, and you should look at each of them individually. By far the safest thing is to block all requests to access your location, camera, and microphone. However, that will break some web sites. As long as Firefox prompts you for permission, you can leave these settings as the default. Just know that you can permanently deny or allow any site here. Below that, you should check all three boxes. This may require you to restart Firefox.

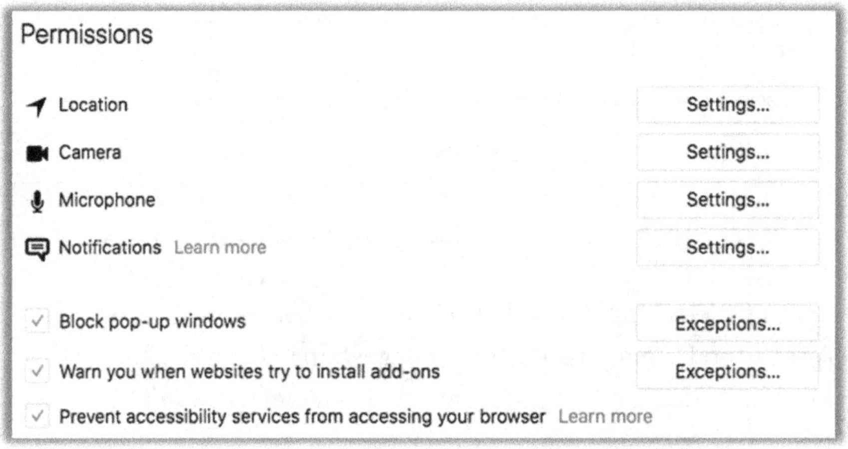

Figure 7-10. *Firefox Permissions settings*

6. Find Firefox Data Collection (Figure 7-11). You can decide what you want here. For maximum privacy, you should share nothing. But for Mozilla to improve its products, it has a legitimate need for some user data. But maybe they can just get that from someone else.

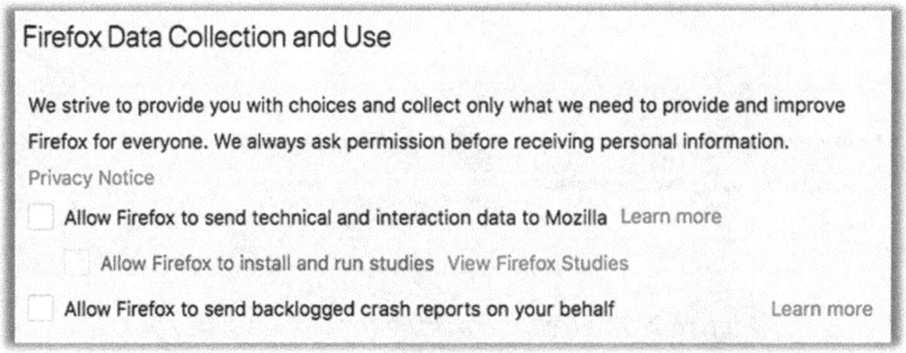

Figure 7-11. *Firefox data collection and use settings*

7. Finally, find the section Deceptive Content and Dangerous Software Protection under the Security section (Figure 7-12). I'm not sure how effective this is, but it's worth a shot. I would check all the boxes.

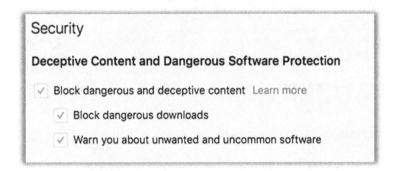

Figure 7-12. *Firefox security settings*

Tip 7-2b. Chrome

1. Open Chrome menu at the upper right and select Settings (Figure 7-13).

Figure 7-13. *Chrome settings*

2. Scroll to the bottom and click the little Advanced button. In the "Privacy and security" section, set the options as shown in Figure 7-14. Many of the options here involve sending information about you to Google—and while they may be helpful services, they give away a lot of information about you.

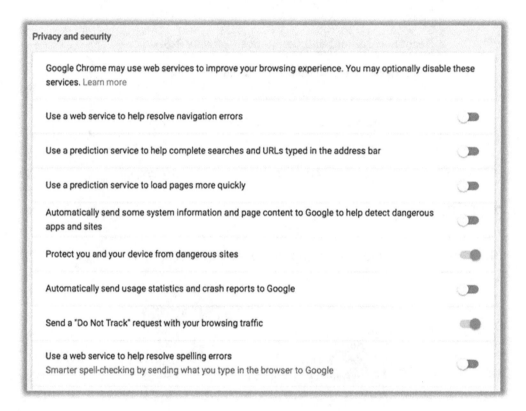

Figure 7-14. *Chrome "Privacy and security" settings*

3. At the bottom of this section, click "Content settings." There are several settings here, and you should look at each of them individually. By far the safest thing is to block all requests to access your location, camera, and microphone. However, that will break some web sites. As long as Chrome asks you before accessing, you should be safe. Just know that you can permanently deny or allow any site here. The setting for Flash should also be defaulted to "Ask first." That's the setting you want here. The whole reason we have Chrome is to run Flash when we have to, but you still want to be asked first to be safest.

4. Also in "Content settings" you'll see Cookies—click to open these settings. Be sure to block all third-party cookies. You'll want to allow first-party cookies, though (the first option in Figure 7-15).

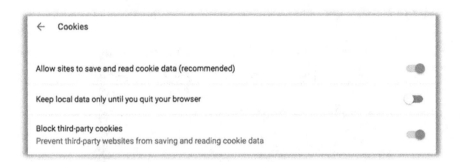

Figure 7-15.   Chrome Cookies settings

5. Back to settings, find "Passwords and forms." You should disable auto-fill of passwords here. And if there are any passwords saved here, you should delete them. (We'll be using LastPass to save your passwords!)

Tip 7-3. Remove (or Disable) All Unnecessary Add-ons

Web browsers have become very flexible, allowing you to add all sorts of fun and useful features via plugins, add-ons, extensions, and toolbars. Unfortunately, these extras, many of which are free or get installed with other software, can open security holes and reduce your privacy. Toolbars are often the worst offenders, but any add-on can cause problems. Avoid them unless you really need them. (In the next section, I'll give you some add-ons that will significantly enhance your security and privacy.) If you have any trouble removing an add-on, try searching for *remove <add-on name>* in your web browser. Some of these add-ons are tenacious and hard to remove (and these are the ones you most assuredly need to remove).

Note that Java is a plugin most people don't need anymore. The Java plugin allows code inside your browser to run Java code *outside* your browser, and that's generally bad. Having Java on your computer is fine, but there are few cases for regular users to invoke Java from within a web browser. So if you find a Java plugin, you can remove it. (Remember that JavaScript has nothing to do with Java, despite the similar names. JavaScript is widely used for good purposes, and disabling it would bring many web sites to a screeching halt.)

265

Tip 7-3a. Firefox

1. To remove an unwanted add-on to Firefox, first open the Add-ons menu from the general Firefox menu, which is off to the right (Figure 7-16).

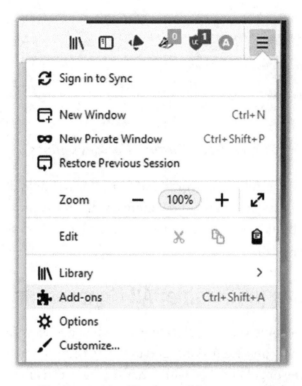

Figure 7-16. *Firefox add-ons menu*

2. Select the Extensions tab at the left. Find the add-on that you want to remove and click the Remove button. (If you're not sure, just click the Disable button for now and remove it later when you're sure.) Figure 7-17 shows an example.

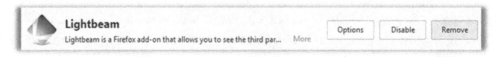

Figure 7-17. *Firefox extension example*

3. You may need to restart your browser to complete this. If you have multiple add-ons to remove, you can remove them all and then just restart the browser once.

Tip 7-3b. Chrome

1. To remove an unwanted add-on in Chrome, first open the Settings menu as we did previously (the menu at the upper right).

2. Select "More tools" and then Extensions (Figure 7-18).

Figure 7-18. *Chrome extensions menu*

3. Click REMOVE under the add-on you want to remove. (If you're
    not sure, you can just disable it using the little switch at the
    bottom for now and remove it later once you're sure.) Figure 7-19
    shows an example.

Figure 7-19. *Chrome extension example*

4. You may need to restart your browser to complete this. If you have
    multiple add-ons to remove, you can remove them all and the just
    restart the browser once.

Tip 7-4. Change the Default Search Option to DuckDuckGo

Even the venerable, ubiquitous Google search can (and will) track you. Think about
some of the things you might search for and ask yourself if you would like that
information saved and made available to someone else. That weird rash on your leg...
how to hack your game console...where to find that special adult content.... If this
idea bothers you, then you should consider changing your default browser search to
DuckDuckGo.

This company is 100 percent committed to user privacy and states unequivocally
that it saves no user data. This web site sums it up well:

`https://duckduckgo.com/privacy`

To set DuckDuckGo as your default web browser search engine, the easiest way is to just
install the DuckDuckGo Privacy Essentials plugin. Not only will this make DuckDuckGo
your default search engine, it will also add some great privacy-protecting features to your
browser. See the next tip for help with installing this and other great plugins.

Tip 7-5. Install Security and Privacy Add-ons

Some plug-ins actually enhance your security and privacy by preventing web sites from loading annoying ads and installing tracking cookies. (In fact, these plugins can significantly increase page-loading speed by avoiding lots of stuff you don't need.) I recommend installing each of the following extensions. They each perform a slightly different function, though there is some overlap. I will walk you through installing one extension. The rest will follow the same procedure.

Note   The nature of most of these plugins is to block or restrict unwanted content. This can sometimes break web sites that haven't been properly designed for the possibility that people might not want annoying ads, tracking cookies, etc. If you find a web site that is not working properly or somehow acting funny, you might try temporarily disabling some of these plugins. Some plugins allow you to "whitelist" web sites, which disables the blocking for sites you choose. Or you could also use the browser provided by Mac OS (Safari) or Windows (Internet Explorer) as a backup.

Let's start with a plugin called Privacy Badger. There are a handful of effective plugins to block third-party tracking, but Privacy Badger is the only one I know of that was created by a purely nonprofit organization—and it happens to be a group that is strongly committed to protecting people: the Electronic Frontier Foundation (EFF).

Tip 7-5a. Firefox

1. Open the Add-ons menu, as we did in the earlier tip.

2. Using the Add-ons search bar (not the regular browser search bar), search for *Privacy Badger* and hit Enter.

3. The top choice should be Privacy Badger from EFF. Click it to select it. Then click Add to Firefox. This will bring up a confirmation dialog; click Add.

Tip 7-5b. Chrome

1. Installing it on Chrome is a little different. First, go to the Chrome Web Store, either by searching for that or by going to this link:

    ```
    https://chrome.google.com/webstore/category/extensions
    ```

2. In the search box at the upper left, search for *privacy badger* and hit Enter.

3. Click the + Add to Chrome button and then click "Add extension" in the pop-up dialog.

Now that you know how to install one of these, you can do the rest on your own. I highly recommend you install all of plugins listed here:

- **LastPass.** Even though we already installed LastPass in an earlier chapter, the browser plug-in was installed only for the browsers you had installed at that time. If you just now installed Firefox or Chrome, then you're going to need to install the LastPass plug-in for that browser.

- **DuckDuckGo Privacy Essentials.** Not only will this install some excellent privacy and security tools, it will set your default web search to be DuckDuckGo. If you just can't stand using anything but Google for search, then you can skip this plugin. The others here will perform a lot of the same privacy functions. You can also change your search engine to something else at any time.

- **HTTPS Everywhere.** Another great plugin from EFF that attempts to use HTTPS wherever possible. Some sites can do HTTPS but won't do it unless you ask—this plugin makes sure that your browser asks for HTTPS by default. Note that some sites with mixed content (HTTP and HTTPS on the same page) may not work properly with this plugin, so you might try disabling this one first if you're having trouble.

- **uBlock Origin.** This plugin blocks web site advertising (and therefore tracking). You should note, however, that most free web sites stay in business by getting money from advertisers. You *may* want to consider enabling ads from web sites that you want to explicitly support. But keep in mind that it's not just about ad revenue for your favorite site—it's also about protecting your privacy and securing your computer from malvertising. (Don't install uBlock; that's different. You want uBlock Origin.)

- **Decentraleyes.** It's a little hard to describe what this one does in a few sentences. But many of the web pages you visit download a bunch of little helpers in the background to do fancy things. Just the act of fetching these little snippets of code can give away information about sites you visit—this plugin contains many of the most popular helpers so your web browser doesn't need to get them.

Tip 7-6. Be Careful on "Shady" Sites

Some web sites are just way worse than others when it comes to malware, and those sites tend to be associated with what some would call vices…porn, gambling, copyrighted movie and music downloading, etc. I'm not here to judge. Just know that these sorts of sites tend to be worse than others, and the ones that are "free" are ones I'd worry about the most.

Tip 7-7. Beware of Pop-ups Offering/Requiring Plugins

Some web sites will ask/offer to install some malware checker or efficiency booster or video codec. If you get a pop-up window that wants to install something, just close the entire tab or window and walk away. If the plugin is something common like Flash, Java, Silverlight, or QuickTime, you should go directly to those web sites to download and install the plugin. Then return to the web site and see if it works. The rule is: *if you didn't go looking for something or request it yourself, don't install it.*

Tip 7-8. Opt Out Where You Can

While it's hard to truly opt out of tracking, you should still take every legitimate opportunity to do so, if for no other reason than to register your disdain. Here are a few sites you can visit and tools you can use to reduce spam, phone calls, and regular post office junk mail. Check out these web sites for information on how to opt out.

- This site has lots of great info: `https://www.worldprivacyforum.org/2015/08/consumer-tips-top-ten-opt-outs/`

- Opting out of credit card offers: `https://www.optoutprescreen.com/?rf=t`

- Opting out of online tracking: `https://www.networkadvertising.org/choices/`

- Opting out of Google "interest-based" ads: `https://www.google.com/ads/preferences/`

- National "do not call" registry: `https://www.donotcall.gov/`

- Opting out of direct marketing mail and e-mail: `https://www.dmachoice.org/#`

Tip 7-9. Use Private or Incognito Browsing

Both Firefox and Chrome have a special "privacy mode" of web browsing. This mode is supposed to remove all *local* traces of your surfing once you close the special window—your browsing history, cookies, and anything else the browser might remember about your session. The key word here is *local* While it may successfully block some cookies from being stored permanently, it doesn't make you anonymous or stealthy on the Web. Its only purpose is to hide what you've been doing from people who have access to your computer by deleting all the locally stored traces. To enable this mode, follow the next steps.

Tip 7-9a. Firefox

1.   Open the Firefox menu and select New Private Window (Figure 7-20).

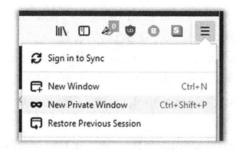

Figure 7-20. *Firefox New Private Window menu*

2.   Do your private browsing in this window. When done, just close this window.

Tip 7-9b. Chrome

1.   Open the Chrome menu and select "New incognito window" (Figure 7-21).

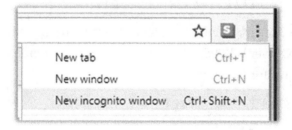

Figure 7-21. *Chrome "New incognito window" menu*

2.   Do your private browsing in this window. When done, just close this window.

Tip 7-10. Change Your DNS Provider on Your Wi-Fi Router

This can be tricky because every Wi-Fi router's admin page is a little different. I can't give you a simple step-by-step for every possible router. In the previous chapter, I told you how to find your router's admin IP address—use that same address to make these changes. You'll need to look for the configuration for Domain Name Service (DNS) server. It should be prepopulated with a couple addresses—a primary and a backup. The first entry is the one it will try most times, but if that one fails, it will try the second one. The default addresses almost surely belong to the DNS provider used by your Internet service provider (ISP).

Once you find these settings, remove the existing entries and add one of the two pairs. Both options listed here are privacy-oriented (and will avoid using your ISP's DNS, which is almost guaranteed to log every site you go to). Note, however, that unless you're using a VPN, your ISP will still be able to see every IP address your computer communicates with and can use that to figure out where you're going if it bothers to do a reverse lookup.

- **Quad9.** This service has some built-in protection against known-malicious web sites. The information is updated constantly.

  - *Primary*: 9.9.9.9

  - *Secondary*: 149.112.112.112

- **CloudFlare.** The main benefit of this site is that it's the only one offering DNS over HTTPS, which will obscure your requests (sort of like a VPN just for DNS).

  - *Primary*: 1.1.1.1

  - *Secondary*: 1.0.0.1

Tip 7-11. Change Your DNS Provider on Your Laptop

If you have a laptop, you should also set your DNS settings there because when you're out and about, you're no longer using your home's Wi-Fi router.

Tip 7-11a. Windows 7/8.1

The screenshots for Windows 7 and Windows 8.1 are nearly identical to Windows 10. I'll show you the first few different steps here and then send you to the Windows 10 instructions.

1. Open Control Panel. Click Network and Internet (Figure 7-22).

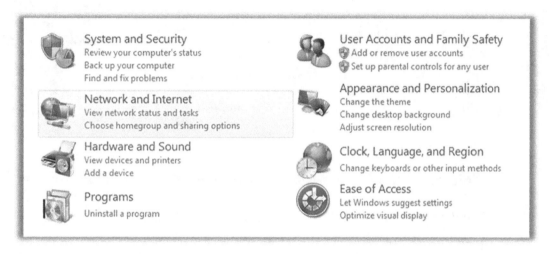

Figure 7-22. *Windows 7/8.1 Network and Internet settings*

2. Under Network and Sharing Center, click "View network status and tasks" (Figure 7-23).

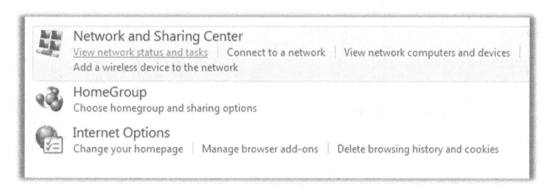

Figure 7-23. *Windows 7/8.1 network status settings*

3.   Click "Change adapter settings" at the left (Figure 7-24).

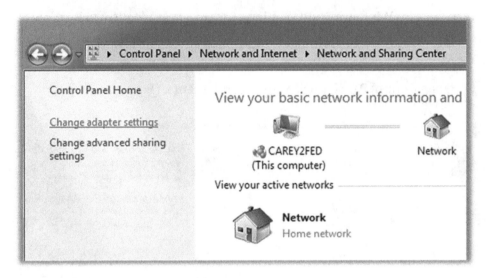

Figure 7-24. *Windows 7/8.1 "Change adapter settings" link*

4.   The steps and screenshots from here out are basically identical to
     Windows 10. Skip ahead to Tip 7-11b, Step 4.

Tip 7-11b. Windows 10

1.   Open Settings. Click Network & Internet (Figure 7-25).

Figure 7-25. *Windows 10 Network & Internet settings*

2. Click Network and Sharing Center (Figure 7-26).

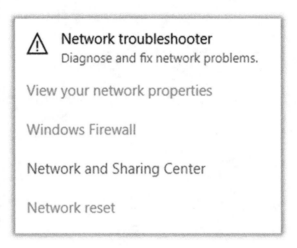

Figure 7-26. *Windows 10 Network and Sharing Center settings*

3. Click "Change adapter settings" at the left (Figure 7-27).

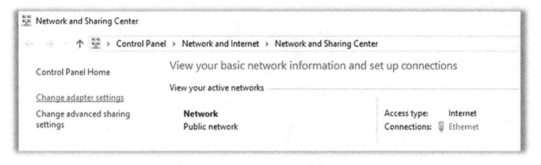

Figure 7-27. *Windows 10 "Change adapter settings" link*

4. You may see more than one connection here. You should probably change them all, but the primary one for laptops will be the Wi-Fi adapter. Repeat the following process for every one you want to change. Start by double-clicking the adapter you want to change.

5. Now click the Properties button (Figure 7-28).

Figure 7-28. *Windows network adapter settings*

6. You're probably going to want to change the IPv4 settings. (Someday we'll all be using IPv6, but that time is a way off.) Find this and double-click it (Figure 7-29).

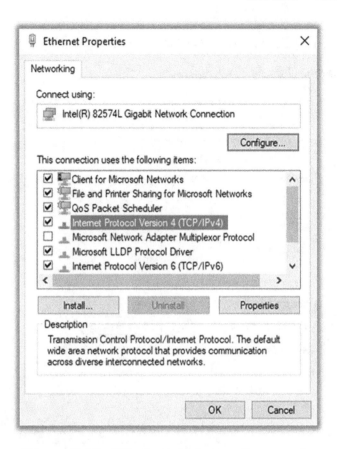

Figure 7-29. *Windows 10 network properties*

7. Change the DNS server addresses to the ones you want (see the previous tip for info). You'll need a primary and a backup pair. In Figure 7-30 I've shown the Quad9 addresses as an example.

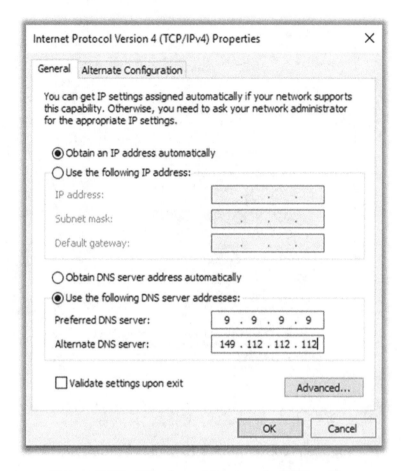

Figure 7-30. *Windows 10 example DNS settings*

8. Click OK or Close on all the windows to save the settings.

Tip 7-11c. Mac OS

1. Open System Preferences from the Apple menu. Find Network
    and click it (Figure 7-31).

Figure 7-31. *Mac OS network settings*

2. If necessary, click the lock icon at the lower left and enter the admin username and password to unlock.

3. You may see more than one connection here. You should probably change them all, but the primary one for laptops will be the Wi-Fi adapter. Repeat the following process for every one you want to change. Start by selecting the adapter you want to change. Click the Advanced button at the lower right (Figure 7-32).

Figure 7-32. *Mac OS network adapter settings*

4. Click the DNS tab. Remove the existing DNS servers at the left using the little minus button at the lower left. (Note that if these entries are automatic, you can't directly remove them—they'll disappear when you add the new ones.) Now add two more entries: the primary and backup DNS servers you want to use. Refer to the previous tip for two good options. Figure 7-33 shows Quad9 servers.

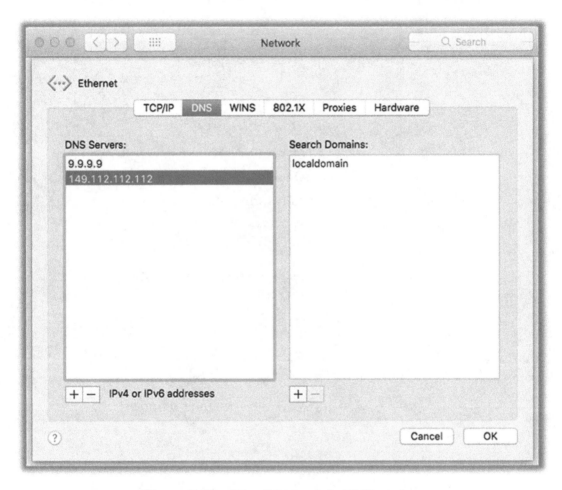

Figure 7-33. *Mac OS example DNS settings*

5. Click OK here and then Apply.

CHAPTER 8

Secure Communication

Web surfing is all fine and good, but it's a decidedly solo activity. When we need to communicate with others, we turn to other methods. Though the younger generation has embraced texting for person-to-person communications, e-mail is still the go-to method for communications in the world of work and for many people who grew up before the era of cell phones and SMS (Short Message Service, the original and official name for "texting"). Instant messaging's popularity has waned with the advent of smartphones, replaced by more mobile-oriented messenger apps. Let's dig into these technologies a little deeper. To understand how to protect ourselves, we need to have a basic idea of how they work. Let's start with e-mail.

E-mail

When you visit a web site with your web browser, you are creating a connection between your computer and a distant server such as your bank, an online retailer, or whatever. This connection may or may not be encrypted. If it is encrypted, then you can be sure that no one else will be able to peek at your messages.

With e-mail, however, the complexity basically doubles. To send an e-mail message, you first send the message to your e-mail provider, and then your provider attempts to send the message to the recipient. This allows the service to "store and forward" the message. If the recipient is not immediately available (i.e., "online"), then the message can be saved for future transmission. Even if the recipient is currently available, the nature of the e-mail system is to keep a copy of the message on the server until the user explicitly deletes it. (See Figure 8-1.)

© Carey Parker 2018
C. Parker, *Firewalls Don't Stop Dragons*, https://doi.org/10.1007/978-1-4842-3852-3_8

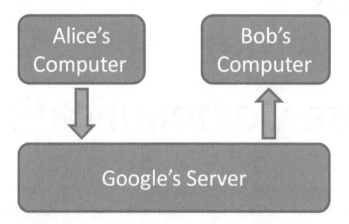

Figure 8-1. *E-mail communication within a single service*

Note, however, that the recipient may use an entirely different e-mail service. For example, if alice@gmail.com sends an e-mail to bob@yahoo.com, then both Google and Yahoo will have copies of that message on their servers—one copy for Alice and another for Bob. (See Figure 8-2.) If Alice deletes her copy, Bob may still have his copy, or vice versa. (Of course, even if both Alice and Bob delete their copies of this message, Google and Yahoo may well still keep their copies on the server for some period of time.)

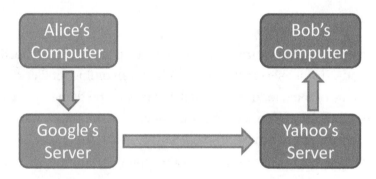

Figure 8-2. *E-mail communication between two services*

When we talked about encryption used for surfing the Web, all of the communications were point-to-point and short-lived. With e-mail, the message is often encrypted only in transit (the arrows in the diagram). The messages themselves are rarely encrypted, meaning that anyone with access to the computers or servers could potentially read the e-mails. E-mails are really more like postcards than sealed letters because anyone involved in transporting the message can read it. Also, while the connection between Alice and Google's e-mail server may be encrypted, she has no way to know or control whether the link between Google's server and Yahoo's server is encrypted or whether the link between Yahoo's server and Bob's computer is encrypted. In fact, until recently, many of these server-to-server links were known to be unencrypted.

So, what can we do about this? The best answer is to encrypt the e-mail message itself, before it ever leaves Alice's computer. Bob would then decrypt it when it arrives, and no one in between would be able to see the contents. Unfortunately, this is not easy for the average person to do, at least not yet. Google and other mainstream e-mail service providers are working hard on providing solutions that will work without a lot of user interaction, but as of the writing of this book, they are not yet available. The process involves generating a public/private key pair using a passphrase, publishing these keys to one or more public key servers, and...I've already given up. Regular people will never do this. We need something that just works. It may be something entirely new, relegating e-mail to an old technology you'll tell your grandkids about. E-mail just wasn't built for end-to-end encryption. Nevertheless, there are some viable options now, and I'll tell you about them at the end of this chapter.

Text Messaging

Short Message Service (SMS), or *texting*, came around with the advent of mobile phones. It's still the lower common denominator today for mobile messaging—all cell phones and cellular service providers support this technology. Texting is similar to sending an e-mail. It supports the store-and-forward function, meaning that the intended recipient doesn't need to be online to get your message—you can send it whenever you want, and whenever they turn on their phone, the message will be delivered. Also, the phone companies have managed to work out the technical stuff to allow someone on Verizon to send text messages to someone using AT&T or T-Mobile. Apple has even integrated SMS with its instant message system (Messages or iMessage) so that you can use Apple's proprietary system if all parties are using an Apple product (in which case the messages are blue) or fall back to regular text messaging otherwise (where message bubbles will be green).

Instant messaging (IM) has been around for about as long as e-mail, believe it or not. They both date back to the early 1960s. IM is similar to e-mail in terms of the communications pathways shown in the diagrams for e-mail, but there are two main differences. First, there's usually no store-and-forward ability. Second, instant messaging is mostly proprietary, so there is usually only one service provider involved. That is, if you're using Google's IM service, you generally can't communicate with someone using Yahoo Messenger or AOL's AIM service.

This is similar to the newer, mobile-oriented messenger apps: WhatsApp, Facebook Messenger, Telegram, WeChat, Discord, and so on. To chat with others, all users must have the same app installed. Unlike older instant messaging, most modern messenger apps will allow messages to be stored and forwarded if the intended recipient isn't currently online.

Spam and Spoofed Messages

Junk e-mails and messages—usually unsolicited advertisements—are referred to generally as *spam*. Many of our most-used messaging platforms are open by default. That is, if you know someone's e-mail address, messaging handle, or cell number, you can send them a message—no permission required. Some messaging systems have implemented a check mechanism whereby you have to first allow the other person to "follow" or "friend" you before they can send you a message; however, this support isn't ubiquitous.

If you're lucky, the spammers will only send you advertisements. However, spam is also a favored delivery mechanism for malware—either with links to bad web sites or with malicious code embedded in attachments. These links and attachments can be sent using e-mail, text messages, and messenger apps.

It's important to realize that it's easy for the sender of a message to be spoofed. That is, just because the "from" on the e-mail or text message is someone or some company you know and trust, you can't assume that it's really coming from them. Also, e-mail accounts are often hacked, so even if a message truly is from where it says it's from, you still have to be very wary of any links or attachments given to you. While antivirus and other safety utilities do an okay job of blocking these things, you can't assume that they are 100 percent effective.

You also need to realize that you can't trust the text of a link. Just because the link says `http://google.com/` doesn't mean that that's really what the link is pointing to. Sometimes if you hover your mouse pointer over the link, your browser or e-mail app will show you the actual link. In fact, if you have the eBook copy of this book and you hover over that link, you'll see that it's actually fake (Figure 8-3).

> do an okay job of blocking these t
>   You al   http://not-google.com/   hat y
> "http://google.com/" doesn't m
> Sometimes if you hover your mc
> show you the actual link. In fact,

Figure 8-3. *Misleading web links in text*

Sometimes the bad guys will try to trick you with web sites that are slightly misspelled, often in a way that is hard to catch like out1ook.com or tvvitter.com.

It gets worse. There's a web technology called Punycode that allows for encoding all sorts of fancy foreign character sets, which is nice. But some of these non-English characters look just like their English counterparts. Bad guys can register web domain names using these characters, and you won't be able to tell the difference no matter how closely you look. Check the example in Figure 8-4.

Figure 8-4. *Example of Punycode misleading web address*

The top value is what you would normally see, but the unencoded version (the real web site) is what you see at the bottom. While this appears to be the English alphabet characters a-p-p-l-e, the web address here is actually using characters from the Cyrillic alphabet that happen to look *just like* a-p-p-l-e in the font used by Chrome and Firefox browsers.

Thankfully, web browser password manager plugins like LastPass will not be fooled by either of these tricks. If you go to a web site that should be familiar but LastPass isn't offering to fill in your username and password, then you might not be looking at the web site you think you are.

Many web links today just immediately redirect you to another web site, so you can't be certain that what you see is what you'll get. There are link-shortening services that will take long, obnoxious web addresses and shorten them to something much easier to type and/or remember. These services perform a redirect from the short link to the real destination. So, for many reasons, you simply cannot judge a link by its text.

Finally, some images and links that come in e-mails can be used to track your movements on the Web and will also help spammers to mark you as a viable target. This is why many e-mail clients will refuse to load the images contained in an e-mail until you say it's okay. For example, a spammer may get a list of a million e-mail addresses from someone who hacked into some databases. The spammer has no way of knowing whether all of these addresses are real and still active. They will also not know if a particular e-mail was able to get through all the various spam filters that are between them and the recipient. But if they put an image in that e-mail with a unique identifier and your e-mail client downloads that image from the bad guy's server, then they will immediately know that the e-mail address works and that it got through to you... in which case you should expect to receive more junk mail.

Many solutions have been proposed for stopping spam, but because the Internet is so driven by marketing and advertising, the key players have been loath to adopt them. It comes down to this: who gets to determine what's junk? We've had the same struggle with regular junk mail delivered by the postal service. The postal office makes a lot of money delivering those ad flyers to you. However, the risks of malware I believe will eventually drive the industry to offer some sort of solution.

One option would be to charge a small amount of money to transmit more than, say, 100 e-mails in a 1-hour period or maybe 500 per day—something that would not affect most people but would cause spammers some grief. Right now, e-mail is essentially free, which leaves it open for abuse. The problem here is that this could hurt small, legitimate businesses and still allow massive, wealthy corporations to continue sending gobs of unwanted e-mails.

The most draconian option would probably be moving to a whitelist system where you cannot send e-mail to someone unless they first approve you as a sender. This could be automated to a certain degree. When you first e-mail someone, you will get a canned response from the service provider saying something like "I only accept e-mail from people I know. Please contact me by some other mechanism first or answer these few questions to prove you know me." Spammers deal with millions of e-mails, so they wouldn't have time to bother with this. This would still allow legitimate companies with which you actually have some relationship to contact you. The process of registering on their web site could automatically add them to your whitelist of approved senders. My gut tells me that this is where we'll end up, unless we come up with a completely new scheme for sending electronic messages.

Until then, we have limited methods of dealing with junk messages. We'll cover those in the checklist.

"So How Do I Communicate Securely?"

Most of the time, you will probably be satisfied knowing that your e-mails and text messages are encrypted in transit, even if the message itself is not. You'll need to realize that your e-mail and messaging service providers are almost surely scanning your messages so they can improve their marketing profiles on you. Most of this is automated (it's not a human reading your stuff), but nevertheless, you're trading your privacy to use these free services.

But there will come a time when something you want to send needs to be really private. Maybe you're discussing something deeply personal, or maybe you're just trying to send financial information to your tax preparer. Remember that copies of whatever you send will likely remain on the servers of your messaging provider, possibly even after both you and the recipient delete the messages.

So, how can you do this? You have at least two options (and to be super secure, you can do them both simultaneously). We're talking about data at rest versus data in motion, that is, encrypting the content of the message versus encrypting the channel that the data will pass through. Think about it this way. You can put your money in a safe—that's security at rest. If you want to then send that money across town, you could hire an armored car—that's security in motion. If you want to be really secure, you would have the armored car transport the money in the safe—that's using both mechanisms at once. If someone hijacks the armored car or follows it to its destination, they'd still have to break into the safe to get the money.

Let's talk first about securing your messages as they traverse the Internet. As we've said, most modern messaging systems will encrypt your message as it travels but will not encrypt the message itself. There are some notable exceptions that offer *end-to-end encryption*. That is, the message contents are actually encrypted at the sender's device and are capable of being decrypted only by the recipient's device. These systems use a form of asymmetric encryption like we discussed earlier in the book—using a public key to encrypt the message and a private key to decrypt it. Apple's iMessage service offers full end-to-end encryption, as do the Telegram and WhatsApp messenger.[1] There are secure e-mail services, as well, including a wonderful service called ProtonMail. Unfortunately, in all of these cases, you'll need your intended recipient to use the same service.

---

[1] Facebook bought WhatsApp in 2014 and has been slowly eroding the strong privacy protections that were the foundation of the original service. A co-founder of WhatsApp left Facebook in early 2018, partially because of these changes in privacy policies.

One way around this is to separately encrypt the contents of your message, and then you can theoretically send it using any communications mechanism you want. This would be like driving your safe full of money across town in the back of your pickup truck. Everyone can see the safe—and may well assume that it contains something valuable—but the contents are perfectly secure, assuming you bought a decent safe.

So, how does one go about encrypting a message or a file? The simplest way is to zip the file or files using a compression utility. These utilities are usually used to shrink the size of a file and/or bundle several files together into a single file. You select the file or files and tell the utility to zip them up, resulting in a single output file that should be smaller than the original(s). In fact, the most common such utility creates a file ending in `.zip`.

But these zip utilities also often have the option of adding a password to the bundle, meaning that the recipient won't be able to unzip the file without knowing the password. Adding the password encrypts the entire bundle.

If what you're sending could be sent as a Portable Document Format (PDF) file, you can also usually create PDF files with passwords. So, if you're sending a single file, you could export that file to PDF format and add a password to that file. (This may require opening "advanced" options when exporting the file.)

Of course, if you have the option, you could combine both techniques: encrypt the contents and send them using an encrypted communications mechanism. But at a bare minimum, you need to encrypt the contents itself. Remember that whatever you send could be saved on a server somewhere for a very long time, possibly unencrypted, just waiting to be found. Encrypting the file is more important than sending the file using an encrypted communications channel.

Note   When sending a password-protected (encrypted) file, you must find a way to securely communicate the password to the recipient. Specifically, you can't just send the password using the same mechanism that you used to send the file. For example, if I were to e-mail my tax docs to my CPA in a password-protected zip file, I should not then send him the password in another e-mail. I should either call him on the phone and tell him the password or send the password using a secure messenger application.

Summary

- E-mail and text messaging add a new dimension to the problem of secure communications. Instead of just having to secure a single channel between you and a web server (as with web surfing), you also need to secure the channel from the server to the intended recipient—and perhaps between your service provider's server and their service provider's server. That is, communication between two or more people is almost never point-to-point—there could be other "legs" along the way that are not secure.

- Furthermore, even if all of these separate channels are encrypted, the messages themselves are almost surely not, meaning that the servers between you and the intended recipient will have copies of your messages that they can read whenever they like. Those copies can remain long after you and the recipient delete them.

- We have to be careful when clicking links and opening attachments we receive, even if they appear to be from someone we know and trust. E-mail in particular can be used to send dangerous, malware-laden files or links to web sites that will attempt to infect your computer.

- If we want truly secure and private communications, we need to encrypt the message itself as well as the channel by which it's sent.

Checklist

Tip 8-1. Create E-mail Accounts for Public and Private Uses

E-mail accounts are free and easy to create. Having one e-mail address for people you actually care about and another "throwaway" address for retailers, web forums, contests, etc., will at least allow you to quickly segregate important e-mails from ones that can wait (possibly forever). If your current e-mail account is already swamped with junk, you should consider creating a new e-mail address that you will give out only to friends and family.

While Gmail, Yahoo, and Outlook are free and easy to use, you might want to seriously consider using a for-pay service to better protect your privacy. Fastmail is an excellent option. Because Fastmail also has the ability to create secondary accounts ("aliases"), you can actually use this one service for both your public and private e-mail addresses.

https://www.fastmail.com/

Tip 8-2. Use an Encrypted E-mail Service

The desire for truly private e-mail communications is definitely increasing as we learn more and more about mass surveillance and hackers liberating embarrassing conversations from poorly secured servers. The marketplace is starting to respond with new offerings that provide true end-to-end encryption.

One such service that was launched in early 2016 is ProtonMail. I use this one myself. There is a free tier of service, so you can try it without paying a dime. For truly end-to-end encrypted e-mails, you'll want the recipient to have a ProtonMail account, as well. There are options for sending encrypted messages to other e-mail services, though—they will receive a link instead of a message and will have to click the link to view the message. This is the problem with secure e-mail today—it requires a lot of coordination.

https://protonmail.com/

Tip 8-3. Send Sensitive Info Securely

You should never send sensitive or highly personal information via e-mail or text message. Again, most of these messages should be thought of as postcards, not sealed envelopes. And copies of these messages may remain on servers long after you and the recipient delete the message. Sensitive info would include Social Security numbers, credit card numbers, passwords, medical or financial data, and anything else that you wouldn't want someone else to see.

Regardless of how you plan to send this information, you should take the precaution of encrypting the data before you send it. This means somehow locking that data with a password. The gold standard for this is a system called Pretty Good Privacy (PGP), but it's hard to set up. An easier and more universally accessible method is to create a password-protected zip file. While you will need some special tools to create this encrypted zip file, your recipient should be able to open this file without needing a special application. (Even if they do, the applications are free and easy to use.)

Your first step is to pick your password. Since this is something you'll need to be able to communicate to someone else (your recipient will need this to open the file), consider how you will send it. You can't use the same mechanism for sending the zip file and sending the password. Will you have to call them on the phone? Can you send them a secure text message? Will they be able to copy and paste it, or will they have to type it by hand? You want something they can handle without too much trouble, but it can't be easy to guess. Once you have your password, proceed with the following steps to create your file.

Once you've created your file, you can send it via e-mail. You might also use a cloud storage service like Dropbox, which allows you to create a "share link"—a unique download link. Once the file has been downloaded by the recipient, you should remove the file from your cloud service (or at least disable the share link).

If this whole process is too complicated, you might try the next tip.

Tip 8-3a. Windows

The default zip function build into Windows, particularly older Windows versions, is not very secure. The best, free zip utility for Windows is called 7-Zip.

1. Download and install 7-Zip (you probably want the 64-bit version unless you have a very old computer): `https://www.7-zip.org/`.

2. Put all of the files you want to encrypt into a single folder, say My Private Files. Then right-click this folder and select 7-Zip ➤ Add to archive (Figure 8-5).

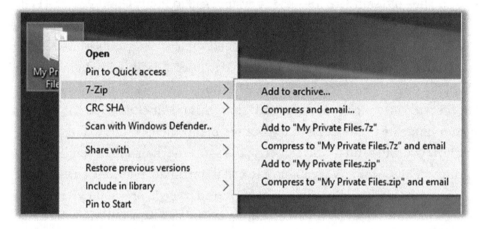

Figure 8-5. *7-Zip archive creation*

3. Don't let all the options scare you. In the window that pops up (Figure 8-6), you only have to check three things.

   a. Set "Archive format" to 7z (upper left).

   b. Set "Encryption method" to AES-256 (lower right).

   c. Enter your chosen password.

4. Click OK to create your password-protected file (it will end in .7z). Send this file to your recipient. If they have trouble opening it, have them download 7-Zip (Windows) or Keka (Mac).

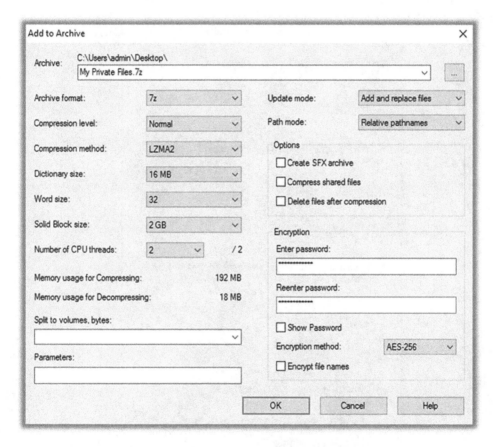

Figure 8-6. *7-Zip password-protected archive settings*

Tip 8-3b. Mac OS

1. Download and install Keka. Ideally, you would do this via the Mac App Store. But you can also find it here: `https://www.kekaosx.com/en/`.

2. Keka is handy but a little odd to work with. Launch Keka (Figure 8-7). If not already selected by default, choose the tab for 7z. Fill in your chosen password. I usually also select "Exclude Mac resource forks" (harmless and invisible to Mac users but confusing for Windows users).

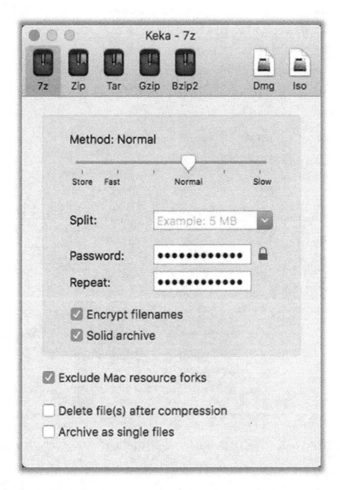

Figure 8-7. *Keka password-protected archive settings*

3. Put all of your files into a single folder, say "private files." Drag that
    folder on top of the Keka window and it will change (like Figure 8-8).
    Just let go and your encrypted 7z file will be created (by default, it
    will be in the same location as the original folder).

Figure 8-8. *Keka creating an encrypted archive*

4. Send this file to your recipient. If they have trouble opening it,
    have them download 7-Zip (Windows) or Keka (Mac).

Tip 8-4. Send Files Securely Using the Web

All that encrypted stuff can be a real pain in the butt. We have to just build this stuff into
everything so that it's the default. But there's one other new option you might want to
consider if the previous tip was too hard for you. It's a free web transfer service from
the good people at Firefox (though it can be used with any browser—Chrome, Safari,
Internet Explorer, Edge, etc.).

1. This service currently supports sending single files only. If you have multiple files or folders, you should first zip them all up into a single file. When you do the following, you'll end up with a file ending in .zip that you can send. This is *not* encrypted! But the sending process will protect it.

   - On Windows, right-click the main folder and select "Send to..." and then "Compressed (zipped) folder."

   - On Mac, right-click the main folder and select "Compress (folder name)."

2. Go to https://send.firefox.com/. Simply drop your file onto the web page to upload the file securely (Figure 8-9).

Figure 8-9. *Sharing a file with send.firefox.com*

3. This will result in a unique web link that you can send to your
    intended recipient for secure downloading (Figure 8-10).
    Simply click the "Copy to clipboard" link and then paste this
    link in an e-mail or text message. Note that by default, this link
    will expire in 24 hours. It will also be good for only the specified
    number of downloads. After successfully being downloaded or
    after 24 hours (whichever happens first), the file will be deleted.
    You can also delete the file manually using the button on this
    page. I *strongly* recommend setting a password. Anyone with
    the link will be able to download the file—adding a password
    will add another security step.

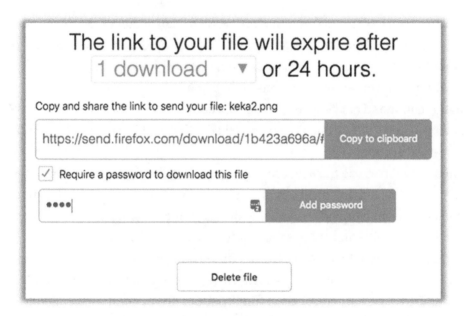

Figure 8-10. *Settings for sharing a file with send.firefox.com*

Tip 8-5. Read Your E-mail Using the Web

While e-mail applications like Windows Mail and Apple Mail have some really handy
features, sometimes it's better to use the web-based e-mail client. Many web e-mail
clients are quite good actually, including some features you can't even get on a more
traditional application you would run under Windows or Mac OS. If you've received
a sketchy-looking e-mail, using the web client to read it can provide another layer of

safety. Most popular web e-mail clients have built-in virus and link scanners. These clients also have much more limited access to your local files and operating system—they're "sandboxed" to help contain bad things within your browser.

The one downside to strictly using a web-based e-mail client is that you don't have a local (downloaded) copy of all your e-mails. If your e-mail provider is inaccessible for any reason, you won't have access to any older e-mails. So I generally recommend that you use a regular mail application periodically, which will download your messages locally for offline access and backup. Examples of this would be the Mail applications that come built in to Mac OS and Windows 10.

Tip 8-6. Don't Abandon Unused E-mail Accounts

Over the years, you may have accumulated several e-mail accounts. Sometimes your ISP will create an automatic e-mail address for you, for example. Or perhaps you had to set up an e-mail account for some special occasion and now have no need of it. If you never check it, you may never realize that it has been taken over by spammers or other ne'er-do-wells. I recommend checking in on your old accounts from time to time. Look in the Sent folder and make sure it hasn't been hijacked. (If so, see Chapter 12 for dealing with a hacked e-mail account.)

If you don't plan to use the account anymore, you have two options. If this account was rarely used, I would delete all e-mail in all folders, clear out any saved contacts, and then contact the e-mail provider on how to delete your account.

If you want to delete an account that you've used a lot and is well known to your friends and family, I would instead consider just leaving it alone. E-mail providers will sometimes recycle old e-mail addresses, meaning that someone else could end up with your address (like someone else getting your old phone number). This can lead to confusion and could even be abused. So, you might delete all the e-mails and contacts and then just check it from time to time to keep it active (from the perspective of your e-mail provider). Make sure this account has a strong, unique password, too.

If you've forgotten the password, you can usually find a "forgot my password" link that will send a reset e-mail to whatever your backup e-mail account was for that account. (I know... it's a vicious cycle, right? Do you have access to that account?)

Tip 8-7. Keep an Eye on Your Account Activity Info

Many e-mail providers will alert you if they detect suspicious activity on your account. This often means accessing your account from unusual locations. (Remember, each computer has a unique IP address, and this address can be used to find your general location on the planet.) Every so often, you might take a peek at your recent activity to look for this yourself, especially if you have some reason to believe your e-mail account may have been hacked. Here are links to three of the most common e-mail account services. However, you can probably find similar "activity" information under your profile/account settings for most services.

Google

1. Sign into your Google account: `https://myaccount.google.com/security#activity`.

2. At the left, click "Device activity & security events."

Outlook.com

1. Go to this link: `https://account.live.com/Activity`.

2. Sign in to view your activity.

Yahoo

1. Go to your Yahoo profile: `http://edit.yahoo.com/config/eval_profile`.

2. Click "Recent activity."

Tip 8-8. Don't Forward Something Without Verifying It First

We've all gotten those e-mails about dying children wanting to get e-mails from around the world or Disney giving away free passes or some celebrity dying. There are many hoaxes and "fake news" out there that sound very real. Do your part by verifying anything before sending it to all your friends and family. How do you do that? You can always just search the Web using a key phrase from your e-mail plus the word *hoax*. Or you can just go to `snopes.com`, whose whole purpose is to document these chain letter claims (as well as common urban legends). Some of them are even true. They do the homework for you.

Tip 8-9. Don't Click Links, If Possible

Links can be faked or tweaked ever so slightly so that a human might not notice. For example, out1ook.com instead of outlook.com or tvvitter.com instead of twitter.com... did you catch the difference? It may depend on the font you're using to view this book. It gets even worse, though. There's a web standard called Punycode that allows the creation of web addresses using all sorts of foreign language characters that often look just like their standard English keyboard counterparts.

Whenever possible, leave the e-mail be and go straight to the source in your web browser. For example, if you get a suspicious e-mail from your bank that says "click here to verify your account," just log into your bank directly and check your account for any notices (or call them). Note that it doesn't really matter if the e-mail comes from someone or some company you trust—the sender can be forged, or their account could have been compromised.

The main rule here is: don't click any links that you didn't ask for. For example, if you just reset your password, then you would expect an e-mail shortly thereafter with a link to click.

If you're worried about a link or button that you really need to click, you can try testing it on this web site first:

```
https://www.virustotal.com/#/home/url
```

Tip 8-10. Don't Open E-mail Attachments, If Possible

While images are usually safe, things like Microsoft Office documents (Word, Excel and PowerPoint files), PDF files, or compressed files (like zip files) should be avoided—or any file with an extension you don't recognize. At work, follow whatever policies your company specifies. You can't get very far if you don't trust e-mail from your co-workers. But at home, you should be very wary about opening any attachment that you didn't explicitly ask for. If you're not sure, contact the sender first (via phone or some other means) to make sure they did actually send it.

Tip 8-11. Check Files Before Sending

As a matter of Internet hygiene, you should consider scanning files before you send them on to someone else (particularly if you got the file from someone else). If you don't have an antivirus program installed (or if you just want to be super sure), there's a great web site that will scan a file for viruses using several tools. Of course, be aware of privacy issues here. While this site is trustworthy, your company might not like it if you were to upload proprietary information (and you probably already have antivirus on your work computer that is checking all your files).

`https://www.virustotal.com/#/home/upload`

Tip 8-12. Deal Properly with Spam

If you get an e-mail that you're pretty sure is junk, don't even open it, and certainly don't reply to it. You don't want the sender to know your e-mail address is active and valid. Don't try to "unsubscribe," unless you're sure the sender is reputable. If your e-mail application has the option to mark the message as junk or spam, do that—it will help them to filter these messages out in the future (not just for you, but for others, as well). If there is no such option, just delete the message. If the sender is a company you have an account with, then log into your account and find your e-mail preferences. You should be able to turn off (or at least reduce) their e-mails there.

Tip 8-13. Use Secure Messaging Apps

Most text messaging today is not very secure. The messages might be protected *en route* but not at the various servers in between—that is, segments of the path are protected, but it's not encrypted end to end. The following apps are encrypted from end to end and will work on your computer as well as on your mobile devices. Note that whoever you're communicating with will also need these same applications installed.

- Signal is my top choice: `https://www.signal.org/download/`.

- Wire (use the free "personal" account): `https://app.wire.com/`.

CHAPTER 9

Online Accounts and Social Media

We've talked about how to surf the Web safely and covered the basics of digital communications. Now we need to cover a few other related topics that have to do with your online behavior in general. We'll cover online banking and shopping, social media, cloud storage services, and just commonsense tips for living in the digital age.

Banking and Shopping Online

As we discussed in previous sections of this book, the security standards used by almost all banking and shopping web sites are sufficient for protecting your credit card information, at least during the transaction. As long as you see the little lock icon to the left side of the web address box, your communications with the far end are encrypted and secure. The real concern is saving your credit card information for future use. While most large online retailers do a good job guarding this data, there have definitely been situations where hackers have managed to steal users' credit card information from these sites. But, as I said earlier in this book, fraudulent credit card charges are not a huge issue for the credit card owner—the credit card companies will not hold you liable for these charges, and you will never actually be out any money (assuming you report the charges in a timely manner, of course). This is *not* the case with debit cards, however. Debit cards provide immediate access to the funds in your bank account. If those funds are taken, they're gone until you can convince your bank to reimburse you. This is why it's always best to do your online shopping with a credit card instead of a debit card, if at all possible.

But the issue we're discussing here is whether you should store your credit card information on a given web site to make future purchases easier. You should feel safe doing this with any major, reputable retailer, if you plan to do a lot of shopping there.

© Carey Parker 2018
C. Parker, *Firewalls Don't Stop Dragons*, https://doi.org/10.1007/978-1-4842-3852-3_9

But know that you can also put your credit card information in a password manager like LastPass and rapidly fill in all the relevant info on any online shopping site. So, instead of trusting the retailer with this info, you can just trust it to your password manager. Since the risks are fairly low, it's really a matter of personal preference. I tend to save my credit card info on sites where I do a lot of shopping and use LastPass to fill in my credit card info on other sites.

Online banking is another practice that makes some people very nervous. Because banks are doing everything possible to reduce the need to hire human beings, it's actually becoming expensive to avoid online banking. Banks are now charging their customers for mailing paper statements and in-branch transactions that require a live person. Like it or not, online banking is here to stay, and it's the only way to avoid the growing list of banking fees. Like online shopping, interacting with your bank online is perfectly secure and safe. You should feel at ease checking balances, making transfers, and paying bills using your computer or smartphone. I know it seems scary, but financial institutions have been sending trillions of dollars in financial transactions over computer networks for decades, and they have a vested interest in doing it securely.

However, what you may want to do is to set some reasonable limits on what someone can do with your accounts. I say "someone" because we're talking about the case where someone other than yourself has gained access to one or more of your accounts. This is true whether you use online banking or not, actually. For example, overdraft protection can be helpful for you if you accidentally write a check that your primary account can't cover, but if you allow *unlimited* overdraft protection, this could also allow someone who manages to steal your checkbook or debit card to drain multiple accounts! So, you should talk to your local bank representative about putting commonsense limits on your bank accounts and be careful about how your various accounts are linked together. This is similar to creating a regular, nonadmin computer account. You're guarding against the case where someone gets access to your account and limiting the amount of damage they can do.

It pays to be vigilant, as well. You should check in on all your online financial accounts from time to time, looking for suspicious activity and verifying the account balances. Many online banking sites offer automatic notifications for all sorts of specific activities on your account like transfers, withdrawals, and purchases over a certain amount. You can also be notified of things like password and account changes, overdrafts, large deposits, and so on. This is a great way to keep tabs on your account activity.

Credit Bureaus and Identity Theft

Identify theft is one of the nastiest problems you can deal with because it can negatively affect you for years, even if you do everything right. If someone manages to open a line of credit in your name and runs up a huge bill and these bills go to collection agencies, they could hound you for a long time.

Much of this hinges on some shadowy but powerful organizations called *credit bureaus*. The "Big Three" credit bureaus—Equifax, Experian, and TransUnion—know all about you. And yet you are not their customers; you're their product. You can't take your business elsewhere if you don't like their service. You indirectly agreed to give these companies your information by agreeing to terms of service with your banks, credit card companies, utility companies, and loan agencies. The bureaus track all of your spending and debt and then generate a single score that supposedly determines your creditworthiness. The precise algorithm for calculating your credit score is a closely guarded secret, and even your access to your own credit history is strictly limited (one copy of your report for free, per year, per bureau).

In 2017, Equifax suffered a massive security breach, and the records of almost 150 million customers (nearly half the U.S. population) were stolen. Equifax's response was slow and insufficient, and yet to date there have been no real consequences for the company, or even the industry as a whole.

While many financially savvy people are aware of the Big Thee credit bureaus, many are less aware of the Work Number and the National Consumer Telecommunications and Utilities Exchange (NCTUE). The Work Number is a service provided by Equifax that collects wage information from employers on about one-third of the working U.S. population. This information is being used to do things like verify your employment history for prospective employers and validate your income for loans and social services.

The NCTUE is a sort of specialized credit bureau that is focused on cellular services but is also being used by utilities companies. While this company appears to be a consortium of agencies, most of them appear to ultimately be owned by (wait for it) Equifax.

To be fair, these agencies do provide a valuable service that many consumers and lenders rely on. The problems are that they are not responsive to consumers and their security mechanisms have proven to be abysmal.

You can't currently opt out of these credit services entirely, meaning that they will still collect and sell your data, and it will therefore remain at risk of being stolen or abused. However, you can at least protect yourself from someone opening new credit in your name (i.e., identity theft) by implementing a *credit freeze*. The process is painful (and we'll go over this in the checklist), but at least now it's free everywhere thanks to some legislation passed in 2018. Freezing your credit means that your credit score and credit history will not be available to anyone for any reason. This means you can't get a new credit card or a new loan without first "thawing" your account. But realize that your credit history is also often checked for other reasons: signing up for utility services, getting a new cell phone, applying for a job, and so on. When this happens and you need to grant access to your credit report, you'll have to find out which credit bureau they use and temporarily thaw your account.

Cloud Storage Services

Everything today is moving to "the cloud." That is, more and more of our services and data are going online. As we discussed in Chapter 5, Apple and Microsoft have made it nearly mandatory to sign up for their cloud accounts to use their products. However, in this chapter I'm focusing on cloud storage services. These services give you a virtual hard drive somewhere out on the Internet where you can store just about any type of computer file.

There are dozens of cloud storage providers these days, all claiming to protect your data with "military-grade" or "unbreakable" encryption. As we discussed with online backup, you need to understand who holds the keys to your encrypted data. In most cases the answer is "them," unless you explicitly take steps to change that behavior.

The simplest analogy for this is renting space in a physical storage facility, like U-Store-It or PODS. You buy a certain size container (the larger it is, the more it costs to rent), and then you put your excess stuff in the box. When you're ready to leave, you lock it. But who keeps the key? Would you be comfortable leaving the only key with the owner of the rental facility? That would mean anyone who could convince the owner to open that container would have full access to whatever is stored there. Most places allow you to keep the key (or perhaps there are two locks on the door and you each keep one key). This isn't only for your protection; it also neatly absolves the rental facility from responsibility for protecting access to the key and deciding who should be allowed to check out that key. The owner knows that if necessary, they could break your lock and gain access, too—for instance, if you die or lose the key or if a law enforcement officer comes knocking with a warrant.

However, the default key arrangement for cloud storage is usually the exact opposite—the storage provider keeps the key, not you. Again, this means anyone who can convince (or coerce) the owner into coughing up the key can gain full access to all your digital stuff. It also means the owner (or any of employees) has complete access, as well. However, some of these cloud storage providers will give you the option to provide and manage your own key. You have a password manager, so you can use it to safely store these keys. There are also applications you can use that will manage this encryption for you, in the case where the storage provider doesn't offer the option for you to keep the keys. They will encrypt all your data before it's stored and decrypt it when you need it. You can think of it as a second lock or a container within a container.

Sometimes, though, this is just too much hassle. Encrypting your data in the cloud means that it's harder to share with other people, and it may break some nice features (like searching by file name or content). The thing to keep in mind if you're not going to hold the encryption keys yourself is that whatever you put in the cloud could potentially be seen by someone else. As long as you don't care about that, then you can forget about pre-encrypting the data. It's important to realize, however, that just because you've deleted a file from this cloud service, they may still have a copy. For example, when you delete a file from Dropbox, you can actually log into your Dropbox account on a web browser and *undelete* it! That means it was never really deleted in the first place. These services may keep multiple copies, as well—so that if you change a file, they may retain a copy of what it looked like beforehand. They do this not to be sneaky (probably) but to help you recover something if you accidentally alter or delete it.

Social Media

Now we finally come to the web services that we lovingly refer to as *social media*. This includes things like Facebook, Twitter, Instagram, LinkedIn, and Pinterest.[1] The stated purpose of these services is to allow people to find, connect, and share things with other people. However, I'm here to tell you that the actual purpose of these sites is to compile massive dossiers on as many people as possible and sell that data for money. The profit model for all of these "free" services is to provide companies with highly targeted advertising on the principle that catering to an individual's tastes, income, education, religion, and so on, will make them much more likely to buy. Social media services are

---

[1]Note that Microsoft owns LinkedIn, and Facebook owns Instagram.

the most colossally effective trojan horses ever created by humans. People willingly provide hordes and gobs of extremely personally information on these sites. Even if you try to restrict access to your closest friends and family, you've already given the service provider permission to share this information with third parties (this is buried somewhere in your "terms of service").

This was brought to light most recently by the Cambridge Analytica scandal. It's a long story, but basically a political research and marketing company wanted to learn about as many U.S. voters are possible. Working with a psychology researcher named Aleksandr Kogan, Cambridge Analytica (CA) created a fun little Facebook survey called "This Is Your Digital Life" that attracted 270,000 people to respond. When you take these surveys, you're granting the third-party survey maker access your Facebook data. However, Facebook also allow third parties to gain access to all of your Facebook friends' information, too. This allowed Cambridge Analytica to amass a database of highly personal information on nearly *90 million* Facebook users. Using this data for marketing purposes was against Facebook's policy, but CA lied and said it was using it for academic research.

But the real problem isn't policy, enforcement, or even security. The problem is that this data is being collected in the first place. The mere *existence* of so much highly personal information begs for it to be stolen and/or abused. On a personal level, people will invariably use this data to stalk love interests, check up on spouses or ex-lovers, dig into the lives of celebrities and politicians, and so on. It's just human nature. At the corporate and government level, the potential for abuse is almost limitless. *The only way to prevent this is to not collect the data in the first place.* Since we can't prevent these companies from collecting the data, the next best option is to just never use these services.

Yeah, yeah, I know. That ship sailed a long time ago for most of you. You can argue that it won't really do you much good to quit at this point, and frankly most people just can't give it up. These social media services are wildly popular because people truly enjoy using them to share all sorts of information with friends and family. So, let's just acknowledge that and move forward. In the checklist for this chapter, I will give you some specific advice on how to lock down access to your social media accounts and how to avoid giving out the wrong types of information. But if you're ready to make the break, I'll also tell you how to delete your accounts. (You can do it! I did. In the wake of the Cambridge Analytica debacle, I deleted both my Facebook accounts.)

Summary

- Online banking and shopping are actually very safe, in most cases. As long as you deal with a reputable retailer, make sure your connection is secured, and use a credit card from a major bank, you should be fine.

- Identity theft is one of the most difficult attacks to recover from. To prevent someone from opening new credit in your name and sticking you with the bill, your best option (and it's not an easy option) is to freeze your credit.

- Cloud services provide extremely convenient ways to access and share your files, pictures, and other data, but you need to understand who holds the keys to that online storage and know that your storage provider may save copies of your files long after you "delete" them.

- Social media services like Facebook and Twitter collect unprecedented amounts of information on their customers, and they make money by selling that information to advertisers. You need to be mindful of what information you give them and what you share with others.

Checklist

The checklist for this chapter sort of covers the "rest of the Internet"—things like online banking and shopping, social media, and online behavior in general. The items here are a bit of a hodge-podge of online safety guidelines, tips, and tricks.

Tip 9-1. Lock Down Your Apple/Microsoft Accounts

It's almost impossible to avoid setting up Apple and Microsoft accounts. These cloud services are deeply embedded into most recent versions of Mac OS, iOS (iPhone and iPad), and Windows. But you can still tweak the settings on these accounts to better protect your privacy.

As a general rule, when signing up for these accounts, give them as little information as possible. Also, feel free to give them incomplete or even incorrect data. Instead of signing up with John Doe, try just using John D. Instead of giving your correct birthday, just give them something close enough. For child accounts, which often enable parental controls and age-based content, you can give a date that's closer to the actual birth date. Don't give them your full address. Often a ZIP code is sufficient.

However, if they ask for a mobile phone number or other e-mail address, you need to give them a real one. These are often used to verify your identity or to help you unlock your account if you forget your password.

In this section, we lock down the settings on your computer. (In Chapter 11, we show you how to lock down your iOS and Android cloud settings.) There's no way to sugarcoat this... there are a ton of settings here. I'm not going to go through every single one of them, just the key ones. Regardless, I suggest you poke around and at least familiarize yourself with what's there. The other hard truth is that these settings change often. The settings for Windows 10 changed while I was writing this book. And when new settings show up, they're often "on" by default (i.e., set to the least private option). This is the world we live in now.

The following steps apply to settings on your computer. For Microsoft, you will want to review your online Microsoft account settings, as well. Go to this web site:

```
https://account.microsoft.com/
```

Find your Privacy Dashboard and take the time to poke around in all of these settings. Realize that all of the talk about "personalization" and "interests" and "history" is really about building up a profile on you that may be shared with others (on purpose or via hacking). Just say no wherever you can.

Tip 9-1a. Microsoft Windows 7/8.1

There aren't a lot of settings for privacy on Windows 7 and Windows 8.1. The following screenshots are from Windows 7, but the Windows 8.1 screenshots are nearly identical.

There are also several Knowledge Base (KB) software updates that are all about tracking. Unfortunately, removing all these software updates is rather involved. For that, you might try this web site for help, if you're up to the task:

https://spreadprivacy.com/windows-7-privacy-tips/

1. Open your Windows Control Panel. Search for *Action Center* and click it (Figure 9-1).

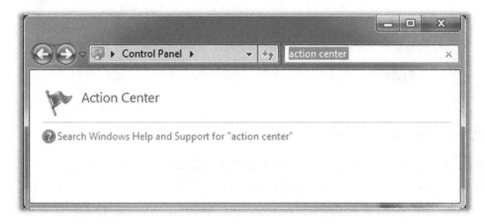

Figure 9-1. *Windows 7 Action Center settings*

2. Click the link "Change Action Center settings" at the left.

3. At the bottom, click "Customer Experience Improvement Program settings" (Figure 9-2).

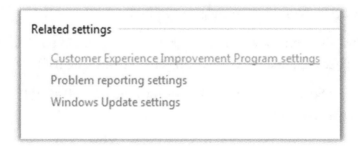

Figure 9-2. *Windows 7-related settings*

4. Click No on the next screen (Figure 9-3).

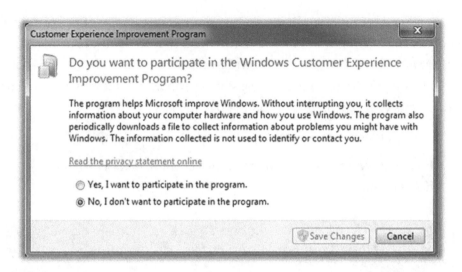

Figure 9-3. *Windows 7 customer experience settings*

Tip 9-1b. Microsoft Windows 10

There are many, many settings here. Most of them involve sharing some sort of information with Microsoft directly or with certain applications on your computer (which may then share that information with the owner of the application). Many of these services are handy—and if you know you want to use them, then just be aware that you may be sharing data. For anything you are not using or are not sure if you're using, turn the setting off (set it to "don't share"). You can always come back and change the setting later. Note also that the admin account can enable/disable entire services for all accounts, if you really want to lock things down.

1. On your computer, open Settings. Open Privacy.

2. Start with the Windows Permissions section.

    •   Under General, I would uncheck everything, but in particular, uncheck the first option ("let apps use advertising ID").

    •   Under Speech, Inking and Typing, I would turn off everything, unless you really plan to use it.

- For "Diagnostics and feedback," you may not have an option to send nothing. You may only be allowed to choose "basic" or "full." I would choose "basic."

- Below this are other settings, including "Tailored experiences." Doesn't that sound so desirable? Again... these are euphemisms for "allow us to track you." Disable this.

- Now go to Activity History. Turn this off. While you're there, you might want to also click "Clear activity history."

3. Under "App permissions," there are a gazillion settings, but they basically fall into the same pattern. You can enable or disable a particular feature for all people and all applications, or you can enable/disable a feature on a per-application level. Unfortunately, the descriptions are not always clear—but again, you can change your mind later. Disable things where you can, and when you find that you need them, you can turn them back on.

Tip 9-1c. Mac OS

There are two areas you'll want to check: your iCloud settings and your Security & Privacy settings. To control what information is stored in iCloud, you need to go to the iCloud settings. The more you sync or put in iCloud, the more Apple knows about you: it's that simple. That said, these are handy services, particularly if you have multiple Apple devices. Despite my concerns, I sync my contacts, notes, and reminders through iCloud because I have many devices, and I like having them stay in sync automatically.

1. Go to System Preferences and find your iCloud settings (Figure 9-4).

Figure 9-4. *Mac OS iCloud settings*

2. Once you open this preference, you'll be shown several options for services to sync or back up in iCloud. You'll want to make your own choices for each of these, but here are some specific things to consider:

-   iCloud Drive is Apple's built-in cloud storage service, like Dropbox but with more Apple-centric features. Apple pushes you to use this constantly, which is annoying. I avoid it. For one thing, it's expensive—if you use it at all, you'll use up the free 5GB of storage in a hurry and need to buy more. If you enable this, all of your documents will automatically be stored in the cloud. (If Apple ever lets you use your own private encryption key, this might be a more attractive service.)

-   Turn off Photo cloud backup. You should already have one if not two different backup solutions for your computer, and those solutions have a lot more privacy control. Click the Options... button next to Photos and deselect iCloud Photo Library at a minimum. You may also want to disable the other options, though iCloud Photo Sharing can be handy if you have a friend or family member that you often share photos with.

-   Disable Keychain backup to iCloud. You have LastPass for managing your passwords. While this can be convenient because it's built into all of Apple's products, it's currently not as secure as LastPass. (This may change with time. Apple is becoming very serious about its security and privacy.)

-   If you have a laptop (MacBook), I strongly encourage you to enable Find My Mac. It's less useful for desktop computers that never leave the confines of your home, but if you're at all worried about your computer being stolen, you should enable this feature that can help you find it.

-   You need to decide how much information you want to put into iCloud. Look at the other settings here and disable anything you don't need to synchronize with other Apple devices.

3. Next open Security & Privacy settings under System Preferences
    (Figure 9-5).

Figure 9-5. *Mac OS Security & Privacy settings*

4. If necessary, unlock the settings by clicking the padlock at the lower
    left (Figure 9-6). There are several settings here. The basic idea is that
    you want to limit access to potentially private things like location,
    contacts, calendar, and photos to only those applications that truly
    need it. When it doubt, turn it off—you can always turn it back on.

    •   Be wary of apps that want access to Accessibility controls, unless
        you truly need it. These abilities can often give rogue apps a way
        to hack your system.

    •   When it comes to Analytics, I usually turn those off. Yes, it helps
        developers to improve their products, but until we come up with
        real regulations on what data can be collected and how it can be
        used, I err on the side of caution.

Figure 9-6. *Mac OS Privacy settings*

Tip 9-2. Use Throwaway E-mail Accounts

Many web sites will ask you to create an account to view their content or access key portions of their web site. This mainly allows them to send you marketing e-mails or sell your contact info to advertisers. To ensure that you've given them a valid e-mail address, these sites will often block access until you click a special link they send to you via e-mail. If you don't plan to regularly use this site, creating a new, unique user ID and password can be very annoying. To work around this, there are web services that allow you to create a temporary e-mail account—something you can use just long enough to get that one, stupid confirmation e-mail. Other sites have collected some "public" accounts that they share so that other people can use them. While these don't always work, sometimes it's worth trying.

- **Shared logins.** The following sites will give you some pre-existing accounts that people have shared so that you may not have to create an account for yourself.

  - `login2.me`

  - `bugmenot.com`

- **Disposable e-mail accounts.** When you go to these sites, they provide you with a throwaway e-mail account. You can check your e-mail for a short period of time and then abandon it.

  - `10minutemail.com`

  - `guerrillamail.com`

  - `getairmail.com`

  - `mailinator.com` (warning: e-mails are viewable by anyone)

- **E-mail aliases.** Some e-mail services offer you the ability to create e-mail aliases. These are e-mail addresses that will forward directly to your normal e-mail inbox, but you can cancel them at any time, effectively blocking that person from being able to ever reach you again—without abandoning your real account.

  - *Yahoo*: `https://help.yahoo.com/kb/SLN15953.html`

  - *Outlook*: `https://support.office.com/en-us/article/add-or-remove-an-email-alias-in-outlook-com-459b1989-356d-40fa-a689-8f285b13f1f2`

  - *Gmail*: Simply add any set of characters after a plus sign to your e-mail address. For example, if your real address is `joe@gmail.com`, you can give out `joe+alias@gmail.com` and the e-mail will go to the original address.

  - *Fastmail*: `https://www.fastmail.com/help/receive/aliases.html`

Tip 9-3. Use Credit Cards Online (Not Debit Cards)

Quite simply, if someone charges something to your credit card without your permission, you're not actually out any money—the credit card company is. As long as you report the fraudulent charge in a timely manner, you won't be responsible for the charge. With debit cards, that money is actually gone from your bank account, and you then have to fight to get it back.

Tip 9-4. Use Virtual Credit Card Numbers

Some credit cards offer a one-time-use "virtual" credit card number. This is a great option for buying something online from a store that you will probably never do business with again. This is usually done online, through your credit card account web site, but it can be hard to find—call the number on the back of your card and ask about this service. This service will generate a throwaway 16-digit credit card number that will work only one time. It comes with its own expiration date, security code, and everything. The charge will show up on your regular bill. Just be sure to save that temporary card info until you've received the merchandise, in case you need to return it or something.

The Capital One service, Eno, allows you to create cards that act as aliases for your real credit card. Unlike single-use virtual numbers, you assign these cards to a particular merchant. This has at least two benefits. First, if that company is hacked, the card info will be useless to the hacker—it works only for that vendor. Second, if your real card is ever lost or stolen, these alias cards will not be affected. They will still be tied to your account and will be associated with your new credit card number.

Tip 9-5. Give Your Credit Card Company a Heads-Up

Because credit card companies are ultimately the ones on the hook for illicit purchases, they have implemented all sorts of automatic antifraud protections. Their computers are well aware of where you live and what sorts of things you typically buy. If you suddenly buy something in a foreign country or make a large purchase from an online store, they may turn off the card until they can talk to you and verify that the charges were legit. To avoid this, you can give them a call ahead of time to let them know you'll be traveling abroad or will be buying something expensive from a place you don't normally shop.

Tip 9-6. Set Up Restrictions on Your Financial Accounts

Services such as overdraft protection, funds transfers, and linked accounts can be convenient. However, you need to think about what someone else could do if they were to somehow gain access to your checkbook, ATM card, or debit card. Anything you can do with it, they can also do. Don't link two accounts unless you really need to (like with overdraft protection). If possible, put limits on daily withdrawal and transfer amounts. If you need to, you should always be able to go into your bank branch if you need to exceed these limits—but at least in that case you will deal with a human that can verify your identity.

Tip 9-7. Turn On Account Alerts

Many online banks, credit card companies, and financial firms have ways to create alerts on various types of account activity including being able to set trigger levels. For example, you can be alerted whenever someone withdraws more than $200 from an ATM or charges more than $300 on your credit card in one day. These are great ways to keep tabs on your accounts.

Tip 9-8. Freeze Your Credit

The most potent way to prevent an identity thief from opening a new line of credit in your name and sticking you with the bill is to freeze your credit at the Big Three credit agencies: Equifax, Experian, and TransUnion. When you freeze your credit, you prevent banks, lenders, credit card companies, employers, and really anyone from obtaining your credit record. This effectively prevents anyone from getting a new credit card or loan or bank account in your name (including yourself). If you need to do any of these things, you will need to find out which credit bureau is needed and temporarily "thaw" your account. Thanks to recent legislation, this process is now completely free (as it should be). For a freeze, you will have to individually contact all three agencies.

If you know you will be needing to access your credit report, you might instead set a fraud alert on your account. It will require that they contact you before opening any new credit lines in your name. This is also free but will expire after a year. You only need to contact one of the Big Three agencies for this—that agency will contact the other two for you.

You can freeze your credit online using the following links. They will mail you a PIN that you will need to unfreeze your accounts. When you get this, be sure to save the information somewhere safe (like in LastPass).

- *Equifax*: `https://www.freeze.equifax.com/Freeze/jsp/SFF_PersonalIDInfo.jsp`

- *Experian*: `https://www.experian.com/freeze/center.html`

- *TransUnion*: `https://www.transunion.com/credit-freeze/place-credit-freeze`

Equifax operates a totally different database of employment and salary information called the Work Number. They work with many employers to actually record your paycheck information and employment history. Originally, this information could be accessed online by providing a Social Security number and date of birth, but when exposed by KrebsOnSecurity, this portal was shut down. You can opt out of this collection, but it's tricky to do. The following article will give you more info and help you through the process:

`https://krebsonsecurity.com/2017/11/how-to-opt-out-of-equifax-revealing-your-salary-history/`

Tip 9-9. Use Secure Cloud Services

Cloud storage providers may encrypt your data, but if they also hold the key, then it's possible for that data to be viewed by employees, hackers, or legal authorities. And you should assume that your data will be saved forever (even if you delete it). This also applies to anything you post on social media sites.

Sync.com is an encrypted cloud service where you set the password. Your files are encrypted before they leave your machine, and Sync has no way to decrypt them. However, you're still trusting them to do this correctly and honorably.

`https://www.sync.com/`

You can add this ability to any cloud storage service by using Cryptomator. This application allows you to create "vault" folders that are encrypted locally using your own key. It's like putting a safe inside a public storage locker.

`https://cryptomator.org/`

Tip 9-10. Don't Broadcast Your Travel Plans

While it's good to give your credit card company a heads-up on travel, you shouldn't be broadcasting this information on Facebook or Twitter. Criminals actually monitor social media sites looking for people who will be away from home for extended periods of time. You should also refrain from posting vacation pictures during your vacation to a public location, as well. Post them to a private service or just post them when you get home.

Similarly, you should never post pictures of your airline tickets or boarding passes online. You should also be careful how you dispose of your boarding pass and presumably your airline-printed luggage tags, even after your flight. These codes can contain things like your name, frequent flier number, record locator number, and other personally identifiable information. This information could be used to alter or even cancel your next flight or be used to gain access to your frequent flier account, among other things.

Tip 9-11. Don't Sign In Using Facebook, Google, Etc.

You'll see many sites now offering to let you sign in using your Google, Facebook, or Microsoft credentials instead of setting up a dedicated account for that site. Sure, this is convenient (and should actually be secure), but it means that you're allowing Google or Facebook to track you on these sites. Since you have a kick-butt password manager, it's no big deal to set up a dedicated account on each of these sites with unique passwords. Or try using throwaway accounts for one-time access (covered earlier).

Tip 9-12. Don't Divulge Too Much Personal Info Online

This is a tough one. For whatever reason, people love to over-share on sites like Facebook, Twitter, and Instagram. But just remember that this information lasts forever and could be seen by anyone, despite any restrictions you try to put on your account or whatever privacy policy the social media site claims to follow. When you forget your password, how do you recover it? Most sites will ask you to answer three questions that supposedly only you would know the answer to. Where did you go to college? What's your mother's maiden name? What's the name of your first pet or car? This is precisely the sort of information people post on social media. This information can also be used to impersonate you on the phone, as well.

Tip 9-13. Be Wary of Using DNA Services

There are services available today like 23andMe and Ancestry.com that allow you to use your own DNA to track your heritage and perhaps find long-lost relatives. Some services even claim to help you identify possible future health risks. While there is obvious value to these services, you need to realize that there are many scary ways this data can be abused, as well. Law enforcement and intelligence agencies are using these DNA databases to find people—or, importantly, their relatives. Because you share a significant percentage of your DNA with your parents, your siblings, and your children, you are actually also submitting *their* DNA when you submit your own. While we can hope that your DNA will be stored securely and access will only ever be granted to law enforcement when presented with a valid, court-reviewed warrant, I wouldn't count on either. Databases can be hacked. Companies can be coerced. People do things they're not supposed to.

Tip 9-14. Account Recovery Questions: Lie

Since password and account recovery is usually accomplished by providing the answer to a few simple questions, why not protect your accounts by simply providing the wrong answers? Nothing says you have to answer these questions *truthfully*. You just need to be able to faithfully provide the same answers when asked again later. Whoever is trying to hack your account will be trying to give the right answer, and they can't possibly succeed if you lied.

One method would be to alter the real answers in some predictable way. Most of these questions have one-word answers, so just find some method for modifying the answer that only you know. Maybe prefix each answer word with *not* or some other prefix. Or repeat the word twice, or even just the first letter. For example, let's say the question is "What was your mother's maiden name?" If the real answer is Brown, try *NOTBrown* or *nworB* or *BrownBrown* or *BBrown*.

If you really want to kick it up a notch, use LastPass to generate totally random answers to these questions—use the password generator. (You may need to disable special characters.) Just be sure to save these answers in LastPass. I would probably save them in the "Notes" section of the web site's vault entry or, if necessary, create a new secure note just for these answers.

Tip 9-15. Limit Who Can See Your Stuff

Most social media services provide ways for you to reduce who can see what you post, who can view your profile, and who can find or contact you. Take advantage of these settings by dialing them down as low as you can stand. Put your "friends" into groups, granting full access only to the handful of people who really deserve it.

Tip 9-16. Don't Give Out Your E-mail Credentials

Many social media sites offer to help you find friends by looking at your e-mail contact lists. To do that, they just need your e-mail ID and password. Don't worry, we won't use it for anything else, really! *Don't do it.* Just don't. You would not only be giving them access to all of your e-mail contacts but all your e-mails, as well...forever (or until you change your password). On Google, it's even worse—your e-mail account password is also the password for Google Docs, Google Calendar, and dozens of other Google services.

Tip 9-17. Enable Two-Factor Auth Wherever You Can

You might not think that locking down your social media accounts is that important, but it's almost as important as locking down your e-mail and financial accounts. Hackers with access to your account can pretend to be you—and in a virtual sense, anyone who can log into your accounts *is* you. They can send notes to your friends asking for emergency money. They can send them links to infected web sites. They can even lock you out by changing your password. Enabling two-factor authentication is a great way to significantly reduce that risk. Use your favorite search engine to search for *two-factor authentication <service>*, where *<service>* is whatever service you're using. Many offer it now. This handy web site can help you find the sites that do:

```
https://twofactorauth.org/
```

Note that if you have the option of using an authenticator app like Google Authenticator or using a test message (SMS), you should use the authenticator app. Text messaging isn't as secure as it should be. It's better than nothing, however, so if that's your only option, take it.

Tip 9-18. Read the Terms of Service (or Not)

How many times have you actually read the entire terms of service or the end-user license agreement (EULA) before signing up for some online service or installing an application on your phone or computer? No one does. We just check the box that said we read it and click Accept. Sadly, even if you did read it, you probably wouldn't learn much. The use of legalese and pleasant-sounding euphemisms make it really hard to truly understand what you're agreeing to. I encourage you to try it, though—go read Facebook's or Google's or LinkedIn's privacy policy, from top to bottom. See if you can figure out what data they collect and who they share it with.

On the Internet, there's a term for an executive summary: TL;DR, which is short for "too long; didn't read." There's a web site called "Terms of Service; Didn't Read" that attempts to sort through these arcane privacy policies and distill them to quick bullet points. You might give that a look before you click Accept next time.

https://tosdr.org/

Tip 9-19. Know What They Know

Many of the big online services have a way for you to download all of your information in one fell swoop. Every e-mail, every post, every picture, every "like," every friend, every contact...you get the idea. I recommend you try this, if for no other reason than to understand the sheer quantity of information these companies have on you. Pay special attention to any marketing information—the ads they've picked for you, the demographics they've guessed for you, and so on.

Then realize that this is just the tip of the iceberg. They're only sharing what you've given them directly—they are probably not sharing what they have deduced about you or what data they may have been able to correlate with you from other public sources.

- *Facebook*: https://www.facebook.com/help/1701730696756992

- *Instagram*: https://help.instagram.com/181231772500920

- *Twitter*: https://help.twitter.com/en/managing-your-account/
  how-to-download-your-twitter-archive

- *LinkedIn*: https://www.linkedin.com/help/linkedin/
  answer/50191/accessing-your-account-data

- *Google*: https://support.google.com/accounts/answer/3024190

- *Yahoo*: https://help.yahoo.com/kb/account/sln28671.html

- *Pinterest*: https://help.pinterest.com/en/articles/change-your-privacy-settings

Tip 9-20. Lock Down Your Social Media Accounts

It would take an entire book to tell you how to properly lock down all the social media sites, and it would be obsolete the second it was published. There are so many different settings, and they change constantly. But by default, most of the social media sites are configured to be very public. After all, it's in their best interest to maximize the number of connections you have. The following links will help get you started. Most of these links are directly from the source because I want to make sure they're always up-to-date. However, I also strongly suggest doing a web search for *<service> privacy settings* to get third-party articles on how to properly lock down these accounts.

- *Facebook*: https://www.facebook.com/help/325807937506242/

- *Instagram*: https://help.instagram.com/116024195217477/

- *Twitter*: https://support.twitter.com/articles/14016-about-public-and-protected-tweets#

- *LinkedIn*: https://help.linkedin.com/app/answers/detail/a_id/66/ft/eng

- *Yahoo*: https://yahoo.mydashboard.oath.com/

- *Pinterest*: https://help.pinterest.com/en/articles/change-your-privacy-settings

Tip 9-21. Close Accounts You Don't Use

If you're no longer using a social media service (or have had enough of their shredding your privacy), you should delete your account. Many of them will try to talk you into just deactivating your account... but that doesn't protect your privacy. You need to actually delete your account. Here are some links to get you started.

- *Facebook*: https://www.facebook.com/help/224562897555674

- *Instagram*: https://help.instagram.com/448136995230186/

- *Twitter*: https://support.twitter.com/articles/15358-deactivating-your-account#

- *LinkedIn*: https://www.linkedin.com/help/linkedin/answer/63?lang=en

- *Yahoo*: https://help.yahoo.com/kb/SLN2044.html

- *Pinterest*: https://help.pinterest.com/en/articles/deactivate-or-reactivate-account#Web

CHAPTER 10

Parental Guidance

So far, we've been focused on cybersecurity and privacy for adults. If you're a parent, grandparent, or educator, this chapter will help you understand how to better protect the kids in your care.

The Internet Is Everywhere

I'll tell you right off that this was probably the hardest chapter in the book for me to write. Why? While I'm perfectly comfortable giving you advice adult to adult, it feels like lecturing as soon as I try to give you advice on what you should do for your kids. I'm a parent of two high school girls myself, and I know that what makes sense for my kids may not make sense for yours. Every parent, every child, and every family's social dynamic is different. Also, what makes sense for adults doesn't always make sense for kids. In fact, what makes sense for a given child can change drastically just a year or two later. So, it's important to realize that the suggestions in this chapter need to be carefully considered for each child individually and continually reconsidered as they grow older.

All the risks for adults that I discuss in this book apply to kids, as well. However, kids have a lot less maturity and life experience than adults do. Kids are very focused on the now and just don't have the context required to think more than a few days into the future. Furthermore, you are not likely to be there when they have to make a decision about what to do or not do. Access to the Internet is everywhere. Even if your particular child doesn't have a smartphone, you can bet that most of their friends do. According to a Pew study from May 2018, 95 percent of teens have a smartphone or access to one.[1] They probably also have access to other Internet-connected devices: tablets, smart TVs, set-top boxes like Apple TV or Fire TV, and even eReaders like a Kindle. If it has a place to enter a Wi-Fi password, then it can connect to the Internet.

---

[1]https://www.pewinternet.org/2018/05/31/teens-social-media-technology-2018/

© Carey Parker 2018
C. Parker, *Firewalls Don't Stop Dragons*, https://doi.org/10.1007/978-1-4842-3852-3_10

So, while you can certainly take some measured precautions and set reasonable limits on the things you can control, you just have to realize that Internet access today is everywhere. You simply cannot keep your kids from it, unless you want to move away from civilization (in which case you don't need this book).

As just one example, I heard my daughters talking a couple years ago about what someone had posted on their "finsta" account. I knew about Instagram, of course, but I had never heard of finsta. So, I asked what it was, and they casually explained that it's fake Instagram account (as opposed to their "real" account, or "rinsta"). While the rinsta account is wide open and public, the finsta account is much more restricted—usually just very close friends. It's more popular with girls than boys, apparently, too. Was I worried? No, not really. I trusted my girls, but I also knew that at their ages, there wasn't much I could do to prevent things like this short of taking away their phones. It's a fact of modern-day life.

As I said before, most of the security and privacy recommendations in this book apply to people of any age, so in this chapter, I'm really just adding a few other thoughts to consider that apply specifically to children.

The Grandmother Rule

The Internet is forever. Anything that happens in cyberspace has the potential to remain there not just for the rest of your life but for as long as our race survives. Digital information doesn't decay and can be copied infinitely without degrading in quality one bit. (Get it? One *bit*?) Digital stuff just yearns to break free. Once you take that picture or send that message or record that video, you should assume that one day it could be seen by someone you didn't intend to see it. And don't be fooled by any device or software manufacturer that claims they can lock this stuff down, preventing copying or transfer or whatever. Also, don't count on claims that messages will "self-destruct" or that you can delete messages after you send them. If it can be seen by the recipient, then it can be captured and shared with someone else. If you can manage to drill one thing into your kid's head about the Internet, this is it. They should consider that anything they post on social media could someday by seen by college admissions officers, potential employers, and (eventually) their own kids. It's less likely that private messages will be made public, but especially when the recipients are also kids, I would assume that anything is possible.

This leads me to the Grandmother Rule: don't do anything online that you wouldn't gladly share with your grandmother. I don't even have to explain that. Somehow Grandmom is the gold standard on proper behavior. She just is.

Cyberbullying

One of the most amazing uses for the Internet is communication. With our smart devices and computers, we can send messages to dozens of people around the globe simultaneously and nearly instantaneously. We can have a face-to-face chat with anyone on the planet as if they were standing right in front of us. And we can share our thoughts on any subject at any time with friends as well as complete strangers. While the benefits are undeniable, this power comes with a dark side for our kids: cyberbullying.

As long as we've been a sentient species, there have been bullies—kids who take some sort of pleasure in harassing or embarrassing another child. But unlike traditional bullying, *cyberbullying* can happen anytime and anywhere. It's also possible for cyberbullies to act anonymously, making it hard to stop. Finally, as we've just established, it can be nigh impossible to erase this stuff from the Internet. Embarrassing pictures or hurtful messages can live forever.

The original rule of human society, the Golden Rule, applies in cyberspace just as it applies in real life: treat others the way you wish to be treated. The Internet can seem unreal to kids because it's not personal. Something you would never do or say to someone in person is somehow a lot easier to do with a web or phone app. So, tell your children to imagine that they're doing it in person…in front of their grandmother…and then see if it still feels right.

Adult Content

This is a tough one. The Internet is chock-full of adult content—from simple nudity to unbelievably graphic violence and pornography. There are some ways you can try to restrict their devices and your home network (and I'll discuss them in this chapter and the next), but the reality is that kids have many, many other ways to get on the Internet that you can't control. Your best approach here, in my view, is to have The Talk with your kids and include a discussion about the Internet. Encourage them to come to you with any questions they have and counsel them to use their best judgment. If you plan to set up technological restrictions on their phones and computers, explain that you're trying to protect them from seeing things you can't unsee and that there will be plenty of opportunity to explore these things when they're an adult and have the maturity to handle it.

Don't Panic

I'm not trying to scare you. Like I said at the beginning of this book, any powerful tool can be used for good and for evil and everything in between. When all is said and done, the best thing you can do, for yourself and your children, is to get educated. You can't let fear of a few bad actors cause you to deny your children the amazing benefits of a connected world and easy access to the collected knowledge of humanity. The trick is to alert your children to the risks while preserving the sense of wonder and adventure that should accompany such a magnificent and powerful tool.

Summary

- Kids have all the same risks on the Internet as you do, but they don't have the same experience or maturity, which makes it harder for them to weigh the consequences of their actions.

- The Internet is forever. Don't do anything on the Internet that you wouldn't gladly do in front of your grandmother.

- Treat others on the Internet the same as you'd treat them if they were standing right in front of you, in front of all your friends (and your grandmother).

- Don't panic! The Internet is just a tool, though a powerful one. The benefits far outweigh the risks, and you should embrace it. Focus on education and staying engaged.

Checklist

This list is by no means exhaustive. I strongly encourage you to use the links provided at the end of this checklist to do some further reading. Many excellent web sites have been created to specifically address these issues, and I am just scratching the surface with this list. However, these are some of my favorite tips for helping to keep your kids safe and happy on the Internet.

Tip 10-1. Create a Dedicated Account for Each Child

Every child's needs and maturity levels are different. Creating an account for each child will allow you (and the child) to customize the settings, preferences, background images, web bookmarks, and so on. It's not just about custom parental controls, it's also about giving everyone their own space and the opportunity to express their individuality. (It can also contain the damage if they somehow get into trouble.) Use the steps outlined in Chapter 5's checklist to create these accounts. On both Windows and Mac OS, you have the option to designate these new accounts as "family" accounts or accounts that have "parental control." Go ahead and select that option as you create the account.

Tip 10-2. Use Parental Controls for Young Children

Both Windows and Mac OS have built-in parental control settings. This software can be used to limit what web sites your kids can access and how much time they spend on the computer. In my experience, these tools work well until they get to the point where your kids need to use the Internet for school. Many perfectly normal web sites used by schools can be blocked by these utilities. While you can try to approve each of them as needed, you may find that you constantly have to tweak the settings. When I got to that point, I just turned off the web site blocking.

When you get into the parental controls configuration, there are lots of possible settings. Just use some trial-and-error here. You're going to need to tweak these over time anyway as your child gets older and is able to handle more.

Tip 10-2a. Microsoft Windows 7

1. Open the Control Panel and search for *Family*. Click "Set up parental controls for any user" (Figure 10-1).

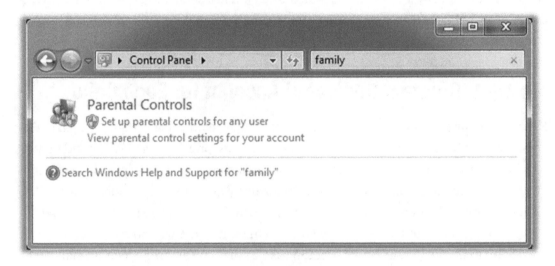

Figure 10-1. *Windows 7 Search for family*

2. Select the user account in the next window (Figure 10-2).

Figure 10-2. *Windows 7 account selection*

3. Click the button for "On, enforce current settings" (Figure 10-3).

Figure 10-3. *Windows 7 parental controls*

4. Click the various links to configure the settings to your tastes.

Tip 10-2b. Microsoft Windows 8.1

1. You should have had the option when you created your child's account to enable Family Safety. But if you didn't do that, follow these instructions to add this feature. This is easier to do as an administrator, so you should log into the admin account that you set up earlier.

2. Open the Control Panel and search for *Family*. Click "Set up Family Safety for any user" (Figure 10-4).

Figure 10-4. *Windows 8.1 Search for family*

3. If you don't have any family accounts set up for anyone, you will
    see something like Figure 10-5 (if not, skip ahead to the Family
    Safety screen that shows all the accounts). You will need to go to
    the Settings app to set up the first one. Click the Accounts link
    here to launch that app.

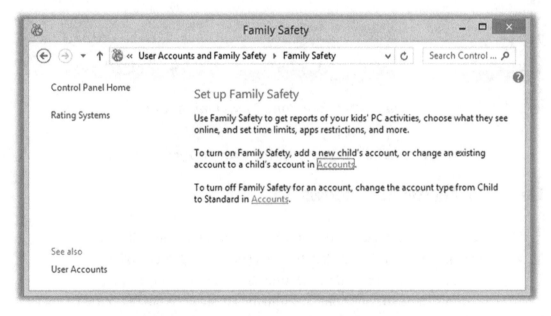

Figure 10-5. *Windows 8.1 Family Safety setup*

4. Select the account you want to change. Then click the Edit button
    (Figure 10-6).

Figure 10-6. *Windows 8.1 "Manage other accounts" menu*

5. Choose Child from the options and then click OK (Figure 10-7).

Figure 10-7. *Windows 8.1 child account setting*

6. This should automatically set up Family Safety for this account, but you may want to review the settings.

7. To tweak the Family Safety settings, go back to the Control Panels. Search for *family* again, as we did earlier. Again click "Set up Family Safety for any user." This time you should see something like Figure 10-8.

Figure 10-8. *Windows 8.1 "Choose a use and set up Family Safety" menu*

8.   Click the various links to configure the settings to your tastes
     (Figure 10-9).

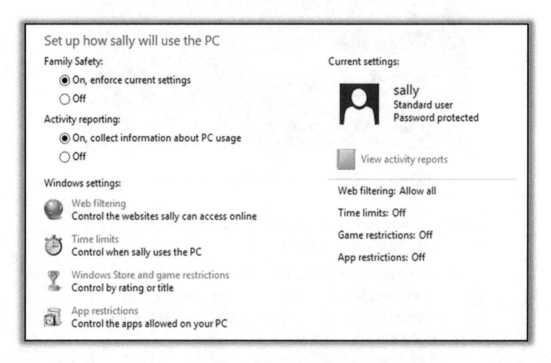

Figure 10-9. *Windows 8.1 Family Safety options*

Tip 10-2c. Microsoft Windows 10

With Windows 10, Microsoft requires both you and your children to have a Microsoft account to use parental controls. I personally find it ridiculous that Microsoft requires children to register to have parental controls on a home computer. If this was an added feature with extra benefits, that would be okay—but requiring it for *any* level of parental control seems to me like a poor policy.

But if you have Windows 10 and need parental controls, you can go to this web site and Microsoft will walk you through the steps to set it up:

```
http://windows.microsoft.com/en-us/windows-10/add-child-
account
```

The basic procedure is as follows:

1. Create a Microsoft account for yourself, if you haven't already.

2. Create a Microsoft account for each child who will require parental controls.

3. Register this child with Microsoft as a member of your family. This will send your child an e-mail inviting them to your family. They must accept this invitation for parental controls to be enabled.

4. Once accepted, you can adjust their parental controls, and you can manage their parental control settings on your Microsoft account on the Web.

5. You can find more information here: `https://account.microsoft.com/family/`.

Tip 10-2d. Mac OS

1. This will be easier to do using your administrator account. I recommend logging in as admin.

2. Open System Preferences and select Users & Groups (Figure 10-10).

Figure 10-10. *Mac OS Users & Groups preferences*

3. If necessary, click the lock icon at the lower left to unlock these controls.

4. Select your child's account from the list. Check the box for "Enable parental controls" (Figure 10-11).

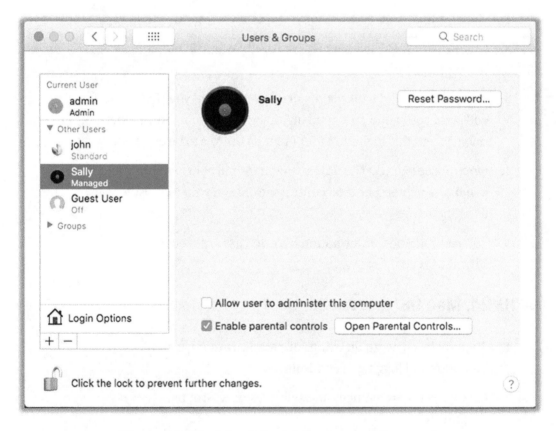

Figure 10-11. *Mac OS enabling parental controls*

5. Click the button Open Parental Controls (Figure 10-12).

Figure 10-12. *Mac OS parent control settings*

6. There are many different options here—click through the various tabs and configure them appropriately for your child. Just be prepared to tweak these as you find cases you didn't consider and as they get older.

7. Apple has a new web site entirely devoted to parental controls and family sharing of applications, movies, and music. Be sure to check it out:

    ```
    https://www.apple.com/families/
    ```

Tip 10-3. Research Before Allowing Your Kids to Sign Up

I can't stress this enough. Don't trust what anyone else tells you because most people really don't know what they're talking about. Spend the time to check out the site yourself and search the Web for parental reviews (see some of the sites I list at the end of this checklist). Also, be sure to check the date on the reviews and favor the ones that are most recent—at least within the last year or two at the most.

Tip 10-4. Teach Your Kids to Protect Their Identities

When signing up for web sites or social media or whatever, enter as little identifying information as possible. Teach your kids to never give out their full name, address, telephone number, e-mail address, or even school name to strangers.

Tip 10-5. Be Able to Access All Accounts and Devices

At least for young children, you should always have the login credentials to all of your kid's accounts and devices (computer accounts, smartphones, tablets, game consoles). If a device has a fingerprint reader, you can just add your fingerprint. They should know that at any point you can log in and see what they've up to. When they get old enough (whatever age that is for your child), you can relax this restriction. At some point, you're going to want to give them their privacy and establish an honor system.

Tip 10-6. Honor the Age Restrictions

Almost all social media sites require that users be at least 13 years of age to join. You have to enter your birthday as part of the registration process, though they have no way to verify this. Nevertheless, it's not good to teach your children to lie about their age in order to gain access to a web site.

Note that you might want to consider using an incorrect date, however—maybe a date that's one to three weeks after the actual date. It's just one more piece of identifying info that you should avoid, if you can.

Tip 10-7. Friends Must First Be Met in Person

Teach your children that people on the Internet may not be what or who they claim to be. A good rule of thumb is to insist that they first know someone in real life (or in Internet-speak, "IRL") before they can "friend" them in social media or communicate with them via chat rooms, e-mail, social media, or text. That is, they must have met this person face to face. You must approve any exceptions to this rule.

Tip 10-8. Lock Down Chromebook Settings

If your school has issued your child a Google Chromebook or if you've decided to give them a Chromebook for home use, you should take the time to lock down the privacy settings. While the Chromebook is a secure option for surfing the Web, it can be a privacy nightmare. The EFF has a great guide to these settings, which I highly recommend. This guide will walk you through protecting your passwords and synchronized data, as well as reducing the amount of information about your child that is shared with Google.

```
https://www.eff.org/deeplinks/2015/11/guide-chromebook-privacy-
settings-students
```

Tip 10-9. Remember the Golden Rule

The Golden Rule applies in virtual realms, as well. But beyond just being good policy, it's important for your children to realize that anything they do on the Internet can potentially be leaked to people they don't intend. That basically means that anything they post online could be seen by anyone, possibly many years in the future.

Tip 10-10. Keep Computers in a Common Area of the House

While children should have a certain degree of privacy in their communications, it's just asking for trouble to allow them to surf the Internet in a closed room. This applies to smartphones and tablets, as well. You can require them to put their phones and tablets on the charger before going to bed (and that charger should not be in their rooms). I don't care how good your kids are; the temptation to respond to the inevitable chat/video requests in the middle of the night will be too great. This rule also ensures that their phones are fully charged at the start of each day.

Tip 10-11. Use OpenDNS

As we covered earlier in this book, whenever your computer wants to talk to another computer on the Internet, it needs to first look up its address. This is done using Domain Name Service (DNS)—DNS is what converts "google.com" to an IP address that is routable. There's a free service called OpenDNS that you can use to block objectionable web sites for individual computers or your entire house. Unfortunately, setting this up can be tricky—and if your kids are savvy enough, they can just change it to something else. If you're interested, you can go here for full info:

```
https://www.opendns.com/home-internet-security/
```

Tip 10-12. Use Device Tracking (Judiciously and Fairly)

If your kid's smartphone or tablet has a tracking feature, you should enable it. You should use it only if the device is lost or stolen or if you need to find your child in an emergency situation. You should also make it clear to your child that you have this ability but will use it only in these special situations.

Tip 10-13. Create a Contract for Your Kids

Using the Internet and having a smartphone are privileges. You are the parent and you have the final say on when, how, where, and how often these tools are used. Come up with a set of simple, clear rules for using these things and print them. If you want to get formal, have your child sign it. Be sure to include things that you promise to do, as well. Here are a few you can look at for reference, but I encourage you to create your own. (The last one here is really funny, too.)

- ```https://www.netsmartz.org/Resources/Pledges```

- ```https://www.connectsafely.org/family-contract-smartphone-use/```

- ```https://www.janellburleyhofmann.com/postjournal/gregorys-
  iphone-contract/```

Tip 10-14. Parental Resources

Here is a list of some excellent parental resources. Bookmark them in your web browser for quick access.

- *Common Sense Media*: `https://www.commonsensemedia.org/`

- *NetSmartz*: `https://www.netsmartz.org/`

- *ConnectSafely*: `https://www.connectsafely.org/`

- *Protecting Kids Online*: `https://www.consumer.ftc.gov/topics/protecting-kids-online`

CHAPTER 11

Don't Be a Smartphone Dummy

Mobile devices have become integral parts of our lives—particularly smartphones like Apple's iPhone and all the variants of Android phones. Smartphones contain unbelievable amounts of extremely personal information including financial data, health data, your personal address book, e-mails, web surfing history, and access to much more data in the cloud. They also track your location pretty much anywhere on the planet, 24/7, because frankly they have to send you texts and phone calls. If that weren't enough, smartphones have built-in microphones and cameras that can record everything you do. Your mobile phone may have more personal information on it than any other device you own, even more than your home computer. And make no mistake—a smartphone *is* a computer, and a very powerful one at that. Do you remember the Deep Blue supercomputer that beat chess champion Gary Kasparov in 1997? The iPhone 8 has more than *20 times* the computing power as Deep Blue, and it fits in your pocket! So, let's talk about how we can secure these wonderful devices.

iOS Is More Secure Than Android

Let's get this out of the way: in my not-so-humble opinion, iOS is way safer than Android. Unlike Mac OS versus Windows, the difference between these mobile operating systems is significantly starker. Google is doing some fantastic work in the realm of security, don't get me wrong. But the Android ecosystem is fundamentally different than that of iPhones, and those differences make Android phones a lot harder to secure.

When Apple came out with the iPhone, it was really in the driver's seat. Steve Jobs knew that this device was going to completely change the smartphone world, and he managed to get all the major cell phone carriers to give him maximum control over the software on this device. The problem with Android is not that it's not secure. The

© Carey Parker 2018
C. Parker, *Firewalls Don't Stop Dragons*, https://doi.org/10.1007/978-1-4842-3852-3_11

problem is that Google gave too much control over the software to the cell phone manufacturers and service providers. I'm sure there were business realities at play here. Perhaps the cell phone folks felt burned by Apple's control over iOS and demanded more ability to control the Android OS on the devices they sold. So, you could argue that this isn't really Google's fault. But however it happened, the cell phone makers and cellular service providers are an integral part of the supply chain and serve as gatekeepers all software updates to Android phones. As recently as a couple years ago, a study found that almost 30 percent of Android phones weren't even capable of getting the latest software. Even if the phone makers and service providers want to allow the updates, they have to go through a lengthy process of testing the changes on each device first.

Google is working on changes to Android that will address these problems, but because of the previous problem, it will work only on the very latest phone models. It could be years before most Android phones will be able to stay as up-to-date as Apple iPhones. A notable exception would be Google's own Nexus and Pixel smartphones. In this case, Google is in full control of both the hardware and the software (much like Apple), allowing Google to keep these phones updated with the latest security software and fixes.

iOS Is More Private Than Android

While the security issues are important, to me the real difference between Apple's iOS and Google's Android operating systems is privacy. There's just no comparison: Apple wins hands down. There are two reasons for this. First, Apple's iOS is a very closed ecosystem, meaning that Apple exerts extreme control over what apps it will allow to run on the phone and what those apps are allowed to do when you can run them. This control is a source of major frustration for a lot of people. They want to be able to do whatever they want to do, even if that means taking more risks. You can have a spirited and healthy debate over the freedom and control aspects here, but the upshot is that Apple's closed system and restrictive permissions ultimately gives you, the user, more protection from malicious and prying apps.

The other reason is that Google is an advertising company. Google's business model is tied directly to knowing as much about you as possible. It's a pure conflict of interest that I just can't reconcile, and it's the same reason I can't recommend Google's Chrome browser. While I firmly believe that Google is doing great things in the realm of security, it has shown time and time again that it will go to insane lengths to track everything you do to command top dollar for its advertising.

Wireless Madness

While laptop and desktop computers have their share of wireless technologies, smartphones have more. Modern cell phones have Wi-Fi, cellular data, Bluetooth, Near-Field Communication (NFC), and now even wireless charging. Every one of these wireless interfaces presents a potential chink in your smartphone's armor—a gap that will allow the bad guys a way into your phone. Let's quickly review each one.

For Internet access, your smartphone has two options: cellular data and Wi-Fi. Cellular data service comes with nearly every smartphone service plan. They usually sell it to you in monthly chunks of gigabytes (GB), with steep fees for exceeding your limits (unless you opt for the expensive "unlimited" plan). Cellular data is your default connection to the Internet from a smartphone and should be available in most populated areas. But because you are charged for what you use, you have to be somewhat careful about how you use it. Regular e-mail and web surfing is usually fine, but you wouldn't want to binge-watch your favorite Netflix series using cellular data. Video services (YouTube, FaceTime, Netflix, etc.) can eat up a lot of data.

So, what if you do want to catch an episode of *Game of Thrones* on your iPhone? That's where Wi-Fi comes in. As we discussed in Chapter 2, Wi-Fi is a wireless networking technology, giving you access to the Internet at home, in coffee shops, in hotels, in airports, in restaurants, and in other people's homes. Wi-Fi service is generally unlimited and free. But as we've also discussed, public Wi-Fi hotspots are notoriously bad when it comes to security and privacy. If you're just going to surf the Web or read e-mails, I recommend avoiding public Wi-Fi and just stick to using your cellular data plan. You can also use a virtual private network (VPN) service to protect your Wi-Fi traffic, but be aware that services like Netflix will now block you if you're using a VPN (to prevent people from accessing their services from outside their home country).

Because the whole point of smartphones is to be unencumbered, they use wireless technologies for everything. This is where Bluetooth and NFC come into play. As we discussed in Chapter 2, Bluetooth is used to connect peripheral devices to your phone like headphones and keyboards without the need for pesky cords. NFC, on the other hand, is used for things like mobile payments and pairing of devices (sometimes Bluetooth devices). NFC tries to limit itself by physical proximity—hence the "near" part of Near Field Communications. The idea is that the user has to place the smartphone near the payment terminal or whatever; it can't just connect while it's in your pocket or purse. In reality, though, any radio frequency (RF) technology can work over longer distances in the right circumstances.

The last cord to cut is the power cord. Some smartphones (and other devices like the Apple Watch) have come up with clever ways to transfer power without cables. However, this usually requires very close proximity—like sitting on a special mat or stand—but hey, there are no wires! The appeal is that you don't have to physically connect the power cord.

Unfortunately, all of these wireless technologies increase your cell phone's attack surface—they're just more avenues for hacking in. While these technologies seem fairly simple to use, they are quite complicated under the covers. To do what they need to do, they are quietly and constantly monitoring the airwaves for signals and often replying to wireless queries from other devices automatically. Most of these technologies require a unique wireless identifier to operate. But this has allowed some enterprising retailers and law enforcement types to track your device using this ID and, by extension, track you. Some stores have devices that monitor Wi-Fi from phones to monitor your movements in their stores—when you enter, how long you linger in front of that sale rack, and when you come back to the store a few days later to buy something. They may or may not be able to tie that wireless ID to your name, but they know it's the same person each time because the Wi-Fi ID of your phone doesn't change. Apple has tried to thwart this tracking by using random, temporary Wi-Fi ID's, but it's not clear how effective this is at defeating tracking.

To Hack or Not to Hack

As we've said, smartphones can be much more restrictive on what applications you can run or even what settings you can change. Cell phone makers and cellular providers do this mostly for security purposes—trying to protect people from themselves. But they also do this because they want to protect themselves and their business interests, often at the expense of their customers. It should be no surprise then that enterprising hackers have found ways to circumvent these restrictions, and they've made them available to the public via easy-to-use tools that you can find all over the Internet if you take the time to look.

The process of circumventing your smartphone's built-in restrictions is a form of hacking called *jailbreaking* or *rooting*. Like regular computers, smartphones have different levels of permissions. Unlike regular computers, the cell phone makers and cell phone service providers reserve the highest permissions for themselves. Needless to say, this rubs some people the wrong way. "I bought the stupid device. Why can't I do whatever I want with it?" If you get the right phone and the right hacking tool off the Internet, you can gain full administrator privileges and do whatever you want. While this sounds very tempting, I'm here to tell you that it's not a good idea.

If you recall, in Chapter 5 I strongly encouraged you to create and use a nonadmin account on your computer. This follows the security practice of "least privilege." You want to restrict what you can do in most cases to be the bare minimum, just in case some bad guy or piece of malware gains access to your account. By using a limited-access account, you can limit the amount of damage that can be done if that account is hijacked.

This is the same basic philosophy at work on smartphones. Apple and Google have created elaborate permission schemes on their smartphones that are designed to let you do everything you need to do while simultaneously restricting the damage that can be done by a rogue application or service. While some of these restrictions are more for their benefit (or the cell phone service provider's benefit), on the whole they are the best mechanism for protecting your data and your privacy. Removing this safety mechanism will allow you to do whatever you want... but it also opens the door for any other application on your device to do what it wants. While I think there's a strong philosophical argument to be made in favor of removing these restrictions—and I hope in the future cell phone makers return more of this power to the user—right now I think it's safer for most users to leave these restrictions in place.

Privacy Matters

For me, privacy is far and away the most important topic related to smartphones today. These devices are with us almost every hour of every day and are in constant contact with the Internet. They know where we are, where we've been, who we know, who we talk to, how to access our bank accounts, what news we read, what we buy, what games we play, what pictures we like to look at, what we text and e-mail, what web sites we use, what's on our schedule...the list is endless. Your phone probably contains or has access to credit card numbers, phone numbers, passwords, PINs, birth dates, passport info, and Social Security numbers. We keep all the information of our lives on our smartphones so that we can access it anywhere at any time.

According to a 2016 Pew poll, 28 percent of people still do not lock their smartphones with a PIN or other access control.[1] While I hope that number has increased since then, I don't doubt that a majority of people still haven't taken this most basic step to secure this treasure trove of information.

---

[1]https://www.pewinternet.org/2017/01/26/americans-and-cybersecurity/

Many modern smartphones now come with the ability to unlock your phone using a fingerprint. This presents an interesting dilemma. As we discussed in Chapter 4 on passwords, fingerprints are a form of biometric authentication. As opposed to something you *know* (a PIN or passcode), biometrics represent something that you *are*. PINs and passcodes are a pain in the butt, there's no doubt. Having to enter even four digits to get into your phone all the time is annoying (and honestly, you should be using more than four). Using your index finger is much, much easier. But is it really secure?

First, realize that there are multiple ways that someone else can use your fingerprint. The most obvious way would be somehow compelling you to do it for them or knocking you out and pressing your finger to the sensor. But it turns out that it's actually not that hard to pull a usable fingerprint from a smooth surface.

Second, there's currently a distinct legal difference between a fingerprint and a password or PIN. This is an evolving area of law, and it probably varies country by country, but a fingerprint is viewed like a physical key. If law enforcement has a warrant to search your home, they can compel you to open the door with your key. But can they compel you to use your finger to unlock your cell phone? Currently, in the United States, the courts seem to be saying that they can. At the same time, the courts in the United States have upheld the Fifth Amendment right against self-incrimination for passwords and PINs—something you hold in your head and would have to communicate somehow to reveal.

And now we have face recognition, such as Apple's Face ID. To unlock your phone, you just need to look at it. Personally, I find this to be inferior to fingerprints. The recognition can happen at a distance, and despite Apple's claims to the contrary, it appears to be easier to fool than the fingerprint reader. This will surely improve over time, however.

So—as is often the case with security and privacy—you need to weigh the trade-offs with respect to convenience. While it's much more convenient to use your finger or your face to unlock your smartphone, it doesn't really offer you any protection from law enforcement or a physical attacker. That's probably not a concern for most people, however, meaning that in most cases, using biometrics to unlock your phone is a worthwhile trade-off between convenience and security (especially compared to not locking your phone at all).

Summary

- Our cell phones hold amazing amounts of extremely personal information. We need to realize this and take extra steps to protect this data.

- Cell phones are wireless in just about every way and come with a bevy of technologies that allow them to function untethered. However, that also means there are extra avenues of attacks for bad guys.

- Cell phone makers and service providers have restricted what users can do with their devices for both security and proprietary reasons. While it's often possible to download tools that will circumvent these restrictions, for the average person this is not necessary and will expose you to a great deal of risk.

- You should always lock your smartphone, either with a PIN, with a passcode, or with biometrics like a fingerprint or face scan. For most people, a biometric lock is a good balance between security and convenience, but if you're really worried about your privacy, you need to use a passcode.

Checklist

The cell phone market—particularly the Android phone market—is extremely fractured. By that I mean there are many variants of the Android operating system out there, not only in the underlying version of the operating system itself (with tasty names like Oreo, Nougat, and Marshmallow) but also with respect to service providers. The cellular service companies like AT&T and Verizon often make their own customizations to the operating system. Even the smartphone manufacturers like Samsung and LG often customize the OS. This makes it difficult to provide a definitive, specific step-by-step guide. Therefore, most of the advice in this checklist is somewhat generic. You may need to search the Web or talk to your cellular service provider to help you find the proper way to do these things.

Remember the following:

- Android is Google's mobile operating system, used on devices from many different manufacturers including LG and Samsung (and of course Google).

- iOS is Apple's mobile operating system, used on iPhones and iPads.

Tip 11-1. Back Up Your Phone

If your phone is lost or stolen, you want to be able to recover the information it held. You can often use these backups to restore all of your apps, settings, and data to a new phone. You can also use the backup to go back to a known-good state if something goes horribly wrong.

Tip 11-1a. iOS

If you have a computer, I recommend backing up your iPhone to the computer using Apple's iTunes application. You can do this on Mac OS (where iTunes is built in) and on Windows (where you need to download and install the iTunes application). You can back up your iPhone to iCloud (covered next), but you currently get only 5GB of free space.

1. If you need to install iTunes (on Windows), do that first.

2. Once iTunes is installed, connect your iOS device to your computer with the included USB cable.

3. The device should back up automatically when connected.

If you don't have a computer, you'll have to back up to iCloud. If you have more than 5 gigabytes of data (which isn't hard to do), you will need to pay for more storage space (a monthly fee).

1. Go to Settings and then click your name at the top to access your account.

2. Find iCloud Backup and click it.

3. Turn on iCloud Backup.

4. Backups will happen only when connected to Wi-Fi.

Tip 11-1b. Android

For Android, there's no one clean way to back up your entire phone. You can back up your basic settings by going to Settings ➤ Personal ➤ Backup and Reset. Select both the data backup and data automatic restore options. However, this will not back up your text messages, pictures, music, etc. There are many backup apps on the Google Play store. You will have to do a little research there to find a good one that meets your needs. If you connect your Android device to your computer with a cable, you should also be able to manually copy files from your Android device to your computer, but this is a pretty clumsy option for regular backups.

Tip 11-2. Keep Your Device Up-to-Date

Security problems are found all the time, and mobile device makers release updates on a fairly regular basis. You should be sure to update your device's software whenever a newer version is available—this includes the operating system as well as applications.

Tip 11-2a. iOS

Apple's iOS is free and easy to update. On your iPhone, go to Settings ➤ General ➤ Software Update to check your current version and see whether you have any updates.

Tip 11-2b. Android

On Android, it's often difficult or impossible to update the OS. To check your version and see whether any updates are available, go to Settings ➤ About Phone. If there is an available software update, you should see it here.

Tip 11-3. Lock Your Device

I know this seems like a pain in the butt, but you absolutely need to lock your mobile devices. Anyone who picks up your device can access tons of personal information, so you need to erect a digital barrier—either a PIN or passcode (most secure) or a biometric lock (fingerprint or face scan). Some devices allow you to enter a full-on password, which is obviously the most secure way to go. However, since unlocking the device requires physical access, a four-digit PIN will be sufficient for most people.

If your phone has the option to wipe all data after a certain number of incorrect attempts to unlock, I encourage you strongly to enable this feature, as well. You can store this PIN/passcode in LastPass if you're afraid you'll forget it. All Apple phones have this feature. Go to Settings ➤ Touch ID & Passcode. Scroll all the way down to Erase Data and enable the feature.

Tip 11-4. Don't Use Biometric Locks for Sensitive Stuff

One of the nifty features on newer mobile devices gives you the ability to unlock it using fingerprint or facial recognition. This is undoubtedly easier than having to type in a PIN or password, but using biometrics is not as secure. Not to sound paranoid, but these techniques work just fine even if you're not conscious. Also, while the law is still not 100 percent settled on this, recent cases have concluded that a law enforcement officer can compel you to unlock a device using biometrics, but they cannot force you to divulge your PIN or passcode.[2]

Tip 11-5. Dial Down What Your Apps Can Access

Both iOS and Android have gotten really good about forcing application makers to explicitly ask for access to various features of your phone such as the microphone, the video camera, your contact list, your location, and so on. Practice the policy of least privilege and deny permission to any app that doesn't absolutely need such access. It makes sense for a weather app to want access to your location because you usually care most about the weather where you are. However, why in the world would that same weather app need access to your address book or the microphone? Usually these apps ask for permission when you install them or perhaps when you first run them. At

---

[2]https://www.digitaltrends.com/mobile/cops-compel-fingerprint-unlock-not-passcode/

the time of this writing, Apple's iOS provides a lot more flexibility on what you allow each app to access and give you the ability to change these options after the fact. With Android, it's often all or nothing, and you may not be able to change your mind later. Apple also allows you to control some things based on whether the app in question is in the foreground (that is, it's the app you're using right now—the one "on top"). Google has announced similar abilities in current and coming updates to Android, but right now iOS still provides the most control.

Note that some applications may fail to work after removing permissions—either because they really do need access to the thing you just cut off or because they didn't design their app to deal with people who want to protect their privacy. So, you may have to go through a little trial and error with these settings.

Tip 11-5a. iOS

For iOS devices (iPhone/iPad), go to Settings ➤ Privacy. There you will find a long list of the things that iOS allows you to restrict. You're going to want to go through each category and carefully select which applications should have access to which services. You can always change your mind later.

Tip 11-5b. Android

For Android devices running version 6.0 (Marshmallow) or later, you can go to Settings ➤ Apps (or Application Manager). You'll see a list of apps where you can enable or disable permissions.

Tip 11-6. Limit Ad Tracking

Sadly, both Apple (iOS) and Google (Android) now have some form of ad tracking. You can turn some of this off or down, however.

Tip 11-6a. iOS

Go to Settings ➤ Privacy ➤ Advertising. Enable the button for "limit ad tracking." From time to time, you might want to also reset your Advertising Identifier (click the link below the tracking switch).

Tip 11-6b. Android

On Android, you can elect not to log into your Google account from your phone. However, this will probably prevent you from getting the most out of Google's services. You should also go to Settings ➤ Ads and opt out of interest-based ads. From time to time, you might want to also reset your advertising ID (in the same settings panel).

Tip 11-7. Remove Unused Apps

How many apps do you actually use on your smart device? If you're like me, you've probably accumulated dozens of "free trial" or "free today only" apps that you never use. You might think it's harmless to leave those apps sitting dormant on your device, but the truth is that those apps are probably getting automatically updated all the time—and who knows what version 2.0 does? Maybe it has a cool new "friends" feature that contacts everyone in your address book or starts recommending recipes depending on your current location. With every software update, there are potential risks of software bugs that bad guys can exploit, too.

The opposite problem may also bite you: the app is abandoned and *never* updated. What if there's a known security bug that goes unfixed?

Bottom line: if you're not using an app, delete it. You can always re-install it later if you find that you want it back. In most cases, once you buy it, it's yours for life, and the app store will allow you to download it again. This will have the added benefit of saving precious space on your device.

Tip 11-8. Enable (Self) Tracking

Similar to Find My Mac (see Chapter 5), Apple phones have a neat feature called Find My iPhone that will allow you to locate (on a map) a lost or stolen device. This feature will even allow you to remotely lock or wipe that device, if necessary. Android offers a similar service called Android Device Manager. You can also find apps on the Google Play Store like Prey that offer similar features, but I would use the Android Device Manager if it's available to you.

Note that for these features to work, the device must be connected to the Internet somehow. For smartphones, this is usually not a problem, but for Wi-Fi-only devices (like many tablets and devices like the iPod Touch), you need to make a tough choice: either set your device to always try to connect to whatever Wi-Fi it can find (not as secure) or give up on this feature. However, if you use the next tip, you should feel better about letting it connect to anything.

Tip 11-8a. iOS

On your iOS device, go to Settings ➤ iCloud and scroll down to Find My iPhone. Enable the feature, including the "send last location" option.

Tip 11-8b. Android

On Android, go to Settings and find the Permissions section. Select Security and then Device Administration. Enable Android Device Manager. If you can't find it here, try launching the Google Settings app, find Security, and then enable Android Device Manager.

Tip 11-9. Use the DuckDuckGo Mobile Browser

DuckDuckGo started out as a privacy-oriented search engine but has since released several new privacy-enhancing tools including a mobile phone browser. While you unfortunately can't replace Safari as the default browser on iOS (that is, change which browser is launched when you click a link in some other app), you can at least install and use DuckDuckGo's browser for direct searches and manually pasted web links. On Android, you will have the option to make DuckDuckGo your default browser.

Tip 11-10. Use the LastPass Browser, Too

If you need to visit a web site on your mobile device that requires a password, you should consider using the web browser that's built into the LastPass mobile app. Just open LastPass on your smartphone and click the Browser button at the bottom.

You can also try using the LastPass extension for Safari and for Chrome. It will allow you to enter usernames and passwords directly in these browsers. See this helpful article to set it up:

```
https://blog.lastpass.com/2018/06/passwords-are-big-news-at-
apples-developer-conference.html/
```

Currently, for all other situations, you will need to copy and paste your password from the LastPass app into other apps where needed.

Apple realized that this is a royal pain and there will be welcome changes coming in iOS 12 (due out in the fall of 2018) that will fix this. You'll be able to automatically fill in LastPass information into any application![3]

Tip 11-11. Avoid Cheap Android Phones

There have been several reported cases of cheap Android phones coming pre-installed with adware, spyware, and even straight-up malware—right out of the box. Some of the best-known manufacturers are ZTE, Archos, myPhone, and BLU. Don't cut corners on buying a smartphone. Stick to well-known name brands.

Tip 11-12. Use Secure Messaging Apps

While Apple's iMessage is relatively secure, there are better apps out there, if you really want your messages to be private (that is, encrypted from end to end). Unfortunately, everyone you want to communicate with will also need to download and install the same app—because we don't have a standard yet. These apps are available for both iOS and Android, as well as for your computer, so you can actually message from any device to any device.

- *Signal*: `https://signal.org/`

- *Wire*: `https://app.wire.com/` (use the "personal use" version)

Tip 11-13. Install (and Use) a Mobile VPN

Virtual private networks aren't just for laptops. While most banking and shopping apps on your phone already use encrypted connections, your e-mail and web surfing may very well be completely open and unencrypted. And when you're using the free Wi-Fi at Starbucks, McDonald's, your hotel lobby, or wherever, all that data is completely visible to anyone else in the area with a simple wireless monitoring application. If you have a VPN app installed, it should automatically kick in whenever your device tries to connect to an unknown (and therefore untrusted) network. Fair warning: good VPN services usually cost money. I guarantee you will find situations where it will frustrate you because it won't connect. This is the usual trade-off between security and convenience.

---

[3]Furthermore, iOS 12 will autofill those six-digit PIN codes that you get via text messages (two-factor authentication codes)—another welcome enhancement.

But if you find yourself having problems connecting and you specifically need Wi-Fi (versus cellular data), you can always elect to temporarily disable the VPN.

One note...don't use Facebook's VPN (Onavo). If you select the Protect option in the Facebook app, it will prompt you to install the Onavo VPN, a service owned by Facebook. This gives Facebook complete information on everything you do on the Internet, and its "privacy" policy explicitly says that it will collect and use this info.

Look at Chapter 6 for recommendations on good VPN services.

Tip 11-14. Know Your Rights When You Travel

For some reason, normal property and privacy laws seem to be thrown out of the window when you cross a border. For example, current U.S. law says that border agents can confiscate and search an electronic device for any reason and for as long as they want. Because of our preoccupation with terrorist threats, border guards have been given a lot of leeway, shall we say. There are laws in the works to curb this, but until then, you can find some great information at this EFF web site:

```
https://www.eff.org/wp/digital-privacy-us-border-2017
```

Tip 11-15. Don't Hack Your Device

Because mobile devices have so many restrictions on what you're allowed to do, what apps you can install, and so on, many people have turned to *rooting* or *jailbreaking* their devices to get around these constraints. Having root privileges on a computer means you can basically do anything you want. The problem is that once you've hacked a device and given yourself root access, you have opened the door for other apps to abuse that same privilege level. This exposes you to all sorts of foul play. I strongly recommend you avoid doing this.

Tip 11-16. Disable Bluetooth and NFC When You Can

Bluetooth is the odd name of a versatile, short-range, low-power wireless technology that allows your mobile device to connect wirelessly to external devices such as speakers, hands free headsets, keyboards, and more. You can even use it to unlock your front door! However, leaving Bluetooth on all the time means that rogue devices can also try to connect to your device without your knowledge. These connections can be used to steal your data and potentially even compromise your device. While Bluetooth is fairly secure and these attacks are not common, it's still a good idea to just disable Bluetooth unless you're using it. It will also help you save your battery.

Near Field Communications (NFC) is another wireless technology built into many mobile devices, though used less often and at much shorter distances. While Bluetooth can work at distances of dozens of feet, NFC generally is limited to maybe an inch or less (hence the "near" part). It's usually used to pair your phone with another device—maybe to get a Wi-Fi password or trigger a mobile payment app or even transfer a file from one phone to another. Like any wireless technology, it can be broadcasting and listening all the time to any nearby device, making it a possible "way in" to your phone. Disable this feature if you're not using it.

Tip 11-17. Erase Your Device Before Getting Rid of It

Like our home computer, our mobile devices are chock-full of detailed personal information. In fact, our cell phones arguably have way more info in (or accessible by) them. So, before you give away or sell or even recycle your smartphone, you should be sure to wipe it completely. If you've encrypted the contents, you're most of the way there already. But it's still good to wipe it clean.

Tip 11-17a. iOS

1. Be sure to run a full backup of your iPhone before you do anything. Connect your iPhone or iPad to your computer and let iTunes back it up (or if you use iCloud Backup, make sure it has backed everything up recently). You can use this backup to transfer all the data to a new device. In fact, if you're going to do that, be sure to do that first before going any further.

2. Go to Settings and click your name/picture at the top. Scroll down to the bottom and sign out. Follow the instructions to delete all your iCloud data from your iPhone.

3. Go to Settings ➤ General and scroll all the way down to the bottom. Select Reset. Then select Erase All Content and Settings. If you've signed up for Find My iPhone, you may have to enter your Apple ID and password to disable this feature. Follow any other prompts to enter passwords, PIN codes, etc.

4. See this helpful Apple article for more info:

   `https://support.apple.com/en-us/HT201351`

Tip 11-16b. Android

Unfortunately, Android devices can be very different from one another in terms of settings. This is partially because of different versions of the OS, but it's also because Android allows service providers a lot of leeway in customizing the device. If you have trouble with any of these steps, go into your local cell phone provider and ask for help.

1. Be sure to run a full backup of your phone or tablet before you do anything. You may need to transfer that data to another device. If you have the new device, do this transfer first before doing anything else.

2. If you have a removable SIM card (the little card the cell phone service provider put in there to identify you), remove it.

3. If you have any removable storage (SD card), be sure to remove it.

4. Log out of any services and accounts you use: e-mail, messaging, social media, cloud storage, music services, etc. You may do this through Settings, or you may have to do it through each application.

5. If you haven't encrypted your device, do that now. It will make sure that even if you miss something here that no one else will be able to find it. This should be under the Security settings.

6. Perform a factory reset. Find the Backup and Reset area under Settings. There may be lots of options here—select the ones that make sense. Then find and click the "Reset device" or "Reset phone" button.

CHAPTER 12

Odds and Ends

At this point in the book, I've covered most of the technical topics that require background and longer explanations. However, there are a handful of other topics that I want to touch on because I feel they're important. In this chapter, each section will have its own checklist with just a brief introduction. It'll be sort of like a lightning round!

When Bad Things Happen

Up until this point, the entire book has pretty much been about preventing bad things from happening. Sometimes despite our best efforts, we still get bitten by misfortune. In this section, I will try to walk you through the recovery process for some common cyber-calamities, or at least point you to web sites that can help you.

Tip 12-1. E-mail Account Is Hacked

When bad guys manage to guess your e-mail password, they usually use it to distribute spam and malware. If you don't use your account often, you may first be notified of the problem by a friend or relative who suddenly gets an e-mail from you trying to push pills for male enhancement. Here are some things you should do:

- Immediately change your password and use LastPass to create a strong, unique one. Until you change your password, the bad guys can continue to use your account for their nefarious purposes, all the while pretending to be you.

- You might want to change your security questions.

© Carey Parker 2018
C. Parker, *Firewalls Don't Stop Dragons*, https://doi.org/10.1007/978-1-4842-3852-3_12

- Look in your inbox for any e-mails about password changes or password reset requests that you did not initiate. As I discussed earlier in the book, most password recovery procedures involve sending you an e-mail to reset your password. If you find evidence of a successful password change, you should assume those accounts are compromised. Inspect them closely for bad transactions and change the passwords on those accounts, as well.

- Look at your Sent folder to see whether any spam or scam e-mails were sent on your behalf. You may also want to contact any recipients of those e-mails to let them know they did not come from you and may be malicious.

- Check your e-mail settings to see whether anything looks amiss. For example, make sure someone didn't add or change your e-mail signature (an optional bit of text that is automatically included at the bottom of every e-mail you send). Check your autoforwarding and vacation/away settings, as well.

- You should probably inform your e-mail provider that your account was hacked but that you have changed your password. They may be able to take some action against the attackers.

- Finally, this would be a good time to enable two-factor authentication, if it's available. If you had had this in the first place, your account probably would never have been hacked.

Tip 12-2. Web Site Password Breach

If you get a notice from a web site where you have an account saying that there has been a "security breach," they will usually tell you that you should change your password. That's precisely what you should do, right away. As a further precaution, don't use any links in the e-mail (just in case it's a fraud). Log in to your account by manually entering the web address or using a bookmark or favorite.

What the e-mail may not tell you is that if you use this same password on any other web site, then you better change your password on that site, too (and make it unique this time). If the web site breach e-mail says that credit card numbers were also lost, you should keep a close eye on your credit card account, looking for purchases that you didn't make.

There's a nifty web site that helps people figure out whether their account info has been leaked in a breach:

`https://haveibeenpwned.com/`

That's "have I been pwned." The term *pwn* (rhymes with "own") is hacker lingo for dominating or defeating someone. If you've been pwned, you've been successfully hacked. This site maintains an up-to-date catalog of all the known server breaches, indexed by e-mail address. You enter your e-mail address and the site will tell you whether that address was part of a known breach.

Tip 12-3. You Suspect You Have a Virus

Your best move here is to just not get the virus in the first place because getting rid of something once your system is compromised can be really tricky. How do you know if you have a virus? Well, it's hard to say, generically, but some symptoms might include the following:

- If your files are held hostage for money, see the next Tip.

- Your computer is suddenly more sluggish or less responsive.

- Your computer appears to be working hard even when you're not using it. For example, the fans are blowing full tilt or the hard drive light is flashing constantly.

- Unwanted windows or applications are popping up all the time.

- Computer or web browser settings change without you doing it.

If you think you might have a virus, try the following remedies, in this order:

1. If you haven't already installed antivirus software, do that immediately (see Chapter 5) and run a full scan.

2. You can download and install special, on-demand virus checkers.

   - Malwarebytes "for home" version (Mac or Windows): `https://www.malwarebytes.com/mwb-download/`

   - If you have a Windows machine, you can also try downloading and running Microsoft Safety Scanner: `https://www.microsoft.com/en-us/wdsi/products/scanner`

3. If you can't seem to shake the virus, you might have to completely delete this user account. (If the account was your admin account, you might even need to completely wipe the entire computer and start over.) If you are pretty sure you know when things started going haywire, you can try using your backup software to bring your entire computer back to a point in time prior to the suspected infection date.

Tip 12-4. You've Got Ransomware!

If you get a pop-up message or big scary screen telling you that all of your files have been encrypted and you must pay money to fix it, you're the victim of ransomware. If you have a full backup of your system (see Chapter 3), you can simply restore your system to a point in time prior to the ransomware infection and you're done. That's why the backup is so crucial.

If your backup is only for your files (and not your entire system), then you'll need to delete the infected user account and then restore the files from backup.

If you do not have a backup, then you really have just one hope remaining: that the bad guys screwed up somehow. It happens more often than you'd think. There's an entire web site devoted to helping victims of ransomware, usually by finding flaws in their software that will allow you to recover your files without paying. Before you pay the ransom, check out this site:

```
https://www.nomoreransom.org
```

If all else fails and you really need those files back, then you can always pay the ransom. In most cases, you will get your files back. If you didn't, word would get around, and no one would pay. It's in their best interests to bend over backward helping you. Some of these guys actually have tech support that you can call...I'm not kidding. You will probably be asked to pay with Bitcoin or some other anonymous payment method. Again, they should provide with all the help you need to do this.

Tip 12-5. Restoring a Lost or Messed-Up File

Back at the beginning of this book, we talked about setting up an automated backup for your most important files. This allows you to recover files that you accidentally delete or screw up. We discussed two ways do this this: either an external hard drive plus a backup program built into your OS or using a cloud backup utility like Backblaze. Use the following links to find detailed steps for recovering individual files:

- *Mac OS Time Machine*: http://support.apple.com/en-us/HT201250

- *Windows 7/8.1 Backup and Restore*: https://support.microsoft.com/en-us/help/17127/windows-back-up-restore

- *Windows 10 File History*: https://support.microsoft.com/en-us/help/17143/windows-10-back-up-your-files

- *Backblaze*: https://www.backblaze.com/restore.html

And When I Die...

So, what happens to all your various online accounts when you die? That's a question most people probably never ask themselves until it's literally too late. While most people are aware that they should have a will and maybe some healthcare directives, most people don't often get these documents created unless they're very wealthy or particularly fastidious. But how many people take the time to handle their digital estates? What should happen to all your e-mails, photos, music, forum posts, dating site info, social media accounts, and so on? In this section, I'll give you some tips on how to manage your digital affairs.

Tip 12-6. Get a Will

I can't stress this enough. If you have a spouse or children, you really need to have a will in place. Every state has different rules about what happens to your stuff if you die without a will, but these processes can take a long time, and the default rules may not suit your needs at all. When you go to get your will, talk to your lawyer about handling your digital assets, as well. They should at least be able to tell you what your state law says about this subject. Be aware, however, that this area of law is very new and evolving quickly.

Tip 12-7. Add a Backup to Your Safety Deposit Box

Again, this is not really a digital thing, but it's important. Many banks will not honor a will or power of attorney to allow access to a safety deposit box. I have no idea why this one thing is treated specially, but apparently it is. So, make sure that your spouse and perhaps one of your children have been approved to access your safety deposit box.

Tip 12-8. Save Your Passwords Somewhere Safe

Your successors may need immediate access to things like bank accounts, investments, insurance, computer accounts, and so forth. You should therefore print off a list of your most important passwords and keep them in a safe place. Better yet, print off some one-time passwords for LastPass, which will work even if you change your master password. You might put these printouts in your safety deposit box or in a fireproof safe. LastPass also has a Family Plan that can allow access after a period of time—sort of dead man's switch. If you don't respond within a time period, your chosen successor will be given access to your password vault. Just make sure that whoever needs these passwords knows where they are and knows how to get to them.

Tip 12-9. Ensure Access to Two-Factor Device

If you've followed my advice on setting up two-factor authentication where you can, that means your successors will also need access to your two-factor authentication devices. This will most likely be your cell phone. So, make sure that your cell phone account can remain active (so your phone can receive SMS messages) and that your authenticator app is accessible (write down your phone's PIN somewhere).

   If by some misfortune your loved one dies without doing this, your best bet will be to try to access their accounts from known devices and in known locations. This might prevent the two-factor code from being needed, at least for a period of time.

Tip 12-10. Appoint a "Digital Executor"

While you might want to simply hand over all your passwords to your beneficiaries when you die, you might actually have some parts of your digital life that you want to die with you. The only way to accomplish this is to appoint some third party who you trust to take care of this for you after your death. Your lawyer might be a good choice. You will need to carefully document what you want done with each account. You will only want these passwords and instructions to be opened after your death, which is something your lawyer should be able to arrange for you.

   If you do a little Googling, you can find that people are starting to write articles about what to do with your digital life when you die. Search for *digital estate planning*. These services are in a massive state of flux. I had links to two of them in the first edition of my book, and they're already either out of business or merged with some other company.

Here are a few articles you can start with:

- Catey Hill, "5 Steps to Creating Your Digital Estate Plan," Next Avenue, May 6, 2012, `https://www.nextavenue.org/5-steps-creating-your-digital-estate-plan/`

- Mariella Moon, "What You Need to Know About Your Digital Live After Death," Engaget, December 10, 2014, `http://www.engadget.com/2014/12/10/online-life-after-death-explainer/`

- Leigh Anderson, "You Need to Deal With Your Digital Legacy Right Now," Life Hacker, November 15, 2017, `https://lifehacker.com/you-need-to-deal-with-your-digital-legacy-right-now-1820407514`

Gold Stars and Tinfoil Hats

We've covered well over 150 different tips on mostly simple and mostly free things you can do to improve your computer safety. While some of these tips involved some effort and some of them may have impinged on your convenience, they were quite tame compared to the items in this section! Just for fun, I'm going to lay out some truly "pro" tips for taking things to the next level. These are for the tinfoil hat and black helicopter crowd.[1] I am by no means recommending that you need to do *any* of these things. For that reason, I'm not going to painstakingly lay out the steps required to do them. However, I thought it would be fun to show you the lengths that some people go to in order to be super secure. These are roughly in order of effort and cost or just plain paranoia level.

Tip 12-11. Install NoScript

This plugin for Firefox will completely block just about all "active" content in your web browser: JavaScript, Flash, and so on. You can selectively tell it that certain things and/or particular sites are okay (and it will remember your decision in the future). However, most web sites have many sources of active content, and it can be quite daunting to

---

[1]These are terms associated with overly paranoid people. Search the Internet for more information.

manually enable only the parts you need for the web site to function properly. This plugin has grown to include other great security features, as well. Just be prepared to go through a lot of initial pop-ups asking for permissions.

`https://addons.mozilla.org/en-US/firefox/addon/noscript/`

Tip 12-12. Install Haven on an Old Android Phone

Investigative journalists, human rights advocates, dissidents in repressive regimes, and whistle-blowers are constantly looking over their shoulders. Being discovered or having their data stolen could result in being jailed or even "disappeared." Love him or hate him, Edward Snowden knows a thing or two about this situation, and he has created a free Android application called Haven that acts as a super-duper intruder alarm. Using the smartphone's sensors and communication links, the app will monitor your room or personal space for movement, lights, sounds, and power loss, and report these events securely to people who may be able to help, should you become incapacitated. Or just use it as a kick-butt baby monitor.

`https://guardianproject.github.io/haven/`

Tip 12-13. Add a Dedicated Guest Wi-Fi Router

While most modern routers provide a "guest network" option, you still have to trust that the router software maker implemented that security feature properly. If you have some Internet-enabled devices in your home that you don't fully trust (like Internet of Things devices) or if you have a lot of strangers in your house who want to use your Wi-Fi, you might want to consider beefing up your security and having a dedicated Wi-Fi router for your guests and IoT devices. Having a dedicated router for this untrusted traffic is the safest way to make sure that guests and rogue devices cannot access your private home network.

To do this right, you actually need *three* routers. You'll hook them up in a "Y" pattern. You'll have one wired router connected to your cable modem (or whatever box you use to connect to the Internet), and then you'll hook two Wi-Fi routers up behind that wired router. This will guarantee that devices on the guest Wi-Fi router will have zero access to the devices on your private Wi-Fi router. Confused? Check out this video podcast for the full details:

`https://twit.tv/shows/know-how/episodes/315`

Tip 12-14. Install Little Snitch (Mac OS Only)

Sometimes the apps you install on your computer like to "phone home," providing the software maker or some third party with information you'd rather they not have. Remember that firewalls only prevent unsolicited network connections coming in from the outside. If you've installed software on your machine, that software is free to communicate freely with anyone or anything on the outside. Little Snitch is sort of like a reverse firewall, notifying you of all outgoing connections and giving you the opportunity to allow or block them. Fair warning: shortly after install, you're going to find out that many of your apps want to access the Internet, and you're going to have to go through a lengthy initial process of allowing those apps to communicate.

```
https://www.obdev.at/products/littlesnitch/index.html
```

Tip 12-15. Use Top-Shelf Security and Privacy Tools

When I want to see which tools that truly paranoid types would use, there's one web site that I always go to for reference:

```
https://www.privacytools.io/
```

More than any other web site I've found on privacy, this one always goes the extra mile and doesn't screw around with half measures. Many of the tools I've recommended are listed here, but there are many more. For this book, I've tried to find the right compromise between security and convenience. Not these guys. If you really want to take things to the next level, this is the web site for you.

Tip 12-16. Install Custom Wi-Fi Router Software

When you buy a Wi-Fi router, you're actually getting two things: the hardware and the software that controls it. Like a computer, it's actually possible to replace that software with something better. There are three main projects out there for this purpose: DD-WRT, OpenWRT, and Tomato. (The guys at Tomato definitely won the marketing war here... DD-WRT and OpenWRT just do not roll off the tongue.) These projects offer completely free, open source software that you can install on many modern Wi-Fi routers. This isn't for the faint of heart, but if successful, you can actually add lots of great security features to your router that would normally be found on more costly routers. The security of these products is probably better, as well.

- *DD-WRT*: https://dd-wrt.com/

- *OpenWRT*: https://openwrt.org/

- *Tomato*: https://www.polarcloud.com/tomato

Tip 12-17. Install and Use PGP

Though PGP stands for "pretty good privacy," that's actually being extremely modest. PGP is industrial-strength encryption, mostly used for sending secure e-mail. Unfortunately, it's a real pain in the butt to set up and use. To make matters worse, everyone you need to communicate with must also set this up. I would actually recommend looking into GPG (GNU Privacy Guard), which is a free, open source implementation of the common OpenPGP standard. Alphabet soup, I know. But if you're at all curious, check out this web site:

https://emailselfdefense.fsf.org/en/

Tip 12-18. Use Tor to Protect Your Identity

Tor was started specifically for the purpose of providing anonymity on the Internet. Tor uses an impressive array of technology to hide the location and identity of its users. While Tor is well-known and trusted by many, it's also a magnet for authorities because they pretty well assume that if you're using Tor, you're up to no good. However, it's still worth checking out, even to just understand how it works and how hard it really is to protect your anonymity. You can get a lot of the Tor functionality by using the Tor Browser (a super-private browser based on Firefox). You can find all of this and more at the following site:

https://www.torproject.org/

Tip 12-19. Need to Blow the Whistle? Use SecureDrop

While you can debate whether people like Edward Snowden are heroes or traitors, there's no denying that whistle-blowers have exposed some pretty egregious behavior by governments and corporations. SecureDrop is a communication system specifically designed to protect the anonymity of whistle-blowers and confidential news sources, allowing them to securely communicate with news organizations. For more information, visit this site:

`https://securedrop.org/`

Tip 12-20. Set Up a Virtual Machine

One way to contain some secret activities is to have a whole separate computer specifically for this purpose (see the next tip). However, this will obviously incur some significant costs. You can get many of the same benefits by having a virtual computer running on your regular computer. This is called creating a *virtual machine* (VM). A VM runs its own operating system that is separate from the OS running on the host computer. So, all the web surfing, file downloads, e-mails, and so on, will exist in a sort of container. VMs have the interesting capability of creating snapshots. You can basically take a picture of the virtual computer in some state and return to that state at any time. So, you can do your dirty deeds and then revert to the snapshot…it's like it never happened! While you can pay money for VM software, there's a perfectly good free alternative called VirtualBox. This software runs on both Mac OS and Windows. Note that you'll need to install some sort of operating system on this VM, and Windows generally won't allow you to reuse a license key for free (meaning you would need to buy another copy of Windows for the VM). I recommend Ubuntu, which is a totally free operating system with plenty of security features. See these web sites for more info:

- *Installing VirtualBox*: `https://www.virtualbox.org/`

- *Installing Ubuntu*: `https://www.wikihow.com/Install-Ubuntu-on-VirtualBox`

Tip 12-21. Use a Dedicated Secure Computer

While a VM is cheap and easy, you can never really be certain that there won't be some sort of information leakage between your VM and your host operating system. If you want to go full tilt, you really need a dedicated machine that is completely separate from anything you would normally use. You can save money by buying a used machine, but of course you can't be 100 percent sure that the person you bought it from hasn't somehow compromised it, so you'd better just get a new one from a big-box store.

If you want to really go the cheap route, you can buy a Raspberry Pi 3 minicomputer. For just $35, you can have a fully functional Linux computer that's about the size of a deck of cards! Of course, you'll need to buy a case and a power supply for it, plus an SD card for the "hard drive"... but you can get all of that for about $60. All you need is a monitor, keyboard, and mouse, and you're set!

If you go the laptop route, you'll want to replace the operating system with something secure. Look no further than Tails![2] If it's good enough for Edward Snowden, it should be good enough for you.

```
https://tails.boum.org/
```

Tip 12-22. Go Silent

So far we've focused on computers; what about your phone? Well, never fear, the folks at Silent Circle have a product for you! This company claims to provide a mobile device that offers completely secure communications: phone, e-mail, web browsing, and texting. It also offers a portable box that combines a VPN, firewall, and Wi-Fi to protect your other mobile devices and computers.

```
https://www.silentcircle.com/
```

Tip 12-23. Completely and Securely Erase a Hard Drive

If you have a computer that whose hard drive was not encrypted or if you're just that paranoid that you want to be *really* sure, you're going to want to use a nifty little free utility called DBAN (short for Dave's Boot and Nuke). With this app, you will boot your computer from a CD or USB drive and then scribble all over the hard drive. When you're done, all the data will be completely unreadable—in fact, the computer won't even boot because the operating system will be wiped, too.

```
http://www.dban.org/
```

---

[2]As of this writing, Tails is only supported on standard X86 computers, not ARM computers. Raspberry Pi is an ARM-based computer. But keep checking—the RPi is very popular, and Tails may eventually support it.

CHAPTER 13

Parting Thoughts

Congratulations! You have just read an entire book on computer security! I hope I managed to teach you some things you didn't know, in a way that wasn't boring. More than anything, I hope I've convinced you of the importance of computer security and helped you to implement some basic safeguards to protect your computer castle. Before I wrap things up, I wanted to share with you a few last thoughts.

Keep Calm and Carry On

While the picture this book paints might seem bleak, I don't want you to go away feeling overwhelmed or despondent. Armed with the tips and techniques in this book, you can protect yourself and your family against the most of the common threats out there. Imbued with this knowledge, you should feel confident about using your computer, your smartphone, and the Internet. These tools have already changed innumerable things for the better, and we have truly only just scratched the surface of the potential.

Remember that you don't have to do every tip in this book. I haven't. Not every tip makes sense for every person. But I've given you the information you need to make the right decisions for you and your family—it's up to you. Don't feel like you have to rush through all of these tips, either. The most important things you can do are these:

- Back up your files.

- Keep your computer and smartphone software up-to-date.

- Use strong, unique passwords for important sites.

- Turn on two-factor authentication where you can.

- Surf the Web safely using a good browser with security plugins.

- Don't open unrequested/unexpected attachments or links.

Do those things first. Do the rest when you can.

© Carey Parker 2018
C. Parker, *Firewalls Don't Stop Dragons*, https://doi.org/10.1007/978-1-4842-3852-3_13

The Case for Optimism

In the past decade or so, as the bad guys have turned to the Internet for their nefarious deeds, computer and software makers have been forced to focus more on security and privacy. However, with the revelations from Edward Snowden and all the massive data breaches at big-name companies in the last few years, security and privacy concerns have increased exponentially. Google and Apple in particular have kicked things into high gear. Google is using its dominance in web search and cloud services to push web sites into adopting secure communications by default, as well as creating tools to make it easier and cheaper for them to do so. Apple has already included some great tools on Mac OS for encrypting your data and securely backing it up, but in the wake of recent events, they've taken effective steps to lock down their mobile devices against prying eyes, as well. Global companies like these and others need to be able to sell their products worldwide, and that requires convincing their customers that they are willing and able to secure their data. There are already multiple competitors cropping up to fill this need. This competition should light a fire under the existing corporations to get their respective acts together. Or maybe they'll just end up buying up some of these security-focused startups. But either way, we should be seeing a lot of innovation in the area of security, and this will benefit everyone.

While there have certainly been some colossal security breaches lately, this is causing people to wake up and take notice. Unfortunately, things often need to get worse before they can get better. I don't think we've bottomed out yet—it takes time to implement security changes at large corporations and in computer products—but I think things have already gotten bad enough that we're on the road to recovery. While the U.S. government seems incapable or unwilling to protect the privacy of its citizens, the European Union is taking bold steps with the General Data Protection Regulations that will benefit all of us. Furthermore, the private sector has profits to protect, and they won't be waiting around for legislation. We've already seen this happening, and I expect to see a lot more in the next year or two. The case involving the FBI and Apple that hit in early 2016 is a prime example. When these high-profile security incidents occur, they will force us to finally debate these issues and take action. So, while we are not out of the woods yet, I think we've turned the corner.

Don't Take This Lying Down

Despite the market pressures that are driving increased security, there are still plenty of places where maximizing corporate profits does not directly align with maximizing consumer protections—particularly in the area of privacy. For this reason, it's absolutely essential that regular people like you get educated and get involved. If consumers and citizens don't demand security and privacy, then corporations and governments will be free to put their own interests first, protecting their profits and power.

Regardless of what you believe is the proper balance between freedom, privacy, capitalism, and democracy, you can't really participate in the debate or make informed choices unless you understand the underlying issues. I don't mean you have to understand all the deeply technical details, but you need to know enough to evaluate different products and different policies. I've tried to give you a good foundation with this book, but I urge you to seek out more information and stay informed. See the previous section of this chapter for some ideas.

I encourage you to take it one step further, however. Don't just get educated; get involved. I'm not encouraging every reader to put down this book and put up a protest sign (though that would be wonderful). There are many simpler ways you can make a difference. For one thing, you can pay others to do it for you. That is, you can donate to groups that are already fighting for your rights and putting pressure on corporations and governments to do the right thing. You don't have to donate a lot, either—even a little money can make a difference, if enough people do it. Just being a member of these groups helps to give them more clout; it gives them a long list of everyday people who made a point to say, "I agree with what these guys are doing; please listen to them." Again, see the list at the end of this chapter for some ideas.

You can also spread the word to others (maybe give them a copy of this book). As these issues inevitably hit the news, discuss and debate them with co-workers at the water cooler, at home with the family over the dinner table, or with friends at the next party or sports event. It doesn't have to be confrontational—keep it friendly and informative. But it's essential, as a society, that we address these issues. We can't ignore them any longer.

Of course, in a representative democracy, the people who are supposed to be your advocates are the people you elect to represent you in the halls of government. However, with campaign finance laws being what they are, these folks are unfortunately much more likely to listen to the needs of their largest donors. Nevertheless, you cannot let that stop you from trying. The real problem in the United States is that people have given up. Voter turnout in this country is abysmally low. I think people are just tired of the mudslinging and backroom dealing. To paraphrase an old hippie mantra, they've tuned out, turned off, and dropped out. The problem with disengaging is that it leaves the more extreme factions and wealthy people in charge. Security and privacy are not partisan issues; they affect us all, no matter what your particular leanings may be. I encourage you to stay involved and to vote every chance you get—not just in national elections but in local ones, as well. If we could get just 5 percent to 10 percent of the people who have given up on voting to get back out there, it could easily turn the tide.

In the meantime, write your elected representatives. For those of you in the United States, you can use the following link to find out who represents you and how to contact them. While online notes are convenient, real "snail mail" letters and phone calls still hold more sway—precisely because they take effort.

```
http://whoismyrepresentative.com/
```

Finally, as you see companies trying to do the right thing and bringing new products to market, support them with your pocketbook whenever you can. We need to shift away from an Internet economy that is based on advertising. That's going to mean paying for things that used to be "free." Also, when given the choice, we need to favor products that do a better job of protecting our privacy and enhancing our security.

Similarly, you should support politicians who stand up for individual privacy and stand against the rampant, unregulated gathering of personal data by corporations. The first step is awareness—these companies simply must be 100 percent transparent about what data they collect, what they do it, and who they share it with. Once we understand the true breadth and depth of this campaign to hoover up all our highly personal data, I think we'll find the political will to make necessary changes.

Going Further

There are several other ways for you to make a difference and gain further knowledge. In this section, I've gathered together some key resources for going beyond the tips in this book. You can use these resources to continue your education and get a different perspective on the topics I've covered in this book. I'll also tell you about organizations that you can support that are out there working hard to protect your rights.

Books

If you liked this book, you should seriously consider reading some of the following books:

- *Data and Goliath* by Bruce Schneier (W. W. Norton & Company, 2016). Schneier literally wrote the book on cryptography but in recent years has become a leading voice on public policy. He's testified many times before Congress. His (recent) books are easy to read, extremely insightful, and compelling. If you like this book, you might also try *Beyond Fear*.

- *No Place to Hide* by Glenn Greenwald (Metropolitan Books, 2014). Glenn Greenwald was selected by Edward Snowden to manage the release of highly sensitive information regarding warrantless NSA mass surveillance. This book chronicles this engagement and helps to explain the importance of Snowden's bombshell revelations.

- *The Code Book* by Simon Singh (Anchor, 2000). If you find the concept of cryptography as interesting as I do, this book traces the history of ciphers and cryptanalysis in an engaging and entertaining way.

- *Little Brother* by Cory Doctorow (Tor Teen, 2010) (fiction). If you prefer to be entertained while you learn about cryptography and why it's so crucially important to democracy and society, this is a must-read. This book talks about a not-too-far-fetched future where law enforcement agencies overreact to a terrorist attack and trample civil liberties in a quest for "security." Seriously, just read it.

Documentaries

If you prefer to learn by watching, here are some excellent documentaries about privacy and cybersecurity:

- *Terms and Conditions May Apply*: This is about online privacy and what sorts of things you're signing away in end-user license agreements (EULAs).

- *CITIZENFOUR*: This is about Edward Snowden and how his initial information was given to reporter Glenn Greenwald.

- *Frontline: The United States of Secrets*: This is a great two-part show from PBS.

- *Code 2600*: This is a great film about the humble beginnings of the hacker culture and how cybersecurity has become much more serious with the advent of the Internet.

Blogs and Web Sites

The following web sites are chock-full of useful information and not super technical:

- *Firewalls Don't Stop Dragons*: My blog! I will be pulling info from many sites, so by following me, you will automatically get some of the rest of this stuff. See `https://www.firewallsdontstopdragons.com`.

- *Naked Security blog*: This is a great source for security info, written in accessible language. See `https://nakedsecurity.sophos.com/`.

- *Spread Privacy blog*: This is another great blog that's very accessible, put out by DuckDuckGo. See `https://spreadprivacy.com/`.

- *Schneier Blog*: Bruce Schneier has a wonderful blog that provides truly insightful analysis of current events, looking beyond the immediate impact and giving much-needed long-term context. See `https://www.schneier.com/`.

- *Microsoft Digital Skills*: Microsoft has an extensive web site, full of many resources for security and privacy. See `https://www.microsoft.com/en-us/digital-skills/online-safety-resources`.

Podcasts

If you haven't tried podcasts before, they're basically periodic radio shows that you can download from the Internet. Most people listen to them using a smartphone app while they commute or travel or do some mindless task. Some podcasts have video, as well, making them more like TV shows. There are thousands of them out there on every topic imaginable, for every taste and education level.

- *My podcast!* It's also called *Firewalls Don't Stop Dragons*, and you can find it on my web site (on the Podcast tab) as well as the usual podcast outlets (iTunes, Google Play, Stitcher, etc.). The show comes out once a week on Mondays and runs 30 to 60 minutes. See `http://www.firewallsdontstopdragons.com`.

- *Security Now!* This is where I really got into security, and I listen to this podcast religiously. While it can get a little technical sometimes, it's always fun—and full of random other fun stuff like sci-fi books and movies. It comes out once a week, usually on Tuesdays, and runs at least two hours. See `http://twit.tv/show/security-now`.

Fighting the Good Fight

The following organizations are doing some excellent work on behalf of everyday people. Take a look at their web sites, and if you like what you see, send them a little money. If they send you a sticker or magnet, proudly display it where others will see.

- *Electronic Frontier Foundation*: `https://www.eff.org/`

- *Electronic Privacy Information Center (EPIC)*: `https://epic.org/`

- *Center for Democracy and Technology (CDT)*: `https://cdt.org/`

Glossary

application. Pieces of software that you launch on your computer to help you do something. Examples include Microsoft Word, Internet Explorer, Firefox, iTunes, Photos, and Outlook.

bandwidth. Used to describe how fast data can travel over a given connection. You most often see this when your Internet service provider tells you how fast you can download something from the Internet.

bit. The smallest piece of computer data. This can be either a zero or a one, making it binary.

Bluetooth. A short-range, low-power wireless technology mostly used to remove the need for wires. Commonly used with wireless headsets, computer mice, keyboards, and sometimes remote controls.

byte. A chunk of computer data equal to eight bits. When talking about many bytes, we use metric prefixes like kilo- (thousand), mega- (million), giga- (billion) and tera- (trillion).

cloud, the. Refers in a general, vague way to all the services and servers out on the Internet. When you store data "in the cloud," it's stored on some big computer on the Internet that's run and owned by a company or service provider.

Ethernet. The technical name of the standard used to connect computers to a network using wires. Ethernet cables look like home phone cables, but the rectangular clip connector at the end is wider.

file manager. The name for the operating system tool that lets you view, move, copy, rename, or delete files. On Windows, this is called the Windows Explorer or File Explorer; on Mac, it's called the Finder.

hardware. The parts of a computer that you can see and touch: the computer, monitor, keyboard, mouse, printer, webcam, and so on.

ISP. Internet service provider. This is the company that gets you connected to the Internet. Examples are Comcast, Spectrum, Verizon FiOS, and Google Fiber. When you connect to the Internet with your smartphone, your ISP is your cellular provider.

© Carey Parker 2018
C. Parker, *Firewalls Don't Stop Dragons*, https://doi.org/10.1007/978-1-4842-3852-3_14

LAN. Local area network. Your home network is a LAN, as is the network at the office where you work. LANs are smaller, private networks (as opposed to the Internet).

malvertising. Web advertising that contains links to malicious websites or actual malicious software that runs in the ad itself.

malware. Software that is built to do "bad" things, ranging from giving you annoying advertisements to actually corrupting or controlling your computer. Examples include viruses, spyware, and trojan horses.

modem. A small box that converts your Internet service provider's special type of connection (cable, phone line, fiber optic, or satellite) to a standard network connection (Ethernet). You usually rent this box from your ISP. Sometimes these modems will also include a built-in Wi-Fi router.

net neutrality. A concept that says everyone should have equal and fair access to everyone else on the Internet—companies with more money shouldn't be able to get privileged access.

network. Two or more computers or devices that are connected and communicate using a common language, or protocol. Networks today use Internet Protocol (IP).

operating system. A special piece of software that runs the entire computer. Examples include Microsoft Windows and Mac OS X.

ransomware. A particular type of malware that surreptitiously encrypts all of your computer's files and then demands payment to decrypt them.

router. The box on your network that separates your local area network (LAN) from the Internet. In most homes today, the router is a Wi-Fi router.

server. Fancy name for a big computer out on the network whose job it is to do something for you. It might hold your e-mail or let you buy something online or stream you a movie. Your computer (the one requesting something) is the *client*.

software. The general term for any program that runs on your computer, including applications and the operating system.

spam. Unwanted or junk e-mail.

WAN. Wide area network. This usually refers to the Internet, but it may also refer to a large corporate network that spans many sites.

Wi-Fi. The wireless communication standard used by computers and smart devices to connect to the network. This is also referred to by the technical name 802.11.

WLAN. Wireless LAN. This is the type of network created by a Wi-Fi router.

Index

A

© Carey Parker 2018
C. Parker, *Firewalls Don't Stop Dragons*, https://doi.org/10.1007/978-1-4842-3852-3

CPSIA information can be obtained
at www.ICGtesting.com
Printed in the USA
LVHW061837181119
637700LV00004B/57/P